FOURTH EDITION

Communicating
With
Parents and Families
of Exceptional Children

Roger L. Kroth and Denzil Edge

University of New Mexico   University of Louisville

LOVE PUBLISHING COMPANY®
Denver • London • Sydney

To Jane Kroth and Sharon M. Edge

Published by Love Publishing Company
P.O. Box 22353
Denver, Colorado 80222
www.lovepublishing.com

Fourth Edition

Library of Congress Control Number: 2006920931

Copyright © 2007, 1997, 1985, 1975 by Love Publishing Company
Printed in the United States of America
ISBN 0-89108-314-6

Contents

6 Parent–Teacher Conferences 77

7 Informational Formats for Parents 95

8 Reporting Progress 113

9 Parent Group Meetings 125

Part Three: Resolving Problems With Parents 135

Part Four: Technology and the Future of Parent Involvement 187

14 Assistive Technology and Devices 189

15 Wrapping Up and Looking Ahead 205

Preface

In 1973, during a Council for Exceptional Children (CEC) convention, Stan Love and I sat across the table from each other at a breakfast meeting. He was a publisher, and I was a "wannabe" author. I had a dream, and he had the means to fulfill it. I saw a real need for a textbook for teachers and other professionals who were working with—or planned to work with—children who had special needs. Specifically, I saw a need to improve communication between teachers and parents of children with disabilities.

From the beginning, many of these parents were lost in the system, having found themselves with a child who had needs they had not expected to encounter and were not prepared to deal with. Then, when their children entered school, these families encountered another set of challenges in communicating with many different educational and related professionals. A counselor by training myself, I wound up in the field of special education. Could my counseling skills and experience be useful to parents and professionals in the school system?

Much has happened in the three decades since that breakfast meeting. Some of the families I have known for years through our mutual association with the educational community have watched their children grow up and enter the marketplace. Other families have grieved as their children have passed away. All of these families have a story to tell. And I have learned from them how to help bridge the gap between school professionals and families.

A short while ago, I ran into Ray Armenta, the father of a young boy I had come to know in school. Ray and I shared a cabin during a summer camp for children with disabilities and their families. When the boy, Andre, was young, he was nicknamed Lazarus because he kept "coming back from the dead." Finally, as an adult, it caught up with him, and he passed away.

Now Ray was with one of his daughters and a grandchild. We talked a while, and I asked his daughter about her children. She told me that one was named Andre, after her brother. I have a hard time keeping dry-eyed when I hear stories like these.

On another occasion, at an Optimist Club meeting in El Paso, some deaf and hard-of-hearing students were presenting speeches in sign language. I was impressed. After the speeches, a teacher and her student came up to me. "I'll bet you don't remember me," the teacher said, then quickly spoke her name. Although I confess to having problems remembering everyone I've encountered, this is one lady I certainly *did* remember. She was another parent I had come to know in one of our camps for families with children who had severe and profound handicaps.

Reminiscing

These chance meetings reminded me of where we'd been and where we were now—and what had happened in between. Significantly, both of these chance meetings highlighted the lasting effects of our introducing camps for families with special-needs children as a way to foster communication between families and educational professionals. Jeanelle Livingston did most of the front-end work for our camps. Attending each camp was an occupational therapist, a physical therapist, a physician, a school psychologist, one or more educators, some University of New Mexico students, and, of course, the special-needs children and their families. In New Mexico, when you say "bring your family," you can expect to see grandparents, aunts, and uncles arriving with the immediate family.

At one of these early camps, a mom, Tammy, related that when her daughter was born, it was immediately apparent that she had a severe handicap and that it was just a matter of time until she would die. The baby cried and cried, she required constant attention, and death seemed imminent. To top it off, her husband left for good. There was no relief for Tammy, and she seemed alone with her burden. At some point, she carefully selected a pretty little dress and a white Bible. She purchased a burial plot. After she was ready, she okayed pulling the life supports.

But the baby didn't die right away. Tammy waited and waited, and finally the baby passed away. As Tammy told her story, there wasn't a dry eye among the group of parents and professionals.

As time went on, Tammy lobbied the legislature for a bill to provide in-home care for children who were in the same circumstances as her daughter. The legislature passed what came to be known as the Fragile Child Act. After that, Tammy applied for, and was accepted into, medical school. Since then, she has become a doctor. This is another of the many stories that bring our work to life.

Meeting Evolving Needs

When we first started our Parent Involvement Center in the Albuquerque Public Schools in the late 1970s, few (if any) such programs had been instituted around the country. Our mission was straightforward: Teach parents how to work with the schools and school personnel how to work with parents. It took some time and practice to produce the "how" of it. Upon observing the results, parent centers began to spring up around the country. Some of these centers unfortunately took on an adversarial rather than an advocacy role, staffed with lawyers whose primary concern was with children's rights. Although rights certainly are a concern, centers need to continue to help parents and professionals to have good personal relationships. Listening and negotiation skills can be taught.

Other changes have transpired over time, too. The thrust of the federally funded Bureau of Education for the Handicapped in the late 1960s was to train teachers and other support personnel. There was—and still is—a paucity of teachers in programs for teachers of children with emotional disturbance, physical handicaps, mental retardation, speech therapy, visual impairments, and hearing impairments, as well as school psychologists. Programs for children with learning disabilities and for giftedness emerged later, along with teacher training programs for these categories identified in the legislation. Among the initial components of the individualized education program (IEP) was a requirement for a conference to include the parents and the child, if the latter was able to provide and receive input. A need for educational diagnosticians arose simultaneously, along with training for this specialty.

The 15-Minute Hour

With the passing years, professionals and parents alike seem to have less and less time, so they are looking for ways to use their time more effectively and efficiently. I call this the *15-minute hour*. One of the aims of this book is to help professionals respect families' limited time and meet the time challenges while establishing rapport, paying attention to the family's environment, studying family backgrounds and values, and developing good listening skills. I think of it as "planning your work and working your plan." The better you hone your skills, the better prepared you will be to make the most of your 15-minute hour.

Parent involvement and parent participation are consistently high priorities in polls and surveys among parents and teachers. Therefore, engaging parents in conferences and planning for their children's education is a worthwhile endeavor. To do this, educators and other professionals who come in contact with students and their families need to develop good skills, and to impart these in an efficient way.

Some things remain the same as before. We still mouth the need to prioritize family and community involvement in children's education. But often the people who espouse these values do not practice them in reality. Not long ago I visited an elementary school with a good reputation for parental involvement. When I asked the principal about parent conferences, she replied that she had to limit the time to 20 minutes—yet her school is recognized as one that keeps the community involved.

What must our training programs look like given administrative and time constraints such as these? Here are two tried-and-true suggestions:

1. *Consider parents as vital to the educational process.* Come to every parent meeting with an attitude and belief that parents are an important resource, from whom you can learn a lot about how to improve your educational role.

2. *Be prepared.* It has helped me to have questions and concerns ready and written down, and invite parents to do the same. Parents can't assume that the teacher knows about the tantrums Dana started throwing before bedtime last week. Teachers can't assume that parents heard about the crying spell Danny had in class a couple of weeks ago.

Policies and Passion

Over time, the friction between home and school has hung on. Too often, educators can be overheard saying, "If it weren't for the parents, I'd like my job." And parents are frequently heard to say, "Tonya's teacher ignores her. She needs much more attention than she's getting. Where are the educators with 'fire in their bellies' who want to go to bat for parents?"

Three decades seems like a long time—plenty long to see changes. Some things have gone around and come around, and some won't come around again. Some things we have learned, and some things we have ignored. All too often, we haven't learned how to instill a level of enthusiasm that will carry teachers and parents over times of crisis and stress. With this book, we hope to incite some fire in your belly.

Roger L. Kroth

ACKNOWLEDGMENTS

Every edition of this book has been supported through the many parent involvement efforts developed and implemented at the Parent Involvement Center in Albuquerque, New Mexico. Beginning with the development of the third edition, I decided to collaborate with an old friend, Denzil Edge, who had written extensively in the area of parent involvement. His vast experiences with grant development, research, and development of school-based programs on parent involvement blended well with my experiences and research. He continues to be a valuable coauthor, particularly in updating changes in technology.

We credit many people in this effort—particularly our wives, Jane and Sharon, for their tolerance of our numerous, early-morning telephone exchanges about the book. Also, we acknowledge the invaluable support of many professionals and parents devoted to building better programs for children and youth with special needs who contributed their efforts to this book. For their many ideas, long hours developing parent involvement programs, and their continued support for higher-level materials for parents and teachers, we thank the following: Paula Parks, Marcia Bumkens, Catherine Senn, Paulette Logsdon, Nat McKay, Jan Lowe, Jackie Austin, Jan Deeb, Judy Elmer, Matt Benningfield, Stephanie Hoover, Sandy Poe, Barbara Chittick, Cathy

Schroerlucke, Linda Seimons, Judy Mullins, Mary Veasey, JoAnn Paroz, Gwenlynne Pike, Jerry Dominguez, Meave Stevens-Dominguez, Lauren Moss, Bobbye Krehbiel, Janeen Kirk-Taylor, Joe Sievert, Kay Haney, Suzanne Robinson, Rudy Montoya, Carla Gibbs, Sharon Solomon, Emily Salazar-Marcum, and Betsy Williams.

Sprinkled throughout this book are many names of those who served on the original advisory board of the Parent Involvement Center at the University of New Mexico, and on the Advisory Board of the Parent Education and Resource Center, University of Louisville: Ray Dembinski, Northern Illinois University; Jennifer Olson, University of Idaho; Richard Simpson, University of Kansas; Bill Wagonseller, University of Nevada at Las Vegas; Kay Hartwell, Arizona State University; Lou Doty, formerly of University of Louisville; Bernie Strenecky, University of Louisville; Jay McLoughlin, Dean, Cleveland State University; Rebecca Jackson, County Court Clerk, Louisville, Kentucky; Pearl Mann, Special Assistant on the Development of the "PEP Talks for Parents" Program; Donna deSpain, Kentucky State Department of Education; Mike Franken, Project Pipeline, Ohio Valley Educational Cooperative; Bob Pillay, University of Melbourne; Dorothy Rich, Home & School Institute; and Don Davies, Schools Reaching Out Project.

We especially acknowledge the patience and support of a good friend, Stan Love. His gentle guidance and well-placed prodding enabled us to accomplish a difficult task. Also, great appreciation goes to the able editors for their long hours devoted to this book.

We've been blessed to have so many good friends and contributors to our own growth and development. It is with great appreciation that we extend to you our heartfelt thanks for your friendships and support over the years. In some small way, we hope this book contributes to your personal growth and professional relationships.

Roger L. Kroth
Denzil Edge

Introduction

In the fast-paced technological world of today, time is a precious commodity. In many schools, communication with parents has been reduced to computer printouts, voice mail, a report card every two months, and an open house once a year. When parents feel rebuffed and left out of their children's education, the school–home relationship can become adversarial. School systems and educators have been taken to court over issues of due process, procedural rights of children and parents, and lack of adequate programming for children with disabilities. In response, schools have tended to become wary of communicating with parents.

Specifically with regard to students with disabilities, federal legislation beginning with the Education for All Handicapped Children (PL 94-142) in 1975 has recognized the importance of involving the parents/guardians of children and youth with disabilities in their education. In subsequent legislation, parents are considered partners with teachers in educational assessment, placement, and programming for children with disabilities.

By law, children with disabilities are to be included in educational environments with their nondisabled peers to the greatest extent possible. Parents are mandated to participate in the development and implementation of individualized education plans (IEPs) and individualized family service plans (IFSPs).

The legislation supports the research literature as it has developed over the years, which clearly indicates that children perform better, both academically and socially, if parents are actively involved in their children's education. Even though most parents want their children to be successful in school, they do not realize the vital role they play in their children's academic and social achievement. Parents too often assume that the school is supposed to take over the role of educating their children.

This book suggests ways by which teachers can convey to parents how important they are to their child's educational growth and development. An abundance of research indicates that parent involvement is the strongest factor impacting the child's academic and social performance. The benefits of parent involvement in education include higher grades and test scores, long-term academic achievement, positive attitudes toward school and improved behavior in school, better attendance and less tardiness, heightened parent–teacher communication, and improved schools.

In summary:

> ➤ Families provide the primary educational environment for children.
> ➤ The involvement of parents is associated with improved student achievement.
> ➤ Parent involvement is most effective when it is comprehensive and well planned.
> ➤ Parent involvement has lasting effects on young children and youth.
> ➤ Parent involvement contributes to improved schools.
> ➤ When parents are involved, children from low-income and minority families improve the most.

In an increasingly diverse and complex educational environment, along with the sweeping changes brought by technology, traditional interactions between school and home are no longer viable. Now, more than ever, collaboration between families and schools is needed to educate our children for a rapidly changing world. Teachers must understand the parents' perspective and value the role of parents in their child's education.

We view parents as partners, not adversaries, and in this book we suggest ways by which educators can improve school–home communication. This is not a book of theories. It is a book of practical techniques and strategies, based on proven theories and on the premise that all parents have strengths to contribute to their child's education. Although the content is aimed primarily at special educators, the ideas are applicable to general educators and general education parents and students as well. We obtained most of the information in this book by talking with teachers and parents, observing teachers in their work with parents, and holding conferences or group meetings with parents. We are sharing techniques that other educators have found to be effective and suggesting additional ideas to try.

This book is organized into four parts, each covering a specific set of issues. Integrating these concepts under an overall umbrella will foster school–home communication to students' benefit. All chapters conclude with practical, resourceful activities, directed toward inservice teachers, student teachers, or preservice students, and all activities can be easily adapted to other settings and for other audiences.

Part One: Understanding the Child and Family (Chapters 1–4)

We lay the groundwork for establishing positive, productive relationships with parents by presenting the Mirror Model for Parental Involvement, developed by the Parent Center in the Albuquerque Public Schools. Still effective, the four levels in the model are based on strengths and needs, with consideration to parents' available time, energy, and skills.

Part Two: Strategies for Involving Parents (Chapters 5–9)

Involvement of parents in the educational process requires planning and effective communication. Parents want professionals to communicate to them without using educational jargon, and they want to feel at ease when attending conferences and meetings. They want information on their child's social as well as academic behavior. Teachers need to be prepared to share this information effectively through conferences, meetings, and telephone conversations. They have to be able to explain the various reporting systems and school policies. This section introduces the parent group as an excellent way to share information.

Part Three: Resolving Problems With Parents (Chapters 10–13)

Successful problem solving requires skill in obtaining the necessary information from parents and must be based on establishing mutual trust and respect. This section presents strategies for pinpointing problems and techniques to obtain the needed changes.

Parent-to-parent activities have become popular because parents sense that other parents understand their situations better than educators do. This section presents strategies for sharing information at parent-to-parent events and developing parents' active participation in educational programs.

Part Four: Technology and the Future of Parent Involvement (Chapters 14–15)

Today's society requires us to competently navigate the world of technology—which may be easier for children than their parents. These chapters present strategies for accessing resources and connecting homes to schools electronically, and they look ahead to the future of parent involvement.

The Hope

In many respects, this book represents a model for all parent–teacher interactions, not just those involving families with disabilities. First, teachers obtain as much information from parents as is necessary to plan educational programs for their children. Second, teachers seek to establish contact that is comfortable and nonthreatening to the parent, using effective human relations skills. Third, teachers provide the information parents need so they are able to work with teachers toward common goals for the children. Fourth, cooperative planning between teachers and parents may prevent, alleviate, and solve many problems that arise. Parents and teachers who recognize their roles as complementary rather than supplementary, who approach their interactions enthusiastically and not apprehensively, and who view the relationship as a partnership will be rewarded with happy, achieving children and warm, personal feelings of mutual respect.

Parents who have children with disabilities need a great deal of positive reinforcement. Teachers who are mature, secure adults can help parents become productive change agents by providing that support.

Parents' involvement in their children's educational life is the key to good learning. This book provides guideposts for enhancing home–school partnerships. Encouraging and enabling parents in this common goal is crucial. The rewards to parents and teachers alike will be gratifying.

Part One

Understanding the Child and Family

1

The Family in Today's Society

A series of federal legislative initiatives, most recently the No Child Left Behind Act, enacted in 2001, clearly mandate that parents of children with disabilities be included in all aspects of education. From their initial involvement in early childhood education programs, parents have input in decision making for the educational assessment, placement, and programming for their children with disabilities. Parents participate in developing and implementing individualized education plans (IEPs) and individual family service plans (IFSPs). They are involved in leadership programs, workshops, technical assistance projects, information and training networks, and conferences.

The Office of Special Education and Rehabilitative Services (OSERS) is committed to improving results and outcomes for people with disabilities of all ages:

> In supporting President George W. Bush's No Child Left Behind agenda and the New Freedom Initiative, OSERS provides a wide array of supports to parents and individuals, school districts, and states in three main areas: special education, vocational rehabilitation, and research. By providing funding to programs that serve infants, toddlers, children, and adults with disabilities, OSERS works to ensure that these individuals are not left behind . . . in school, in employment, in life. OSERS also provides funds to programs that offer information and technical assistance to parents of infants, toddlers and children with disabilities, as well as members of the learning community who serve these individuals. (U.S. Department of Education, 2003)

Parent advocacy groups and organizations have argued for years that the family be an integral part of the decision-making process for educational purposes, and the resulting legislation has heightened awareness of parents' and children's rights, including due process, assessment, instructional placement, and related service needs. Furthermore, the research literature over time has indicated consistently that children perform better, academically and socially, if their parents are actively involved in their education (Henderson, 1987, 1988; White, Taylor, & Moss, 1992). Their learning transfers to real-life situations in the home and community.

Family support programs aimed at strengthening all aspects of children's development (a) emphasize parent education at home, and (b) help parents connect with natural support systems (Davies, 1991; Hall

& Henderson, 1990). The common themes of parent involvement programs are that

> ➤ all children can learn, and they should be provided opportunities for success;
> ➤ the whole child is best served by linking his or her social, emotional, physical, and academic growth and development; and
> ➤ the school, family, and community should share the responsibility for the child's development.

The research also indicates that too many parents of children with disabilities have not been integrally involved in their children's education (Bailey, Buysse, Edmondson, & Smith, 1992; Coulter, Johnson, & Innis, 1991; White et al., 1992). The reasons are many and varied. Some researchers (Davies, 1991; Hodgkinson, 1992) have suggested that families have changed tremendously in recent years and that educational institutions have not adapted well to these changes. In this chapter, we will discuss

> ➤ the changing family structure,
> ➤ some barriers to parent/family involvement,
> ➤ new definitions for parent involvement,
> ➤ ways to involve parents and families,
> ➤ implications for delivering educational programs, and
> ➤ new directions for parent and family involvement.

CHANGING STRUCTURE OF FAMILY AND SOCIETY

During the past several decades our society has undergone quantum shifts, and children and families have been caught up in this movement (Hanson & Lynch, 1992; O'Connell & Sontag, 1992). As stated by Harold Hodgkinson (2000), director of the Center for Demographic Policy at the Institute for Educational Leadership, the composition of the American family has changed dramatically. According to 2003 statistics, more than 1 million public school children now are the responsibility of their grandparents; in 1998, 5.4 million children lived in households headed by a relative other than a parent (Children's Defense Fund [CDF], 2003). But the structure of the family is constantly in a state of flux.

Poverty

In 2004, more than 13 million children (17.8%) younger than 18 lived below the poverty line, defined as household income below $19,157 a year for a family of four with two parents. Black and Hispanic children were approximately three times as likely to be poor as non-Hispanic White children. In 2004, more than 71% of children in poor families lived with a family member who was working. Two in five children (41.8%) in female-headed families were poor, in contrast to only 9.7% of children in all other family types that were defined as poor. Median incomes have been declining since 1999, and the prices of goods and services have steadily increased since 2003 (Children's Defense Fund, 2005).

Ethnic Composition

In the early 1990s, minority children represented the greatest proportion of new children living in poverty (Carson, Huelskamp, & Woodall, 1993). This immense demographic shift has been compounded by the language differences of children and the lack of preparedness of schools to address these changes (Carson et al., 1993).

In an article in the *New York Times*, Lynette Clemetson (2003) commented that Hispanics have edged past blacks as the nation's largest minority group. The Hispanic population in the United States is now roughly 37 million, surpassing the black population of about 36.2 million. "The Latino population grew by 4.7 percent, while the black population grew by just 1.5 percent. The white, non-Hispanic population, estimated at roughly 196 million, grew by 0.3 percent during the same period."

In the same article, Roberto Suro, director of the Pew Hispanic Center, a Washington-based research and policy analysis organization, said, "It is a turning point in the nation's history, a symbolic benchmark of some significance. If you consider how much of this nation's history is wrapped up in the interplay between black and white, this serves as an official announcement that we as Americans cannot think of race in that way any more."

According to the same *Times* article, the explosive growth in the Hispanic population is a result of higher birth rates and the huge wave of immigration during the last decade. The Census Bureau counts all people residing in the United States, whether they are legal immigrants or not. These figures carry important implications for the allocation of resources. In recent years, blacks and Hispanics have often been in opposition in seeking financing and political representation, and the new numbers could bring fresh tensions.

Some Latino advocacy organizations, perhaps anticipating possible difficulties, are playing down the significance of the shift. "Rather than comparing groups, we should be looking at the status of communities," said Sonia Perez, deputy vice president for research at the National Council of La Raza, a national Latino organization. "When you look at Latino and African-American communities, the elements of the agendas are not that different. We share many of the same issues, interests and values."

The *Times* article went on to state that, in many ways, the new figures indicate the growing multiculturalism in American society and the changes in the way the Census Bureau allows people to classify themselves. The 2000 census, for the first time, allowed respondents to choose more than one race in identifying themselves. In addition, Hispanics, a cultural and ethnic classification, can be of any race.

Although the general African American population is slightly smaller than the general Hispanic population, the number of Americans who declared themselves as black "in combination with one or more other races" is now 37.7 million, slightly higher than the overall figure for Latinos. "The statistics are in the eyes of their beholders," said William H. Frey, a demographer at the University of Michigan. "What these numbers reveal is a bit of a conundrum. But advocacy groups, policy people, and politicians will pick the interpretation . . . that works best for them at any given time."

The article continues that much of the social and political impact of the population surge may not be immediately apparent. Roughly one quarter of Latinos living in the United States are noncitizens. And, though there has been a significant migration of Hispanics to cities in the South, Midwest, and central plains, more than half of the Latino population remains concentrated in Texas, California, and New York.

The rapidity of population shift, though anticipated, has taken some demographers by surprise. "It came sooner than we thought," said Martha Farnsworth Riche, director of the Census Bureau during the Clinton administration. Among the factors that contributed to the faster than anticipated growth, she said, was greater cooperation between the

Census Bureau and Latino organizations, which helped undocumented migrants feel safer cooperating with census takers.

The slim numerical gap between blacks and Hispanics is expected to widen significantly over the next decade. Deteriorating economic conditions across Latin America are expected to continue to spur immigration. The birth rate among Latinos is also higher than that of blacks. Demographers expect the spurt to level off in a generation or so as Hispanics intermarry with other ethnic groups and some choose to identify as black, some as white, and some as a combination of one or more ethnic groups or races. "It will only get more broad and more complicated," according to Suro. "It's a reminder that we will increasingly, as Americans, need to find new ways of categorizing people and talking about their differences."

Hodgkinson (1992) agrees that the composition of the American youth population in the future will look very different from the composition of the youth population during the middle part of the 20th century. He projected that by the year 2010, four states (New York, Texas, California, and Florida) will be home to about one third of the nation's youth, and that more than half of these youth will be "minority," according to the current definition of the term. Hodgkinson emphasized that the real "minority" in these four states will be non-Hispanic White youth. Hodgkinson urged the business and government sectors to respond to the rapidly increasing demand for child care while the single-parent family becomes the new "typical American family."

The middle-income level of our society is declining while the rich and poor levels are increasing. We are creating two workforces: one in minimum-wage jobs and the other in well-paying jobs. For every new job created for the engineer, eight new jobs are created for food service workers. This leads to an "information-rich" and "information-poor" split in our society.

BARRIERS TO PARENT AND FAMILY INVOLVEMENT

In 1992, the National PTA (1992) first attempted to identify the problems associated with involving parents and families in education by conducting a survey of more than 27,000 local PTA presidents. These presidents were asked about barriers to getting parents involved with

Spotlight on Diversity

Comanche School is user-friendly. Parents are in and out, visiting classrooms and volunteering their services in a variety of ways.

"Buenos dias, estudiantes. Good morning, students," Shelly Campbell announces over the PA system to start the day. The blue-eyed, blonde-haired principal uses both Spanish and English in an easy manner. In the past, she was selected as Elementary Principal of the Year.

She has the advantage of being able to converse with parents and families who use Spanish as their primary language. The school has a student population of speakers of 10 different languages, among them Greek, Spanish, Vietnamese, and Urdu.

States on the southwestern border—Texas, New Mexico, Arizona, and California—have become minority states; Anglos are now in the minority. In addition to the growing Hispanic population, these states are home to many recently arrived Asian and other populations. And New Mexico in particular has students from different American Indian tribes with their own languages, dialects, and cultural differences—largely, Navajo, Apache, Zuni, and Hopi.

As one can imagine, IEP development can be quite a challenge. Translating materials from the IEP Regulations in English into Spanish or Navajo is done at one's own peril. Literal translation just doesn't work, and trying to use a translator can be a daunting experience. In a workshop conducted in English and translated into Navajo, for example, the speaker might say a few words followed by the translator's saying many words, and then the speaker will talk for a long time and the translator will speak only a few words. Some concepts just do not translate easily.

In addition, the Comanche School attempts to integrate students with special needs into the basic curriculum, using an inclusionary model. Identified special education students are welcome at schoolwide events and activities. A number of the older children serve as peer mediators to ease problems on the playground. A group of children identified as SAK (Socially Active Kids) interact with at-risk children, among other philanthropic activities. Parent volunteers help the special-needs children become involved with music and art programs in the school. All students learn technology skills to the level at which they are able to achieve.

Source: Albuquerque Public Schools, New Mexico.

school activities, and the parents in the National PTA survey gave their opinions about why parents and families are not more involved in their children's education. The reasons for lack of involvement included the following:

> *Time.* Single and working parents have difficulty finding time to get to meetings, conferences, and school functions.

> *Perceived intimidation.* Some parents feel intimidated by principals, counselors, and teachers.

> *A confusing system.* Parents do not understand the workings of the general and special education systems.

> *Childcare needs.* Parents often have other children at home, and they feel burdened by having to bring their children to school events.

> *Language barriers.* Parents who speak and write English as their second language sometimes have problems understanding the printed materials or speeches at meetings.

> *Cultural differences.* Manners and courtesies are different in different cultures. School personnel can unintentionally offend or embarrass parents from cultures different from their own. Associated with this barrier are family observances of different religious and other holidays, which may conflict with school events and activities.

> *Transportation needs.* Some parents lack transportation to attend meetings, conferences, and school events.

> *A feeling of not being welcome.* Parents sometimes do not feel welcomed in the school. The school personnel do not make them feel comfortable.

Ramirez (2001) offered additional reasons for the lack of parental involvement. He suggested that many parents and families feel lost in the maze of educating children. There are three support systems—family, school, and community. Some parents do not have support from any of these. They fear the school system and what it may do to their children if they complain. They don't know how to access the systems and how to get services.

The family, school, and community systems operate in isolation of each other. None of the three is attending to the others' needs. Bonnie Benard (1991), a noted researcher in the area of social change, stated that before any significant change for helping children will occur, the following must be present:

1. care and support,
2. high expectations, and
3. meaningful participation among the three systems of family, school, and community.

She maintained that we must aggressively pursue working with the family to build healthier, more resilient children. If this does not occur, the barriers to teaming and supporting each of the systems will increase.

Ramirez (2001) concluded that barriers to parental involvement often are a direct result of teachers' stereotypes of low socioeconomic (SES) families, single-parent families, and at-risk families. "When the issue of parent involvement came up . . . many [teachers] were apprehensive and desired the involvement to be limited to school functions or at-home activities."

Chavkin (2000) suggested that "a school policy can set the direction by clarifying the definition of family and community involvement and setting priorities and guidelines for the various groups from home, school, and community." She developed a checklist that teachers could use to evaluate their school district's policies pertaining to family and community involvement. The checklist is available in her article, "Family and Community Involvement Policies."

NEW DEFINITIONS OF PARENT INVOLVEMENT

Outdated views of parent involvement have been only minimally effective in meeting today's challenges. A new paradigm of parent involvement is evolving. The League of Schools Reaching Out (Institute for Responsive Education [IRE], 2003) defined and expanded the concept of parent involvement, as set forth here (Davies, 1991; Edge & Franken, 1996):

1. For many children, the term *family* is more encompassing than *parent*—the latter of which is too narrow to describe today's reality. Today, a child's primary family may consist of grandparents, aunts and uncles, or others.

2. Involvement goes beyond parents and families to include all social and community agencies that serve children. Urban families under stress because they are having economic difficulties and struggling to find housing, or are running into barriers of language, culture, and social customs, need assistance and support.

3. The new definitions do not require family members to come to the school for services and activities. These can take place in neighborhood settings and at home.

4. The new definitions reach out to include those who lack proficiency in English, self-confidence, or the energy or time to take part in traditional parent-involvement activities, as well as to those who fear schools because of cultural norms or negative school-related experiences.

5. The new definitions focus on families instead of the agendas of teachers and administrators. The definitions extend beyond purely academic functions to all contributions of families to their children's education.

6. The new definitions emphasize the inherent strengths of families instead of the old "deficit" perception of the traumas, troubles, and pathologies of urban families.

In sum, the new definitions of family require us to take a new look at the organization of parent- and family-involvement programs. Schools have to reach out to parents before positive results can accrue (Coleman, 1991). Simply urging parents to participate will likely result in less than agreeable confrontations rather than pleasant exchanges between school and home. Don Davies and his colleagues at the Institute for Responsive Education maintain that schools have to collaborate with parents, other schools, and community agencies regarding parent- and family-involvement issues (Davies, Burch, & Johnson, 1992).

Some of the collaborative activities suggested by Greenwood and Hickman (1991) are to

➤ foster more effective school–home communication,
➤ involve families in learning activities at home,
➤ involve families in governance, decision making, and advocacy activities for schools, and
➤ collaborate with community agencies in fostering family programs.

These areas of collaboration for schools are modeled after Joyce Epstein's (1990) research into parent and family involvement in education. With these new definitions of family, the outreach of schools and community agencies is needed more than ever to help children succeed in school and life.

PRINCIPLES OF FAMILY INVOLVEMENT

To bring the dreams for our nation's children to fruition, better policies for parent and family involvement in education have to be put into motion, along with more opportunities for children to gain full support from families, schools, and community agencies. A set of principles for guiding school systems, state agencies, and educational projects in developing parent- and family-involvement programs was developed by Davis, Kroth, James, and Van Curren (1991) and others, based on the following conclusions, which remain as relevant today as when they were originally proposed.

➤ Because families are not a homogeneous group, services and programs should be individualized, based on families' needs and preferences, and a variety of types and levels of activities should be provided (Kroth & Otteni, 1985).

➤ "Parents have to be recognized as the special educators, the true experts on their children; and professional people—teachers, pediatricians, psychologists and others—have to learn to be consultants." (Hobbs, 1978)

➤ All families and children have strengths.

➤ Most parents *do* care and *do* want to help their children. Sometimes they lack the skills, but these skills are teachable.

➤ Parents' lack of involvement may not reflect a lack of caring or concern but, rather, overriding family needs that take priority.

➤ A variety of legitimate family forms can promote healthy child and family development.

➤ Accepting and respecting diverse cultural, ethnic, and racial heritages, lifestyles, and values is a necessary condition.

➤ Family involvement is critical across the entire span of childhood and adolescence.

➤ Family involvement is not a separate, distinct component but, rather, is integrated throughout the total special education services system.

➤ Successful family involvement is a long-term process. Program development takes time, commitment, and extensive work.

Parent and family involvement in education requires commitment and consistent follow-up. It requires collaborative planning and development by the home, school, and community. Dorothy Rich (2003), founder and developer of MegaSkills, understands this concept better than anyone.

In the early 1990s, Maupin Elementary School in the Jefferson County Public Schools in Louisville, Kentucky, integrated these ideas and principles into a total parent- and family-involvement learning-choice school. The parents and educators at Maupin developed a matrix of activities that reflect home, school, and community environments across the areas of caring and support, high expectations, and meaningful participation (Benard, 1993; Jan Deeb & Judy Elmer, personal communication, January 7, 1993). This matrix is given in Figure 1.1.

Parent and family involvement in education is larger than any single family, school, or community organization. At the Wingspread Conference Center in April 1992 in Racine, Wisconsin, 23 national organizations met to discuss the importance and future direction of parent and family involvement in their respective organizations, and to develop a closer bond for supporting parent and family involvement. Their work resulted in the parent involvement in Goals 2000, the national legislation designed to provide future guidance for educational systems in the United States.

More recently, results of a National Parent Involvement Summit developed and implemented by the National PTA (1992) indicated that parent and family involvement was the number-one issue in education in the 1990s—and continues to be so today. As the nation focuses on educational excellence, parent and family involvement must be pursued aggressively, supported by homes, schools, communities, businesses, nonprofit organizations, and government entities working together in a mutually collaborative effort.

NEW DIRECTIONS FOR PARENT AND FAMILY INVOLVEMENT

In keeping with the dramatic shifts in society and the proliferation of children of low socioeconomic status being referred for special education

Care and Support	High Expectations	Meaningful Participation
H • Health and safety **O** • Basic needs **M** • Promoting education **E** • Motivation	• Homework • Modeling • Values/goals • Parents as teachers • Positive reinforcement	• Parent workshops • Involvement with child • Volunteer/PTA • Classroom involvement • Decision making • Field trips • Opportunity to extend education into home • Help with homework

S • Health and safety
C • Support of family
H • Home-school linkage
O • Childcare
O • Schoolwide MegaSkills
L   Implementation
  • Family resource center
  • Special programs to
    meet needs
  • Academic learning styles
	• Establish goals
	• Rewards/incentives
	• Awards
	• Values/attitudes
	• Positive reinforcement
	• Schoolwide discipline
	• School-sponsored
	  community resources
		• Student/parent
		  involvement
		• Parent workshops
		• Cultural/multicultural
		  activities
		• Technology training/
		  education
		• Family resource center

C • Financial support
O • Mentors
M • Provide services
M • Training
U • Employment
N   opportunities
I • Community
T   connections
Y
	• Financial assistance
	• Partnerships
	• Shared goals
		• Decision-making input
		• Sponsor parent
		  workshops
		• Family resource center
		  advisory council
		• Bacon's in-school store
		• Baptist Fellowship
		  Center
		• Girl and Boy Scouts
		• Parkland Boys/
		  Girls Club
		• Louisville Urban League

Source: Reprinted with permission of Maupin Elementary School, Louisville, KY.

FIGURE 1.1
Matrix of Family-Involvement Activities

services, we need an even stronger commitment to involving parents and families of children with disabilities in the educational process. Schools and community agencies must not function in isolation.

Universities must train educators how to work effectively with parents (Greenwood & Hickman, 1991). Businesses must become involved with schools and community agencies. Government agencies must pursue policies and program development for parent and family involvement. Research, model programs, and demonstration projects must be developed to assure that all children get the best opportunities for an education through the support and care they receive at home and in the school and community.

According to a research study conducted by Mid-South Regional Resource Center at the University of Kentucky, entitled "Issues and Trends in Special Education" (Hales & Carlson, 1992), parents

- ➤ need to be involved in more decision making regarding their children,
- ➤ need to have more educational services delivered to the home and community
- ➤ need more parent and family training on working with their children.

Parents are calling for more nontraditional ways to be involved in their children's special education programs. These services should be oriented to family and child needs rather than toward disciplinary interests and service traditions. Specific needs raised in the study include family-centered services, at-home crisis intervention services, and special training for foster families to meet the needs of children who have serious emotional disturbance.

Clearly, parent and family involvement in education is needed to foster better educational programs for children and families. Following are some suggestions that reflect the current thinking about how to maximize the involvement of parents and families in the education of their children.

1. *Collaborate and cooperate with family agencies, schools, and communities in developing programs on parent- and family-involvement issues.* Parent and family involvement does not function in isolation; it is bigger than any one person or organization. Schools must provide care and support for the family, set high expectations for involvement, and provide meaningful opportunities for family participation (National PTA, 1992).

2. *Adopt an open understanding of what constitutes family.* Involving parents of children with disabilities requires a shift in

understanding what "family" is. And "family member" is interpreted as any significant other in the child's life. The broader context of family consists of significant others in the home, school, and community (Davis et al., 1991).

3. *Develop more nontraditional approaches to parent and family involvement.* Involving parents of children with disabilities goes well beyond addressing parents' rights. Programs must address the more basic issues of parents as teachers of their children, supporters of educational and social changes, leaders in how to educate their children, and advocates for change (Edge, 1993; Epstein, 1990).

4. *Develop a greater understanding of cultural diversity in society.* Involving parents of children with disabilities requires an understanding of the populations served and the programs needed for these diverse populations. Sensitivity toward diverse populations is essential for developing a sound foundation for change. Training of all educators in understanding cultural diversity is essential for success (Hanson & Lynch, 1992).

5. *Train educators to enhance the involvement of parents and families in education.* Involving parents of children with disabilities requires greater commitment by universities and colleges in training educators to involve parents and families. Field activities with parents and families must be a requirement. Problem-solving approaches and leadership opportunities in working with families also should be required (Epstein, 1987; Greenwood & Hickman, 1991).

6. *Support local schools and community agencies in involving parents and families.* The best place for parents and families to be involved in their children's education is at the local school. State departments of education should facilitate policies, plans, and programs that enable support and encourage local schools to foster quality parent and family involvement (Chapman, 1991; Chrispeels, Fernandez, & Preston, 1990; Epstein, 1987).

7. *Plan for comprehensive parent and family involvement in education.* Parent involvement is much more successful when it is planned and implemented at the whole-school level (Henderson, 1987). Involving parents of children with disabilities requires joint planning and development by school administrators, guidance counselors, teachers, parents, social workers, and other

school-related staff members. Providing opportunities for parents to function as learners, teachers, supporters, advocates, and communicators is essential (Epstein, 1987; Henderson, 1988).

SUMMARY

Parent and family involvement in schools has always been important, but the concept has gained more attention in recent years due to research theorists and new legislation. The state of the family is continually changing and evolving, and professionals must look at all types of families in different categories related to demographics, ethnic composition, and level of poverty in order to understand the population they are serving. These new definitions of family require us to reexamine the organization of parent- and family-involvement programs in schools. This chapter outlines the many reasons why parents and families might show a lack of participation and offers suggestions for how to evaluate and encourage involvement. Schools must display a commitment to involving parents and families in education and be willing to put measures in place to strive for success. Better parent and family involvement leads to better educational programs for students.

ACTIVITIES

1. Using the form provided (see "Classroom Data Form" in Appendix C; you can also use the slightly different "Student Census Form" referenced in chapter 3 and found in Appendix C if the students are old enough to fill it out themselves) or one you develop yourself, aggregate the data for children in your class or school. Ask:

   a. What percentage of the children in your class (school) live in a single-parent family?
   b. What is the most frequent month of birth for the children in your class?
   c. What percentage of the families have
      ➤ a phone?
      ➤ a car?
      ➤ a VCR?

➤ a DVD player?
➤ cable television?
➤ a computer?
➤ mail delivered to the home?
➤ magazines delivered to the home?
➤ newspaper delivered to the home?

d. What percentage of the children are living with an uncle, aunt, grandparents, or other family members?
e. For each of the students, how many other children are living in the same home?
f. When you have compiled the results, evaluate them to learn more about the population you are serving. Be sensitive to your students and be aware of their demographic backgrounds.

2. Send home with your students the two parent/guardian surveys found in Appendix C ("Survey for Parents/Guardians: Interest in Parent/Guardian Group Meetings" and "Survey for Parents/ Guardians of Children With Disabilities: Strengths and Needs"). Encourage parents and guardians to fill out these forms so that you can better plan parent/guardian programs. When you have a number of forms returned to you, plan the appropriate programs that will be of interest to the population you are serving.

3. To better understand the level of parent and family involvement in your class or school, fill out "Survey for Professionals: Evaluating Parent and Family Involvement" found in Appendix C. Encourage colleagues to complete the survey as well. When you have a number of forms completed, conduct a meeting in which you discuss the results. Evaluate the level of parent and family involvement your class or school now has and consider suggestions on how to improve the level and encourage more involvement.

REFERENCES

Bailey, D. B., Jr., Buysse, V., Edmondson, R., & Smith, T. M. (1992). Creating family-centered services in early intervention: Perceptions of professionals in four states. *Exceptional Children, 58*(4), 298–309.

Benard, B. (1991). *Fostering resiliency in kids: Protective factors in the family, school and community.* Portland: OR: Western Center for Drug-Free Schools and Communities.

Benard, B. (1993). Fostering resiliency in kids. *Educational Leadership, 51*(3), 44–48.

Carson, C. C., Huelskamp, R. M., & Woodall, T. D. (1993). Perspectives on education in America: An annotated briefing (April 1992). *Journal of Educational Research, 86*(5), 259–311.

Chapman, W. (1991). The Illinois experience: State grants to improve schools through parent involvement. *Phi Delta Kappan, 72*(5), 355–358.

Chavkin, N. F. (2000). Family and community involvement policies: Teachers can lead the way. *Clearing House,* 287–290.

Children's Defense Fund. (2003). Retrieved March 9, 2003, from http://www.childrensdefense.org/

Children's Defense Fund. (2005). Chapter 1: Family income and jobs. The state of America's children ® 2005. Retrieved on December 13, 2005, from http://www.childrensdefense.org/publications/greenbook/Greenbook_2005_chpt1.pdf

Chrispeels, J. H., Fernandez, B., & Preston, J. (1990). *Home and school partners in student success: A handbook for principals and staff.* San Diego: San Diego City Schools, Parent Involvement Programs, Community Relations and Integration Services Division.

Clemetson, L. (2003). Hispanics now largest minority, census shows. *New York Times.* Retrieved February 9, 2003, from http://www.nytimes.com/2003/01/22/national/22CENS.html?ex=1044260100&ei=1&en=421fc205493b7d7b

Coleman, J. S. (1991). *Parent involvement in education: Policy perspectives* [microform]. Washington, DC: U.S. Department of Education, Office of Educational Research and Improvement.

Coulter, M. L., Johnson, J. J., & Innis, V. L. (1991). *Selected Florida counties early intervention project: The family perspective.* Tampa: University of South Florida, College of Public Health.

Davies, D. (1991). Schools reaching out: Family, school, and community partnerships for student success. *Phi Delta Kappan, 72*(5), 376–382.

Davies, D., Burch, P., & Johnson, V. (1992). *Portrait of schools reaching out: Report of a survey on practices and policies of family-community-school collaboration.* Boston: Center on Families, Communities, Schools and Children's Learning; Institute for Responsible Education. (ERIC Document Reproduction Service Center No. ED 353 701)

Davis, D. T., Kroth, R., James, A., & Van Curren, S. (1991). *Family involvement guides* (2nd ed.). Plantation, FL: South Atlantic Regional Resource Center.

Edge, D. (1993). *Understanding the principles of the changing family structure* [videotape]. Greensboro, NC.

Edge, D., & Franken, M. (1996). *Building parent and community involvement in education: Importance of research in parent involvement* (part one of three part series) [video]. Louisville, KY: Kentucky Education Television and University of Louisville.

Epstein, J. L. (1987, July). Parent involvement: State agencies should lead the way. *Community Education Journal,* pp. 4–10.

Epstein, J. (1990). School and family connections: Theory, research, and implications for integrating sociologies of education and family. In D. G. Unger & M. B. Sussman (Eds.), *Families in community settings: Interdisciplinary perspectives* (pp. 99–124). New York: Haworth.

Greenwood, G. E., & Hickman, C. W. (1991). Research and practice in parent involvement: implications for teacher education . *Elementary School Journal, 91*(3), 279.

Hales, M., & Carlson, L. B. (1992). *Issues and trends in special education.* Lexington, KY: Federal Resource Center for Special Education.

Hall, S. J., & Henderson, A. T. (1990). Uniting schools and families. *Community Education Journal, 18* (Fall), 18–22.

Hanson, M. J., & Lynch, E. W. (1992). Family diversity: Implications for policy and practice. *Topics in Early Childhood Special Education, 12*(3), 283–306.

Henderson, A. T. (1987). *The evidence continues to grow: Parent involvement improves student achievement (An annotated bibliography).* Columbia, MO: National Committee for Citizens in Education Special Report. (ERIC Document Reproduction Service Center No. ED 315 199)

Henderson, A. T. (1988). Parents are a school's best friends. *Phi Delta Kappan, 70*(2), 148–153.

Hobbs, N. (1978). Classification options: A conversation with Nicholas Hobbs on exceptional children. *Exceptional Children, 44,* 494–497

Hodgkinson, H. L. (1992). *A demographic look at tomorrow.* Washington, DC: Institute for Educational Leadership, Center for Demographic Policy. (ERIC Document Reproduction Service Center No. ED 359 087)

Hodgkinson, H. (2000). Educational demographics: What teachers should know. *Educational Leadership, 58*(4). Retrieved March 4, 2003, from http://www.ascd.org/readingroom/edlead/0012/hodgkinson.html

Institute for Responsive Education. (2003). Retrieved March 5, 2003, from http://www.responsiveeducation.org/home.html

Kroth, R., & Otteni, H. (1985). Parent education programs that work: A model. *Focus on Exceptional Children, 15*(8), 1–16.

National PTA. (1992, April). *For our children: Parents & families in education. Results of the National Parent Involvement Summit.* Chicago: National PTA. Retrieved March 2, 2003, from http://www.pta.org/

O'Connell, J. C., & Sontag, E. (1992, Spring). Parental choice and early intervention: A proactive policy of reform. *Special Education Leadership Review*, pp. 97–113.

Ramirez, A. Y. (2001). Parent involvement is like apple pie. *High School Journal, 85*(1). Retrieved January 13, 2003, from University of Louisville's Psychology and Behavioral Sciences Database http://library.louisville.edu/

Rich, D. (2003). MegaSkills® education online: Academic development & character education. Retrieved June 1, 2003, from http://www.megaskillshsi.org/default.htm

U.S. Department of Education. (2003). Retrieved January 25, 2003, from http://www.ed.gov

White, K. R., Taylor, M. J., & Moss, V. D. (1992). Does research support claims about the benefits of involving parents in early intervention programs? *Review of Educational Research, 62*(1), 91–125.

2

The Mirror Model

By the 1990s, most special education programs operated by local education agencies had made provisions for systematic parent contact through parent–teacher conferences, group meetings, or advisory committees. These activities stemmed primarily from federal legislation. The Education for All Handicapped Children Act of 1975, along with its later amendments, and the Individuals with Disabilities Education Act (IDEA) of 1990 further influenced the provision of parent-involvement services by local school agencies.

Many school districts always did have policies encouraging parent participation in school activities. Most school districts have set aside time for parent–teacher conferences at least once or twice a year at the elementary school level. Title programs such as Chapter I, Even Start, Jump Start, and Chapter II have required parent participation in school activities, including parent advisory groups, even to the extent of hiring personnel and establishing budgets for parent involvement. Most school systems have encouraged organizations such as the National Parent–Teacher Association or the National Parent–Teacher Organization to become involved in school programs.

Parents and professionals sometimes have questioned the effectiveness of these program activities. On the one hand, parents report that they are not welcomed into the school building and feel intimidated. On the other hand, professionals have reported that many parents are unrealistic and should be more understanding regarding financial matters and program needs. Many of the conflicts are a result of ineffective communication and lack of understanding on the part of parents and professionals alike.

The mirror model of parental involvement defines the parameters of a comprehensive parent-involvement program in a public school setting. The model is based on the premise that teachers are the greatest potential link between home and school and that, until teachers are acknowledged as key factors in the educational process, this enormous resource will not be unleashed for building healthy home–school partnerships. At the same time, this model is based on a philosophy that parents are capable of managing most of their own behavior and that they are willing and able to take responsibility for much of their children's growth and development.

The helping professions, including educators, tend to take ownership of many of the problems of their clientele (students) rather than take the time to help the parents learn to be their own case managers. Many years ago, Nicholas Hobbs (1978) said it well:

> Parents have to be recognized as the special educators, the true experts on their children; and professional people—teachers, pediatricians, psychologists, and others—have to learn to be consultants to parents.

ASSUMPTIONS OF THE MIRROR MODEL

The mirror model of parent involvement was developed with the following assumptions involving money, time, personnel, and the heterogeneity of parents (Kroth & Otteni, 1985).

Money

In designing a program, money is always an issue. Money will be lacking to do all the things parents want or professionals can deliver. Financial constraints inevitably force program personnel into choices. For example, producing videotapes for small groups would be nice, as would providing parents with take-home computers, but few school districts could even consider these possibilities.

Taking another example—counseling or a therapeutic parent group usually involves only a few parents and therefore becomes an expensive component. In a money crunch, in-depth services for just a few people are often the first things to go. Therefore, in developing services, this component must be placed in perspective. In some cases, referral to other community agencies is the best solution. Essentially, this component is a matter of spending the money where the biggest payoff can be achieved.

Time

Even if money were not an issue, time most likely would be. Time is limited for teachers to prepare for interaction with parents and to actually call or talk with parents. The amount of time parents have for attending meetings and talking with teachers is limited, too. In most families, setting aside time for parent–child interaction means rearranging their priorities. The same challenge arises in teachers and related personnel arranging to spend more time to work with parents. There is never enough time!

Personnel

We make the assumption that there are not—and probably never will be—enough trained people to facilitate interactions between parents and teachers and to train parents in strategies to work with their children more effectively. A continuing lack of teacher preparation affects the services that can be offered.

Heterogeneity of Parents

Most professionals recognize that parents of children with disabilities do not comprise a homogeneous group. Still, almost everything designed for parents violates this assumption. Teachers who are adept at individualizing programs for children seldom individualize for parents. In addition to variables of ethnicity, religion, education, and income, a wide variety of attitudes, values, and childrearing practices must be taken into account. And not all people have the same priorities. Some parents struggle to survive. One mother said, "I have eight children, my husband has shot at me twice, I'm on welfare, and I'm having a hard time keeping clean clothes on my kids and food on the table. I just can't come to your meetings. Besides, I don't have transportation."

Even though family structure has changed over time, professionals often act as if the family is as homogenous as it was years ago. The "Norman Rockwell" family—in which the father went off to work in the morning and the mother stayed home with the two children, a dog named Spot, and a cat named Mittens—represents only a fraction of family constellations today (see chapter 1). Meanwhile, too many conferences, IEP meetings, and other meetings still are being held during the parents' workday, when parents have trouble attending.

Parents' educational levels are discrepant, too. Some parents can read, and others cannot. Their primary language may not be English, yet materials sent home unconsciously assume that all parents can read at the upper high school level. Some of the pamphlets sent home to explain services (e.g., diagnosticians, occupational therapy) are written at the college level. Heterogeneity of parents is a complex issue that can confuse and confound attempts at communication between school and home. Recognizing and attempting to provide for the wide variance among parents is an underlying assumption of the mirror model.

NEEDS AND STRENGTHS

The mirror model assumes that all parents have needs and all parents have strengths. Failing to recognize the strength factor in parents ignores a valuable resource. Similarly, all parents have some needs, many of which are addressed in the law, but parents often are unaware of how the laws can serve their needs.

In the mirror model, Figure 2.1, the top half addresses parent needs and the bottom half reflects their strengths. The left side of the model indicates what parents need as well as the strengths they can bring to the school. The right side of the model indicates how these needs and strengths might be accommodated, along with some suggested activities.

The assumption is that all parents need some things but not all parents need all things. Accordingly, the various levels illustrate the relative numbers of parents affected at the different levels. The emphasis of this book is on services and activities at Levels 1 and 2, because these levels influence the greater number of parents and teachers. This is not to downgrade Level 3 and Level 4 activities but, rather, to put them in perspective.

Needs

Level 4 Needs

One of the most expensive services a school district can offer to families is therapy. It is time-consuming, serves only a few families at a time, and usually requires professionals with specialized expertise. The percentage of parents needing this service is unknown but probably is no more than 5% of the total population of parents. For a large district, this could translate to a substantial number, but in terms of overall priorities, it still would rank low in needs. The preferred role of school personnel at this level may be that of referral to other community agencies.

Although the number of parents requiring this level of service is not directly related to the severity of their child's disability, some professionals believe that parents of children with severe emotional disturbance may need more counseling or group therapy than other parents. This might be related to Bell's bidirectional theory (Bell, 1968), which suggests that just as adults influence children's behavior, children influence adults' behavior. Therefore, disturbed children can produce disturbed parents. School personnel should be able to recognize parents'

			What	How
Parent Needs	Few	Level 4	Therapy—intensive education and support	Provide or refer to counseling, group therapy
	Some	Level 3	Skill training in management; interaction with system; child-rearing	Conduct parent education groups; bibliotherapy; parent support groups
	Most	Level 2	Knowledge of child's progress, environment, friends; assistance with parent–home programs	Utilize notes home, daily/weekly reporting systems, conferences, phone calls, home visits
	All	Level 1	Parents' and children's rights, consent to test and place; school policies and procedures; school and class events	Develop newsletters, handbooks; hold conferences
Parent Strengths	All	Level 1	Special knowledge of child's strengths and needs, family characteristics, and aspirations	Conduct intake interviews; hold conferences; utilize questionnaires
	Most	Level 2	Short-term assistance with projects at school, projects at home; special knowledge of world of work	Telephone for PTAs or parent meetings; assist with meeting arrangements; reinforce at-home or school work; talk to classes at school
	Some	Level 3	Leadership skills, with time, energy, and special knowledge to →	Serve on parent advisory groups, task force, as classroom volunteers, tutors; write newsletters; engage in fund-raising
	Few	Level 4	Special skills, knowledge, time, energy, and commitment for leadership training to →	Lead parent groups; work on curriculum committees; develop parent-to-parent programs

FIGURE 2.1

Mirror Model of Parent Involvement

need for therapy and match parents with the appropriate community services.

Another service that relatively few parents need is help with relocation. Educators can help parents access services that will facilitate their move from one community to another. Often, a couple of phone calls can clear up these parents' questions and concerns. Other school services at this level might include preparing community directories, guides to community services, and other handouts for parents. Directing parents to the appropriate service may be the most important service at this level, and this does not drain financial resources.

Level 3 Needs

Parent group work is popular, and teachers can access various resources for designing, implementing, and evaluating parent groups (National PTA, 2003; Popkin, 1993). Well-designed commercial materials are available, complete with leaders' guides, workbooks, posters, and various supplementary materials. Some of these programs are discussed briefly in later chapters. Many programs are available for parents, too, some in kit form.

Over time, perhaps 20% of the parents can be expected to attend skill training or support groups. Thus, with a class of 10 children, a teacher might expect two or three parents to participate in three or four sessions of a parent group. In lieu of offering this service through the school, many communities have established support groups that are publicized in the newspapers or the yellow pages of the phone book.

The parent population should be analyzed for the needs the program is designed to fulfill. For more than 20 years, the Parent Involvement Center in Albuquerque, New Mexico, and the Parent Education and Resource Center at the University of Louisville have developed many parent group programs. These groups were designed to teach parents how to

> ➤ test their own children,
> ➤ write IEPs,
> ➤ make nutritional snacks,
> ➤ help their children in transitions between programs,
> ➤ listen to their children read,
> ➤ conduct meetings,
> ➤ participate in writing grants,

➤ access library resources,
➤ use the Internet,
➤ be active participants in conferences,
➤ understand their rights under law,
➤ be their own case managers,
➤ develop reading programs at home, and
➤ access the school through interactive television.

Parent programs grow out of observed and expressed needs. Educators can carry out a needs/strengths assessment, or they can become attuned to the needs parents express in everyday contacts. One of the best ways to learn is through teaching, so parents and educators alike might benefit most by using their time to teach others to design and run these groups.

Level 2 Needs

Most parents of children with disabilities want to know more about the causes of their children's disabilities, how their children are doing in their school placements, and what they as parents can do to help. They usually want this information from the primary source—the teacher, the doctor, the diagnostician—and they want it in understandable terms.

Because these needs affect about 80% of the parent population, we should spend time determining how best to receive information from parents and how to convey meaningful data to parents. Teacher skill in delivering sensitive information is essential at this level. Effective communication is necessary for building good home–school partnerships and programs. Improving communication between teachers and parents is a primary goal of this book. To this end, these pages include much practical information on handbooks, handouts, conferencing tips and skills, daily report card systems, and similar means to facilitate understanding between parents and teachers. Some tip sheets and informational sheets are included as examples in the appropriate chapters and in Appendix A.

One way to convey information to large audiences is through topical conferences. The Parent Involvement Center in the Albuquerque Public Schools and the Family Resource Centers in the Commonwealth of Kentucky (2003) are two sponsors of topical presentations. Topics that seem to be of widespread interest are discipline, reading to your child, divorce, teen pregnancy, sex education, drug and alcohol use, adolescence, and stress management. Good materials are available to help in workshops on discipline, in particular (e.g., Popkin, 1993).

Many parents regard teachers as their main source of information and support. The more skilled the teacher is in this role, the more satisfaction parents will derive, and the better the programming will be for children.

Level 1 Needs

In keeping with state and federal law, all parents are to be apprised of their rights and the rights of their children. Because this need affects all children and parents, school district personnel must have as a priority allocating time and resources for activities and materials that explain these rights.

Many school district administrators are apprehensive about conveying this information, as it is not simple to put into lay terms. The information does not always get conveyed clearly, and school personnel need to do a better job here. Sometimes parents sign the various permission slips and forms required by law but are unaware of what they have signed.

Many of the handbooks and supplementary materials that schools prepare for parents are not checked for reading level. A sampling of materials was found to be at the 10th- to 11th-grade reading level, and explanatory material on supplementary services was written at the college level. For parents who don't speak English or don't speak it well, even translating the materials into their language may not help. For example, a translation might use textbook Spanish that differs from the regional Spanish the parents use. Because Level 1 needs affect all parents, sufficient resources should be put into developing materials and strategies to fulfill this need.

Strengths

Level 1 Strengths

All parents know things about their children or family structure from which professionals can benefit in their work with children with disabilities. Skilled professionals can elicit this information through good interviewing skills or observational techniques. They should keep in mind that parents of children with disabilities may be working with a large number of professionals—as many as 12 or even more—because the children are assigned to a number of specialists for individual assistance. Sorting out the specializations and the people involved and meeting the time and other demands can be overwhelming to parents. Even well-meaning professionals with exemplary programs may affect the family negatively if the demands of the programs exceed the strengths of the parents.

School personnel can best utilize parents' strengths at this level by putting themselves in the parents' shoes. Teachers and others should do all they can to make parents feel comfortable enough to reveal their knowledge of their children that can benefit programs for them. And they should try to simplify the maze of personnel and services to take the burden off the parents.

Level 2 Strengths

Most parents have the wherewithal to do more than merely provide school personnel with information. For example, parents may be willing to set up a program at home that reinforces what the teacher is doing in the classroom (e.g., reward growth according to the child's daily or weekly report card system). Or parents might be willing to call other parents as part of a telephone tree.

School personnel should be careful not to overuse parents who volunteer, as they can easily get overworked. Just like teachers, parents can burn out. In capitalizing on parents' willingness to help, sensitive teachers allow them to "take a breather" once in a while.

Level 3 Strengths

Parents represent a rich source of potential assistance for children, professionals, and other parents. Some parents are willing and able to assist in the classroom, teaching children directly or helping teachers. Others serve on advisory boards or participate in parent panels.

Sometimes parents are asked to participate in roles for which they have not been prepared. If parents are asked to be an aide in the classroom, for example, the expectations should be made clear. If parents are asked to serve on committees or boards, the roles should be clarified and training offered if needed.

Level 4 Strengths

Parents long have been recognized as the major sources of strength for other parents. Examples of parent support groups are Parents Reaching

Out (2003) in Albuquerque, another in Louisville, Kentucky (see Learning Disabilities Association of Kentucky, 2003), and one sponsored by the Autism Society of Kentuckiana (ASK, 2003). These groups are made up of parents who provide support for each other, produce newsletters, keep an eye on legislative bills, provide speakers for interested groups, and are available for the unique services that parents need from time to time.

Large communities have a wide range of support groups, and school personnel can help parents locate these groups. The number of parents who are not aware of organizations such as the Association for Children and Adults with Learning Disabilities, the Arc, or Parents Anonymous is surprising. See Appendix D for these national organizations and more.

SUMMARY

The mirror model of parental involvement provides the parameters of a comprehensive parent-involvement program. The underlying assumptions of the mirror model of parent involvement are as follows:

> There never will be enough money to do the things that need to be done.
> Time always will be lacking for parents and professionals alike to work toward desired goals.
> Even with training programs, there never will be enough trained personnel to satisfy all needs entirely.
> Parents of exceptional children are a heterogeneous group and should be treated individually.
> All parents of exceptional children have strengths to be utilized, and all have needs to be met.

The top half of the mirror model addresses parents' needs, and the bottom half, their strengths. These needs and strengths are depicted in four levels each, ranging from the strengths and needs of just a few parents to those of all parents. The left side of the model indicates what the strengths and needs are, and the right side gives some suggestions on how these might be accommodated through various activities. The mirror model provides the conceptual framework from which to analyze and formulate comprehensive parent-involvement programs.

Figure 2.2 is a sample analysis form developed by the Parent Center in Albuquerque, New Mexico. This form can be used to check an existing program or to utilize in planning a new program.

ACTIVITIES

1. Conduct a family study of yourself or one of the children in your class. Ask:
   a. What is the family composition?
   b. Where are the family's needs and strengths?
   c. To whom does the family turn for help?
   d. What are the family's expectations?
   e. Are the members of the family assertive enough to get their wishes fulfilled?
   f. What are the child's strong and weak points?
   g. What are the family's strong and weak points?

2. Analyze your own program, using the form provided in Figure 2.2.
   a. Is your program comprehensive?
   b. On which things might you work first?
   c. List the resources available in your community.

3. By reviewing your records and personal knowledge, analyze the needs of a parent in your class or program.
   a. What are the needs for the parent as you see them?
   b. What are the parent's strengths?
   c. Do you spot any parent(s) whose strengths you might utilize to help other parents?
   d. How heterogeneous is your parent population?

4. Conduct a demographic analysis of the families served by your school and classroom.

5. Generate activities that could fit at different levels of the mirror model.

6. Develop the framework for a comprehensive parent-involvement program for your class.

Teacher:	Often	Sometimes	Seldom	Priority	Projected Start Date	Person(s) Responsible
1. Provides written information on consent to test.						
2. Provides written information on consent to place.						
3. Provides written information on criteria to place.						
4. Provides written information on due-process procedures.						
5. Provides written information on availability of child's records.						
6. Has regularly scheduled conferences.						
7. Involves parents in planning the IEP.						
8. Has a newsletter.						
9. Has parent information group meetings.						
10. Uses daily/weekly report cards.						
11. Makes home visits.						
12. Has class handouts.						
13. Makes phone calls systematically.						
14. Uses "good news" notes.						
15. Interprets test results.						
16. Arranges skill training parent workshops (behavior modification, PET [Parent Effectiveness Training], problem solving).						
17. Takes family history.						
18. Elicits child's strengths from parents.						
19. Conducts parental needs and strengths assessment.						
20. Has "room" parents.						
21. Has parents assist on field trips, parties, etc.						
22. Has parent advisory groups.						
23. Has parent volunteers in the classroom.						
24. Involves parents in special-interest task forces (curriculum, discipline, needs and strengths assessment).						
25. Uses parents as co-partners for other parents.						
26. Uses parents as workshop leaders.						
27. Other:						

FIGURE 2.2
Parent-Involvement Program: Analysis Sheet

REFERENCES

ASK. Retrieved 2003 from http://www.ask-lou.org/

Association for Gifted and Talented Students. (2003). Retrieved February 1, 2003, from www.nagc.org

Association for Retarded Citizens. (2003). Retrieved February 1, 2003, from http://www.thearc.org/

Bell, R. Q. (1968). A reinterpretation of the direction of effects in studies of socialization. *Psychological Review, 75,* 81–95.

Family Resource Centers in the Commonwealth of Kentucky. (2003). Retrieved April 28, 2003, from http://cfc.state.ky.us/agencies/FRYSC/

Hobbs, N. (1978). Classification options: A conversation with Nicholas Hobbs on exceptional children. *Exceptional Children, 44,* 494-497.

Kroth, R., & Otteni, H. (1985). *Communicating with parents of exceptional children: Improving parent-teacher relationships* (2nd ed.). Denver: Love Publishing.

Learning Disabilities Association of Kentucky. (2003). Retrieved April 28, 2003, from http://www.ldaofky.org/

National PTA. (2003). Retrieved from http:///www.pta.org/

Parents Reaching Out. (2003). Retrieved February 11, 2003, from http://www.parentsreachingout.org/

Popkin, M.H. (1993). *Active parenting today: For parents of 2 to 12 year olds* (Parent's guide). Marietta, GA: Active Parenting Publishers. (ERIC Document Reproduction Service No. ED 356 055)

3

Family Dynamics

"I just found out my son is disabled."

"Oh, I'm sorry. I know just how you feel."

"Do you have an exceptional child?"

"No, but..."

I n attempting to be helpful to parents of children and youth with disabilities, we may imply that we know how they feel. Unless we have been there, though, we cannot have the same feelings. Even the parents of the same child have different reactions to the birth or identification of a child with disabilities (Hanson & Lynch, 1992). Therefore, when parents of children with disabilities share experiences, they may have a great deal in common with each other but still differ as a result of filtering their messages through their own past experiences, emotions, and thoughts. A parent who has had a sibling with Down syndrome will view the diagnosis of a child with Down syndrome much differently than a parent who has had virtually no experience with exceptional children or adults. When and how the child was diagnosed, the severity of the disability, the visibility of the problem, where the child is in the family constellation, and the culture and mores surrounding these conditions influence parents' feelings.

Despite these differences, most parents and professionals report certain similarities in the reactions parents have when a child is diagnosed as having a disability. Therefore, some understanding of family dynamics surrounding disabilities will aid teachers as they work with the families in parent-involvement programs, IEPs, ISFPs, and other activities.

THEORIES OF PARENTAL REACTION

Two theories that explain parents' reactions to the realization that their child has a disability are discussed here. Both address the same observable behavior, but they define it in different ways. Probably the best known is the *psychological stages theory*. A lesser known but relevant viewpoint is that of *chronic sorrow*.

Psychological Stages Theory

Lamberti and Detmer (1993) proposed that mourning results from any significant shock to the living system (e.g., being in a car accident, divorcing, failing a class, or giving birth to an "imperfect" child). Certain defense mechanisms are built in, however, as natural and normal protection from psychological damage. These defenses follow a fairly predictable sequence of stages. In the context of the diagnosis of a child with disabilities, the psychological stages allow the parents and families to heal and learn to cope.

Elizabeth Kübler-Ross (1969), credited with originating the stages-of-grief theory, is probably best known for her book *On Death and Dying*. In a later interview (1981), she said, "You have to understand I did not learn about the grief-cycle from dying patients. I learned it from all my years of working with blind people and their parents, and multiple handicapped, retarded patients, first in Switzerland and then here."

Duncan (1977) adapted Kübler-Ross's stages of death and dying in grief theory to families of children with disabilities. Various authors (e.g., McCollum, 1984; Moses, 1981; Parkes, 1988; Stewart, 1986; Witcher, 1989) have expanded on these stages as related to the losses attached to disability.

Stage 1: Denial

After a loss, the first reaction is shock, followed by denial. Denial is like saying, "If I don't pay any attention to it, it might go away."

When a teacher has to tell parents that their child is failing or should be referred for special testing, the parents may act as if they did not hear what the teacher said. They may ignore the advice, or they may go doctor-shopping for another diagnosis. Although the professionals may think otherwise, the denial stage is productive. It gives parents some space to think, process, and absorb the reality that their child has a disability.

Many professionals think the denial stage is the most frustrating stage for both parents and professionals alike. Parents may claim they never were told certain things when the professional knows they were. Professionals may feel personally rejected when the parent is actually rejecting the diagnosis. Parents may think the professionals are not being honest, and each may become impatient with the other. Parents, too, may resent the bearer of bad news.

Although the psychological stage theory is sequential, many parents report going in and out of denial, depending on the external environment. One mother said, "Every time we change schools, I think maybe if I don't say anything about it, they won't notice." As long as the denial stage does not drag on, it is considered a natural reaction. Time, patience, and the nonjudgmental repetition of information are essential to working with parents at this stage.

Stage 2: Anger

Anger can take a variety of forms and have a variety of targets. Clearly, being angry at a child with disabilities is not acceptable. And a teacher may wonder why a parent who has been cooperative is suddenly angry with the program or services for their child. Those who are not aware of the anger stage accompanying the frustrations and anxiety of having a child with disabilities might get caught up in it. Knowing the dynamics involved, the professionals should allow parents to express their anger instead of becoming defensive and taking the anger personally (Witcher, 1989). What is really needed is some quality listening to the parents.

Although anger is considered a stage, it does not always go away, or it may appear and reappear. In manifestations of anger, the two parents may fight with each other, and both may fight with their other children. Siblings may feel a great deal of resentment toward their brother or sister with disabilities, which may lead to feelings of guilt. As with the other stages, the professional is urged to show patience and understanding.

Stage 3: Bargaining

During the bargaining stage, the parents have accepted the diagnosis, at least in part, but they have not accepted the prognosis. In this stage the parent may say, "If I work hard, my child will get well." Parents are willing to try a variety of cures, with the hope that one of the programs will prove successful.

At this time, parents often go into high gear, getting involved in causes and programs for children with disabilities. Again, this reaction is normal. It helps to control anxiety and make parents feel productive. It also can further the overall advocacy of services for children with disabilities.

Stage 4: Depression

Feelings of guilt and inadequacy associated with having a child with a disability often lead to depression. The disability does not go away. By now, the parents may have tried a variety of programs and have received second and third opinions, and the child still has the disability.

This stage, too, is a necessary part of the grieving process. Parents may feel both hopeless and helpless and, as a result, seem paralyzed with inaction. From a professional's point of view, this is a difficult stage to help parents through. Encouragement often seems to fall on deaf ears. Professionals often report that they would rather deal with parents' anger because at least they get a response with which to work.

Stage 5: Acceptance (Coping)

The final stage is usually described as one of acceptance, but some authors (Faerstein, 1986; Featherstone, 1980; Moses, 1981; Witcher, 1989) have viewed it as coping rather than acceptance. As Featherstone pointed out,

> There is nothing final about acceptance.... The most important difference between mourning a death and mourning a disability is that the child in question is not dead at all.... While death provides a moment's respite from ordinary demands, disability generates new tasks and necessities. (pp. 231–234)

In any case, this stage reflects coping behaviors suggesting that the parent has come to grips with the reality of the disability. At the same time, parents must maintain hope. This can be the driving force that keeps people going. As a parent once said, "The difference between professionals and parents is that professionals want to talk in terms of probabilities and parents want to talk about possibilities. It is the possibility that keeps us going."

Usefulness of the Theory

In sum, the psychological stage theory suffers somewhat by the implication that parents move neatly from one stage to another and finally arrive at a stable state of acceptance. Reality dictates a different pattern (Lamberti & Detmer, 1993; Perkins & Harris, 1990). Many parents report that they never were in denial that they had a child with a disability. They say that in actuality they were the first ones to identify the condition and actually had a hard time getting a professional to confirm their diagnosis. Also, many parents report having reexperienced some of the stages as their children reached certain milestones, such as moving from middle school to high school. These stages seem to be revisited throughout the child's and the parents' lives. Knowing these limitations, the theory still has much value.

Chronic Sorrow Theory

The second theory suggests that the grieving process is not time-bound but, rather, continues throughout the lives of the parents and the child with a disability. Both theories recognize the initial shock upon learning the diagnosis, but the difference is in the explanation of the subsequent events and feelings (Chapman, 1992).

If one accepts the chronic sorrow view, the implications are that parents need support throughout their lives. This suggests that a continuum of services should be provided and that parents will need services appropriate to the child's transitions. Even well-adjusted parents become anxious when their children reach certain educational or life-change transitions. Anger may resurface, and depression is common. Acceptance may be elusive.

Regardless of the theory one chooses to adopt, parents of children with disabilities obviously go through trying times. Familiarity with the theories and stages of loss and grief give teachers a tool to help them react in appropriate ways.

PARENTAL AWARENESS

Concerned about parents' levels of awareness of their children's disabling conditions, professionals frequently take the role of primary informant. A social worker or a diagnostician, for example, has an intake conference to obtain relevant information. Sometimes the parent is asked to respond to items on a behavior-rating profile or on background information forms.

Some conclusions have emerged in the research over time. The mothers often score their children higher than the children's actual tested scores, although the differences are not always statistically significant. For example, whenever self-concept is the issue, the mothers tend to think their children have a lower self-concept than the children report they do.

The effects of a child with disabilities on family dynamics are difficult to access. Some parents report that the birth of a child with disabilities has strengthened their marriage and brought the family closer together, whereas others report the opposite. Whatever the effect, the diagnosis of a disabling condition certainly will have some effect on the family. Schedules will be altered, finances affected, interpersonal relationships changed. Parents may even decide to move to communities that have suitable programs for their children.

Therapy may take time away from the other children or from the mother or father. One mother reported that she had done "everything you professionals told me to do. I took my child to speech therapy, physical therapy, a special preschool, and worked with him in the evenings and on weekends. In the process, I forgot I had a husband— and one day I didn't." Another mother living in a rural area had to take her child with a disability to a large city two or three times a week. On one of these trips, her other child asked, "Are you ever going to have time to play with me again?"

The divorce rate in families of children with behavior disorders is extremely high, compared to other families. Parents report considerable stress in their marriages and family relationships. Siblings and relatives often add to the stress of rearing a child with disabilities. The extent to which the child's behavior affects family relationships and the extent to which family relationships affect the child's behavior remain unknown. Perhaps it is enough for school personnel to recognize some of the family dynamics so they can improve their communication and services to the benefit of children with disabilities and their families.

SUMMARY

When a child with disabilities is born into a family or diagnosed at a later date, the event is traumatic and has an effect on the family dynamics. From one point of view, the event is regarded as the "death" of a normal child and the parents go through a period of mourning. In this theory, the psychological stages are predictable and are similar to the stages described by Kübler-Ross (1969) in her classic book *On Death and Dying*. After the initial shock, parents can be expected to progress from denial to anger to bargaining to depression and, finally, acceptance, or coping. In reality, parents probably go in and out of these stages from time to time, depending on external conditions and developmental changes.

Another theory is that of chronic sorrow. After the initial event and the subsequent shock, parents are continually affected by the child's disability and still may be angry, or have recurring anger years later. The child is a living symbol of the loss and sorrow they have suffered.

The birth or diagnosis of a child with disabilities affects family dynamics and family structure in many ways, involving finances, schedules, time demands, and interpersonal relationships. Professionals' awareness of these impacts should lead to better communication with these parents and families.

ACTIVITIES

1. Interview one teacher and one parent of an exceptional child, using the questions and topics in item 2 as a basis for their involvement with each other regarding the education of the child with a disability.
2. Convene a panel of parents, siblings, or grandparents of a child with a disability.

   ➤ Possible questions for the panel members:
   a. What is your child's condition?
   b. What is the family structure?
   c. Who informed you of the child's condition, and how was it presented?
   d. What are the most difficult issues for you in rearing (or living or interacting with) a child with disabilities?

   ➤ Possible topics for panel members:
   a. Effects on family members (i.e., parents, siblings, other relatives) and on the marriage
   b. Changes in family lifestyle
   c. Financial concerns
   d. Medical concerns
   e. Employment issues
   f. Transportation problems

3. Read and discuss selected articles in *Exceptional Parent* magazine.
4. Read books authored by parents of children with disabilities. Access the Internet for current lists of books and resources.
5. Analyze the family dynamics of children in your classroom, using "Student Census Form" in Appendix C.

REFERENCES

Chapman, D.A. (1992). Understanding the grief process. *INSCOM Journal*, (Oct.-Nov), pp. 12–14.

Duncan, D. (1977). The impact of a handicapped child upon the family. *Training Model Session*, Harrisburg, PA.

Faerstein, L. M. (1986). Coping and defense mechanisms of mothers of learning disabled children. *Journal of Learning Disabilities, 19*(1), 8–11.

Featherstone, H. (1980). *A difference in the family. Life with a disabled child.* New York: Basic Books.

Hanson, M. J., & Lynch, E. W. (1992). Family diversity: Implications for policy and practice. *Topics in Early Childhood Special Education, 12*(3), 283–306.

Hollingsworth, C. E., & Pasnaw, R. O. (1977). *The family in mourning: A guide for health professionals.* New York: Grune & Stratton.

Kübler-Ross, E. (1969). *On death and dying.* New York: Macmillan.

Kübler-Ross, E. (1981). Interview. *Playboy, 76.*

Lamberti, J. W., & Detmer, C. M. (1993). Model of family grief assessment and treatment. *Death Studies, 17*(1).

McCollum, A. T. (1984). Grieving over the lost dream. *Exceptional Parent, 14*(1), 9–12.

Moses, K. (1981). *Bridging the gaps.* [video]. Chicago, IL: Association for Retarded Citizens.

Parkes, C. M. (1988). Research: Bereavement. *Omega: Journal of Death and Dying, 18*(4), 365–377.

Perkins, H. W., & Harris, L. B. (1990). Familial bereavement and health in adult life course perspective. *Journal of Marriage and the Family, 52(*1), 233–241.

Stewart, J.C. (1986). Counseling parents of exceptional children (2nd ed.). Columbus, OH: Charles E. Merrill Publishing.

Witcher, A. E. (1989). The grief process as experienced by parents of handicapped children. *Principal, 68*(4), 30–32.

Perceptions and Diversity of Values

"How was school today?"
"Fine."
"What did you do?"
"Nothing."
"Why are you an hour late?"
"I had to stay after school."
"Why?"
"For throwing rocks on the playground."

We form perceptions of others, right or wrong, in a heartbeat. Because we really don't know that person, our perceptions are likely to be wrong. A first glance that takes in some non-verbal body language can turn us on or off toward a person.

Messages go home from school every day via thousands of little messengers. Sometimes a child relates the day's events verbally, and other times transmits them nonverbally. A tear-stained face, torn jeans, a paper with a star or a "happy face"—these are messages that parents receive from school daily. From these bits of information, parents paint whole pictures of their child's school day. Simultaneously, teachers gather bits and pieces of information about the child's home from which they form opinions of the family. As a result, neither parents nor teachers are likely to have accurate perceptions of the school or the family.

CROSS-CULTURAL COMMUNICATION

A problem sometimes emerges in meetings with families who speak a language different from that used by educators and related profession-als. Often, the larger school systems, such as the Albuquerque Public Schools, have interpreters available to enable communication with parents.

The changing demography of the United States is presenting new challenges for all aspects of society, so "teachers need to be culturally aware and sensitive toward parents when discussing a child's disabili-ties. Parents may have attitudes and feelings about disabilities based on their cultural values" (Lupi & Tong, 2001, p. 4).

Self-Reflection

We all have our own unique ways of communicating, within a cultural framework. By the nature of their work, teachers, more than many other professionals, communicate with families from various cultural back-grounds. Therefore, teachers can benefit from self-reflecting on how they communicate, verbally and nonverbally, to determine whether they say or do things that parents from a different culture could misinterpret. In utilizing self-reflection, we have adapted the following suggestions from Lupi and Tong (2001).

1. Stay aware of and later jot down in a journal your verbal, physical, and facial behaviors when communicating with parents.
2. Recognizing that parents from another culture may take more time to assimilate and convey information, allow parents sufficient time to respond and to ask questions.
3. Consider how the situation and setting influence your communication and that of the parents. For example, might it be intimidating? Is the setting quiet and private?
4. Modify your language so it is appropriate to the parents' levels of understanding. This means cutting out jargon that may come naturally when conversing with other education professionals but has no meaning to parents.
5. Reflect upon your own cultural background and its influence on your verbal and nonverbal communication strategies.

Assumptions and Misperceptions

Sometimes the father paints a picture that is quite different from the mother's, although it includes the same bits of information. These differences may have a cultural component as well. The father might interpret his son's torn jeans as "all boy," whereas the mother may read the same sign as "poor little boy—he was picked on by school bullies." On the same day, the teacher might have focused on the boy's progress in schoolwork rather than how he gets along with schoolmates and think, "I'm glad Juan did the math himself today. I think he understands how to work the problems now."

The messages that children bring to school are no more complete or accurate than the ones they take home. Forgotten homework, the same shirt four days in a row, only candy bars for lunch, and yawns—these are signs that the teacher sees and interprets in drawing his or her picture of the child's home life.

Jumping to conclusions or making assumptions based on little evidence is more common than one would like to think. Occasionally being correct in one's assumptions may be enough for us to keep making largely incorrect assumptions. Again, keeping the lines of school–home communication open can help dispel misinterpretations.

Many factors influence perceptions—the quality of parent–teacher interaction, the process, and ultimately the outcome. Each participant brings to the exchange certain physical, emotional, and behavioral

Phil, an engaging kid with a big smile, was one of the shortest boys who tried out for basketball, but he made up for size with a lot of enthusiasm. His gym shirt looked as if it belonged to a big brother, and his tennis shoes were held together with broken shoestrings. The coach took a special interest in Phil because of his personality more than his basketball ability and kept him on the basketball team for that reason.

Concerned about Phil's decrepit uniform, the coach began looking into ways to get him a decent pair of basketball shoes to replace the tattered tennis shoes. Discussing the situation in the teacher's lounge one day, one of the teachers asked the coach, "What's his last name?" When the coach told him, the teacher laughed and said, "Why don't you call up his dad and ask him to buy Phil a new pair? He's the manager of Miller's Department Store."

characteristics and past history, all of which have an influence on perceptions and a potential effect on all school–home interactions. In some cases these characteristics generate such strong feelings that two people are not able to enter into a working relationship. One of the major factors affecting the parent–teacher relationship is the value system of each of the participants.

Understanding Differences in Values

> Understanding cultural values of the home and modifying behavior when meeting with family members is important [for teachers] to consider when developing the school-home relationship.
> (Lupi & Tong, 2001, p. 3)

The values that parents and teachers bring to interactions have been developed over the years through personal interchanges and relations with others, reinforcement of their histories, and contemplation. Because these values are so basic to each person, they are not often brought to the surface for reexamination. Knowledge of one's own values and the values of those with whom one is working can sidetrack potential conflicts (Brooks & Kann, 1992). To generalize about any group, societal, or individual values is becoming increasingly difficult.

Because we are a mobile society and have access to radio, television, movies, magazines, and the Internet, we have been exposed to numerous alternative styles of behaving. Trying to generalize a value system across a segment of people is no longer beneficial. To say that "Teenagers believe," "Chicanos value," "Blacks think," "Teachers regard," or "Parents consider" will probably miss as many who fall in the designated category as it will pinpoint.

> "Teachers...in keeping up with the changing demographics of North American schools, need to be aware of whether the school culture clashes with the students' home culture" (Lupi & Tong, 2001, p. 4).

This is perhaps the first major step in values clarification—coming to seeing ourselves as others see us. Then we can try to understand the value system of others and maybe eventually help parents and others understand their own value system.

VALUES CLARIFICATION

Understanding one's values is important because people often do not act on objective information (Chavkin, 1991). Logic suggests that the dieter standing nude on a scale in front of a full-length mirror with a calorie counter in hand would choose the lettuce salad over the hot fudge sundae. And logic prevails, right? Wrong! Even though using a daily or weekly report card system has a positive effect on children's academic and social growth, many general and special education teachers do not use such a system in their classrooms. Graphs and charts as a tool to measure child progress in the classroom have been shown to be effective in evaluating teaching techniques, but teachers often abandon the practice, pleading lack of time and competing responsibilities.

Value systems are complex and individualistic. The church-going citizen who drives ruthless business deals during the week but shuns the town drunk or prostitute who tries to attend church services raises the cry of "hypocrite." The better one understands one's own and others' value systems, the fewer judgments one is likely to make about apparent inconsistencies in behavior.

History of the Movement

The values clarification movement has enjoyed a great deal of popularity from the mid-1960s to the present. Sidney Simon, a pioneer who perhaps is the best known in this area, has coauthored a number of books introducing and explaining the concept and outlining strategies for clarifying values (Raths, Harmin, & Simon, 1966; Simon, Howe, & Kirschenbaum, 1972; Simon & O'Rourke, 1977). Interestingly, the popularity of the movement parallels the popularity of the behavior modification movement in American education circles. According to Simon et al. (1972), "...the values clarification approach does not aim to instill any particular set of values" (p. 20). More important, the various proposed strategies are provided to help participants gain a clearer idea of what values or behaviors they choose, prize, and are willing to act upon.

Those who utilize values assessment techniques are moving into a sensitive area. Governmental agencies have answered the demand to respect the privacy and well-being of students and their families. Although conscientious teachers automatically respect the rights of others, one should also remember that these rights are protected by law.

Self-Assessment of Values

As a counselor once said, "If I don't know who I am and where I'm coming from, how can I help someone else discover this about himself?" If we accept the premise that a teacher, counselor, or other education specialist is going to teach significant adults in the child's life how to clarify their values, it is important to apply these techniques to oneself.

Techniques range from free response to fixed-response strategies. Some of the results may be analyzed by looking at the responses to questions such as, "Who am I?" or responses to fill-in-the-blank sentences. Other measures have elaborate scoring systems. Selected activities that might help one reflect on one's own value system are given in Appendix B. In some cases, these have been adapted from commercially available strategies or assessment techniques.

COMMUNICATION GAPS

In implementing a parent research project, two university students were interested in what parents would remember from a parent–teacher conference that was held to explain testing information and results to the parents. The first student prepared a list of charts and graphs explaining the results of the tests, complete with a set of definitions to terms often used during evaluation and testing. After she made the presentation to the parents, the second student interviewed them to ascertain their understanding of what was presented.

The father responded that he understood that their son had a serious reading problem. The mother retorted that she had not heard any such thing. They had both heard the same message, had been videotaped, and had assured the researcher that they understood what was presented and had no more questions. Yet they had heard two different messages.

This example is not rare. Most people have had similar experiences. They have seen or heard something and then disagreed with other witnesses about what occurred. *Selective perception* means that one hears or sees what one expects to see or hear or what one chooses to perceive. Usually this is based on one's past experiences. This is one of the reasons that parents and professionals often disagree on what was said in a conference.

Without realizing it, educators, like all professionals, have their own language, called jargon. Parents may nod their head as if in agreement even though they really don't understand. They just don't want to appear "dumb."

Also, much is lost in the translation. In analyzing tapes of parent–teacher conferences, teachers typically are found to talk most of the time. Finally, at the conclusion of a meeting, if more than three recommendations are suggested, parents tend not to comply.

DELIVERING SENSITIVE INFORMATION

Educators and other professionals frequently have been criticized for the insensitive manner in which they have informed parents of "bad news." This criticism should not come as a surprise, as few professionals have been taught or trained how to deliver sensitive information. As a result, some are evasive, some are blunt, some are authoritative, some employ jargon, and most talk without listening. Obstacles to communication that become exacerbated in delivering sensitive information include ego involvement, differences in knowledge, social status, purposes of the communication, emotional distance, one-way communication, verbal manipulation, ambiguity of language, the role of jargon, and the pressure of time.

Everyone has to receive and give bad news sometime in the course of life. This may be something as simple as telling your mate that the cat broke a favorite vase to something as serious as informing someone that his or her mother or father has died. With relatives, the conveyor of bad news usually can draw upon considerable background information to gauge the most conducive time and place to break the news.

Watching a child pick the time and place to inform a parent of a bad report card is interesting. The child may go to great lengths to prepare the environment, and these preparations have the effect of alerting the parent that something is going on. ("I wonder what Susie is up to?") Likewise, when a parent goes into the child's room and closes the door, the parent is sending a message to the child that news is forthcoming. In our personal relationships, we learn a great deal about communication with each other if we tune into the verbal and nonverbal messages that are being transmitted.

Joan Guntzelman, a counselor at Presbyterian Hospital in Albuquerque, helped patients and their relatives cope with situations of terminal illness, serious operations, and feelings of helplessness. She emphasized that people who convey bad news or sensitive information should find techniques that are most comfortable to them. Some of her suggestions for delivering sensitive information to parents are summarized in the following list:

➤ Provide a comfortable and private environment.

A number of years ago, a Native American mother gave birth to a child with Down syndrome. At the time, these children often were referred to as "mongoloid." The doctor said to the mother, "You have a mongoloid child. Do you know what that means?" Not wanting to sound unknowledgeable or to challenge the doctor's position, the mother nodded. When she took the baby home, she visited with her own mother.

"Mother, do you know what a mongoloid child is?" she asked.
"I think it's somebody from Asia," her mother responded.
"I wonder how I got an Asian child," the mother thought.

➤ Tell the parents together, if possible. When one parent has to tell the other, misunderstanding and confusion can result.

➤ Be aware of the parents' readiness to receive the information.

➤ Recognize that more information may be communicated non-verbally than verbally and use your body language accordingly.

➤ Try to have some sense of what the diagnosis will mean to the parents and how much explanation may be necessary.

➤ Keep the information as simple and basic as possible while still conveying what has to be said.

➤ Communicate a sense of calm and composure. This means not being hasty and allowing enough time, including time to answer parents' questions.

➤ When delivering bad news, don't give the "heaviest" information during the first visit if more visits are forthcoming. This initial meeting should have as a major goal establishing rapport and trust.

➤ Realize the possibility that a parent may be in the denial stage and may not listen to or accept what you are saying. Don't push too hard, as the parent will likely be more accepting in time.

➤ Try to be honest and straightforward instead of harsh or insensitive.

➤ Avoid jargon whenever possible. If technical or medical terminology is necessary, explain it in a way the parents can understand.

➤ Be accepting of parents' reactions, whether they be denial, anger, or sadness. Awareness of the theories of grieving is helpful.

➤ Try to gauge the proper amount of time to allow for this meeting, both to convey what is necessary and to allow time to accept and answer parents' questions.

➤ Be aware that parents may not process all the information given them, and be prepared to repeat whatever is necessary at a follow-up meeting.

Many times parents receive bad news in the school environment, which can be sterile and intimidating. A counselor's office or the principal's office offers more privacy and fewer distractions than a classroom or the teachers' lounge. Privacy is often limited in a classroom, and certainly is limited in the lounge.

Getting two parents together for a joint meeting is becoming more and more difficult. In the case of a single parent whose former spouse is not available, an alternative might be to suggest that the parent bring a friend. A friend can serve as a sounding board and provide feedback that the parent is unable to give.

School personnel should be alert to how the parent is taking the news. They may have a response quite different from what the teacher anticipated. For instance, one parent whose child was being referred for special testing was noticeably relieved. "I was afraid you were going to tell me that he was going to be suspended from school," she said. "I knew he was having trouble, and I'm so thankful that maybe we'll get some help now." The same information could be devastating to another parent, who might become agitated and say: "Do you think he's crazy? What will his father say? What am I going to tell the neighbors? Why didn't you tell me he was having trouble?"

Depending upon the parents' background and history, the same words may have entirely different meanings to different people. One person may have a concept of learning disabilities or behavior problems based on a stereotype from television. Another person may have developed a concept of these problems from friends, relatives, or school environments. A third person might actually work with children or youth with disabilities. To tell these three people that they have a child with a learning disability or a behavior problem will evoke three different reactions.

Teachers, counselors, doctors, and similar professionals may have the same difficulty as any other parent in hearing bad news. Even though they can intellectualize about the disability, this does not mean they can accept it any better than people with little or no experience with disabilities. A parent who is able to advocate for other parents may not be able to advocate for his or her own child.

In delivering sensitive information, a follow-up meeting is usually a good idea. Regardless of the amount of time set aside for the initial meeting, the recipient of the information needs time to assimilate it and come up with questions.

The conveyor of bad news has to be prepared to accept parents' reactions, whatever they may be. In ancient times, messengers who brought bad news were often put to death. The tendency is for parents to resent the person who has the role of informing them of bad news and blame the informer. A professional's skill in listening is crucial at these times. Giving parents an opportunity to vent their feelings and think aloud will be of tremendous help to them. And professionals remaining calm themselves has a calming effect on parents. In this regard, the teacher may want to ask the parents if they wish to be alone for a while to think and talk together privately. Taking plenty of time at this juncture will help as the situation develops in the future.

As a defense mechanism, professionals often fall back unconsciously on the use of jargon, because they are most comfortable talking in their own professional language. As we've said, this hinders communication and understanding. Periodically asking the parents to explain what they have heard can help the teacher determine whether the message is getting across. Of course, being able to parrot the words may mean only that the parent heard the message, not necessarily that the parent understood it. Finally, if diagnosticians or teachers think they may have just this one chance for talking with the parents about this situation, they may overwhelm the parents with too much information.

A COMPREHENSIVE SUPPORT MODEL

Students who are culturally diverse and who also have learning exceptionalities endure a double burden. How can the key players in education (students, families, teachers, communities, and governments) work together so these students can reach their greatest potential? The comprehensive support model (CSM) provides one strategy. In the past, "culturally diverse learners were disallowed from reaching their maximum potential because of their different ways of behaving, speaking, learning, interacting, and responding to mainstream ideas" (Boykin, 2000, as cited in Obiakor, Utley, Smith, & Harris-Obiakor, 2002, p. 2). Clearly, schools must take a more comprehensive approach to their general and special education curricula.

In the CSM, "the [learner], family, school, community, and government are collaboratively involved in solving educational problems confronting culturally diverse learners with exceptionalities" (Obiakor et al., 2002). The underpinnings of this model are:

1. Assessment and instructional strategies developed in the context of cultural competence.
2. A collaborative system of community support based upon the eradication of social stereotyping.

3. Awareness and appreciation of family forms that value individual differences, disabilities, and strengths.
4. Cultivation of a sense of safety for culturally diverse children and their families.
5. Advocacy of pro-family economic policies and human services.
6. Respect for differences in worldview and learning style.
7. Expansion of affordable and flexible childcare services.
8. Development of collaborative community approaches to problem solving by including students, parents, schools, and community leaders.
9. Recognition of the role of institutional barriers.
10. Reconfiguration of curricula to eliminate culturally insensitive curricular variables.
11. Reinstitution of "rites of passage and service opportunities" to cultivate a sense of belonging.
12. Educational reform should also include economic reform and the investment in human capital (adapted from Obiakor et al., 2002).

SUMMARY

Understanding perceptions and values is basic to what this book is all about—communicating with parents. Each of us picks and chooses what bits of information we want to use from the vast amount of information available to us.

Communication gaps between professionals and parents occur because of the participants' differences in perception, compounded by cultural differences. In a complex society, even individuals who are in constant contact with each other have distinctly different value systems. Individuals' past histories, their physical and behavioral characteristics, and their emotions have the effect of distorting messages.

The classroom teacher probably has to deal with a wider range of differences than do most adults. Children come to school from homes with different religions, different economic status, cultural differences, and different views on the importance of education. To be most effective, teachers must first understand their own values, then try to understand the value systems of other significant adults in the child's life and possibly help those other adults understand their own value systems.

Understanding value systems is complicated because we as individuals do not always act on available data. Even though we are informed that smoking is harmful to our health, we continue to smoke; although we know that obesity is potentially harmful to the heart, we continue to overeat.

All of us have to deliver sensitive information, or bad news, to someone from time to time. If they are aware of the possible effects of this information on the recipients, school personnel can work on improving their skills in conveying this information. The physical setting and environment, including privacy and lack of distraction, should be conducive for parents' receiving sensitive information, Continual "perception checking" of the parents' understanding is necessary. And the conveyors of bad news must realize that no matter how skilled they are in interpreting and presenting information, most parents will not be able to assimilate everything in one session.

A comprehensive support model (CSM) provides an approach that is culturally sensitive and involves collaboration among all personnel and agencies involved in the child's development. Following the 12 prongs of this approach should lead ultimately to students' optimum development by improved communication with the parents and family.

A number of activities are presented in Appendix B. Teachers may select from among these to review their value systems.

ACTIVITIES

1. Select a few of the exercises in Appendix B to assess your values.
2. Divide into small groups of four or five and discuss times each participant has received bad news. How did you respond? Did you listen and retain all that was being said?
3. Discuss the times each has had to give bad news and how it was handled.
4. Give each participant a sheet of plain paper (8½ x 11) and read the following directions to the group:
   "Put your paper in front of you. I'll give you some directions to follow. I want you to work individually. Please don't ask any questions.
   a. Starting about 3 inches from the top of the paper and 1 inch from the left side, draw a straight line about 1¼ inches long toward the bottom of the paper.

b. Where you finished that line, start another line. Make this one about 1 inch long, and draw it diagonally toward the middle bottom.

c. Start now where you finished the last line, and draw another line about 1 inch long diagonally toward the right upper corner of your paper.

d. Where you finish that line, draw another one about 1¼ inches long toward the top of your paper.

e. Where you finish that line, draw another line 1 inch long diagonally toward the upper left corner of your paper.

f. Where you finish that line, draw another one about 1 inch long diagonally down toward the left upper third of your paper.

g. Where you finish that line, draw another line about 1 inch long toward the bottom middle of your paper.

h. Where you finish that line, draw another one 1 inch long toward the right upper corner of your paper.

i. Now, for your last line, come back to the beginning of your last line and draw another line about 1¼ inches long toward the bottom of your paper.

Compare your drawing with the others in the group. Then compare your drawing with this one." Find the drawing at the end of Appendix C and use it for comparison.

Regardless of the "rightness" or "wrongness" of the directions, all drawings should have been approximately the same, because all presumably heard the same directions. Discuss why people hearing the same information draw different conclusions.

REFERENCES

Brooks, B. D., & Kann, M. E. (1992). Value-added education. *American School Board Journal, 179*(12), 24–27.

Chavkin, N. F. (1991). *Family lives and parental involvement in migrant students' education.* (ERIC Digest). Charlotte, NC: ERIC Clearinghouse on Rural Education and Small Schools.

Lupi, M. H., & Tong, V. M. (2001). Reflecting on personal interaction style to promote successful cross-cultural school–home partnerships. *Preventing School Failure, 45*(4). Retrieved April 25, 2003, from University of Louisville's Academic Search Premier Database http://www.echo.louisville.edu/

Obiakor, F. E., Utley, C. A., Smith, R., & Harris-Obiakor, P. (2002). The comprehensive support model for culturally diverse exceptional learners: Intervention in an age of change. *Intervention in School & Clinic, 38*(1). Retrieved April 25, 2003, from University of Louisville's Academic Search Premier Database http://www.echo.louisville.edu/

Raths, L. E., Harmin, M., & Simon, S. (1966). *Values and teaching.* Columbus, OH: Charles E. Merrill.

Simon, S. B., Howe, L. W., & Kirschenbaum, H. (1972). *Values clarification: A handbook of practical strategies for teachers and students* (rev. ed.). New York: Hart.

Simon, S. B., & O'Rourke, R. D. (1977). *Developing values with exceptional children.* Englewood Cliffs, NJ: Prentice-Hall.

Part Two

Strategies for Involving Parents

5

The Art of Listening

To be human is to speak. To be abundantly human is to speak freely and fully. The converse of this is a profound truth, also: that the good listener is the best physician for those who are ill in thought and feeling.

—Wendell Johnson

istening is an active, constructive endeavor (McDevitt, 1990). As we listen, we create a preliminary representation of the speaker's meaning, generate a hypothesis and expectations, and integrate incoming statements based on the interpretation. Skilled listeners work diligently to understand the messages, and when they become confused, they seek to eliminate the confusion by seeking clarification.

After researching the listening skills of fourth-grade students, Barmor (1991) determined that listening skills can be taught to children and thereby improve their performance in both academic and social behaviors. If listening skills can be taught to children, parents and teachers can gain tremendously (Warner, 1991).

A STUDY OF TEEN LISTENERS VERSUS NONLISTENERS

In Barmor's (1991) study, teens classified each other as "listeners" or "nonlisteners." Students' ratings of each other as listeners or nonlisteners were derived from their listening behavior in one-to-one relationships. These ratings didn't comport with teachers' ratings of students' listening skills, in which teachers judged the students' listening behavior according to whether the student paid attention in class.

Some children whom teachers identified as nonlisteners were viewed by their peers as very good listeners in a one-to-one relationship. The students who were identified as being good listeners were those whom other students sought out when they wanted to talk over problems with someone. These students were considered socially sensitive, usually interested, concerned, caring individuals who tended to be nonjudgmental. By contrast, the students who were classified as nonlisteners were often highly verbal and able to give clear directions or commands but apparently were less interested in listening to others.

A LISTENING PARADIGM

To better understand the various listening postures, we propose the paradigm presented in Figure 5.1. The four quadrants are represented by

A—the passive listener
B—the active listener

A	B
Passive Listener	Active Listener
C	D
Passive Nonlistener	Active Nonlistener

FIGURE 5.1
A Listening Paradigm

C—the passive nonlistener
D—the active nonlistener

No one remains in any of the quadrants all the time. Actually, a person may shift from quadrant A to B or from B to D in any conversation. Sometimes you can observe passive listeners (A) slip into the passive nonlistener (C) role when their eyes get that faraway look.

Quadrant A: Passive Listener

The passive listener has a positive role in a conversation. Not to be confused with apathetic listeners, passive listeners are "there" and "with it." They frequently nod their head slightly and smile from time to time to show that they are paying attention to what the speaker is saying.

In a parent–teacher conference, the parent is more likely to be the passive listener. The teacher is likely to do most of the talking, and this means that many of the parents' concerns will go unheard. Before the teacher knows it, time is up.

It is said that nature abhors a vacuum, and the teacher usually is able to fill the silences more rapidly than the parent can. Teachers might practice becoming passive listeners with each other in the teachers' lounge. It's not as easy as it may seem.

Quadrant B: Active Listener

The active listener is animated in facial expressions and body language. In many respects, active listeners can be equated to outstanding dance partners. They feel the rhythm of the conversation and move accordingly.

The teacher as an active listener in a parent–teacher conference listens intently as parents share information about their children and family. Nonverbally, the active-listening teacher may lean forward and maintain intense eye contact during a conversation Verbally, this teacher reflects back to the parent the feelings he/she hears expressed and may reverbalize the parent's statements, saying, "I think you're telling me..." to test his or her perceptions. This type of listening is hard work, and teacher and parent alike may feel emotionally drained after an active listening conference.

A major strength in the teacher's being an active listener is that it keeps the focus where it belongs—with the parent. The teacher does not take over the problem by offering solutions or making the parent feel guilty by moralizing. What the active-listening teacher does is try to clarify the problem and help the parent put it in perspective.

Quadrant C: Passive Nonlistener

The passive nonlistener may seem to "hear" what is being said but is not listening to the "feeling content" of the messages. This can be frustrating to the speaker, as in the following example.

Wife: I'm so tired. I've been to four stores today trying to find a dress for Saturday night.... You're not listening!

Husband: (folding the newspaper): You said you've been to four stores looking for a new dress.

Although the content of the response was accurate, the husband missed his wife's feelings of fatigue and frustration. She couldn't say that he wasn't listening, because he parroted back what she had said. But no real communication took place. These are merely two people physically in the same room—one who is trying to send a message to alleviate some of her feelings, and the other who is submerged in his own thoughts.

A similar situation occurs in some parent–teacher conferences, particularly when the teacher has a number of conferences in succession.

The teacher may be physically meeting with Mrs. Simmons while her mind is on the next conference with Mr. Snyder, which she is dreading because she has to bring up some troublesome behaviors of his child. She looks at Mrs. Simmons and is able to repeat many of her words, but as far as the conference is concerned, the parent feels frustrated in the teacher's apparent lack of real interest as a passive nonlistener.

When an adult's mind slips out of its listening gear and starts to pursue its own thoughts, children sometimes tug on a sleeve or pant leg to call attention to the lack of listening. Parents seldom tug, but they probably are aware when the teacher's own thoughts take over.

Quadrant D: Active Nonlistener

Active nonlisteners come in several forms, one of which is the cocktail-party type. Almost everyone has attended a social gathering where a great deal of talk was going on but virtually no listening. In this conversation, people talk *to* each other but seldom *with* each other.

Mrs. Smith: We're so glad you could come. I heard you were out of town.

Mrs. Jones: We just got back. We were attending my aunt's funeral in California.

Mrs. Smith: California is so pretty this time of year. We were at Disneyland last spring. I enjoyed it so much.

Mrs. Jones: We were in Louisville last spring. Oh, there's Ruby. I must tell her about the dogwood blossom necklace I found.

Neither of the above conversationalists is really interested in what the other has to say. Each merely waits politely for the other to finish a sentence while thinking what she intends to say, and then takes her turn. Although this type of listening pattern is fairly easy to recognize in social gatherings, it may be less observable in a parent–teacher interaction. It happens when the parent and the teacher enter a conference with something in mind to convey to the other rather than wanting to hear what the other has to say. They exchange talk for the 20-minute session and separate, neither having attended to the other's message.

Teacher: I'm so glad you could come. I've been wanting to talk with you about Billy.

Parent: I'm having trouble getting Billy to do his homework. He always wants to put it off, and we have frightful arguments around the house.

Teacher: He's been fighting on the playground. I've had to keep him in from recess twice this week.

Parent: I don't think he understands multiplication. That's probably why he doesn't do his homework. I wish you could do something about it.

Teacher: Do you have any idea why he's started fighting so much? Does he ever talk about it at home? We don't know what to do with him. It's getting to be a real problem.

Parent: We're having a real problem, too. We're open to any suggestions. This arguing is getting both his dad and me upset.

Teacher: We at school want to cooperate in any way we can. If you have any ideas about fighting, call me, will you? It's sure been nice talking to you, and I'm so glad you could come. You're always welcome at school.

Parent: I'm happy to have met you. If you have any ideas how we can help at home, just call. We want to work with the school.

This type of conferring probably happens more often than one would like to believe. Both parent and teacher are trying to communicate and cooperate, but they are not taking the time to listen to what the other has to say. In this example, little is accomplished, but both leave feeling that at least they have had their say about their problems.

Another type of active nonlistener, the wipe-out artist, is probably the most exasperating of all. These active nonlisteners unravel the outer threads of the story and never allow the theme of the story to unfold. They appear to be actively attending but actually are reacting to the incidentals of the message. This can be especially frustrating if the speaker is trying to relate a situation in which he or she is emotionally involved or feels strongly about. Either the parent or the teacher may act as a wipe-out artist during a conference.

Parent: Billy had the neatest thing happen to him on his way home from school.

Teacher: How does he go home from school?

Parent: Down Center Street and...

Teacher: Isn't that past the fire station?

Parent: Yes, and...

Teacher: Last year, five of our boys said they wanted to be fire-fighters when they grow up. What does Billy want to be?

Parent: A nuclear physicist.

Teacher: Isn't that cute? And to think he can't even spell it! What happened to him on the way home?

Parent: Well, he ran into this man who...

Teacher: I hope Billy said "excuse me." We stress good manners in our room. We have a unit on the magic words "please" and "thank you." I hope you notice the improvement at home.

With a little practice, almost anyone can become an expert in active nonlistening.

Again, people do not fit neatly into one of the four quadrants. Most move from quadrant to quadrant depending on the situation. Still, most people have a propensity to be consistently more of one type than another. A good way to analyze one's inclination as a speaker is to tape-record an interview and listen to it.

DETRACTORS TO LISTENING

A number of things can happen before or during a conference that slow or derail communication (Edge, 1993; Maring & Magelky, 1990). The listening behavior of one or both of the participants may be reduced to a point at which the conference is no longer beneficial. From the teacher's point of view, six detractors stand out:

Fatigue

Listening requires effort. If the mind or the body is tired, listening will suffer. We all have had the experience of sitting in a lecture when we have been so tired that we could not mentally follow the speaker. If the teacher has a number of conferences one after the other and has really worked at listening, his or her mind will be wandering toward the end of the day. To maintain good listening, the teacher should take a break, walk around, and perhaps have a cup of coffee.

Strong Feelings

At times a child evokes strong feelings of anger in the teacher for some reason (usually behavioral). The teacher might want to talk with the school counselor about these feelings. Other strong feelings, such as sadness or pity, also can make listening difficult. The teacher would be wise to take stock of any strong feeling before entering a conversation with the parent. Perhaps the meeting could be rescheduled when the teacher has resolved the negative feelings internally.

Words

The children's verse that ends with "but words will never hurt me" is far from true. Consider for a moment the impact of the following:

"You're fired!"
"I'm pregnant."
"Your child has been diagnosed with autism."
"This is the police."
"I love you."

The very words we say and hear can make our pulse beat more rapidly, beads of sweat appear, and our eyes dilate. Teachers must carefully consider the words they use with parents and realize that certain words may detract from listening on the parents' part.

When asked about their response to hearing for the first time that their child has been diagnosed with a disability, many parents indicate that they blanked out everything after hearing the diagnostic term. As discussed in chapter 3, parents often enter the stages of grieving, beginning with shock and denial, and involving subsequent emotions including guilt, rejection, blame, anger, embarrassment, and hostility before they accept (or at least are able to cope with) the diagnosis and begin the productive steps of coping.

Teachers who recognize that parents are having a difficult time adapting to the reality of having a child with disabilities should allow the parents every opportunity to talk over their feelings as these feelings relate to the child. This is a good time for the teacher to take a passive listening role.

Teacher Talk

A high percentage of teacher "talk time" in a parent–teacher conference reduces the listening time. A teacher once asked another teacher to tape-record one of his parent conferences so he could critique it. Using a stopwatch, the other teacher determined that the teacher had talked 80% of the time during the conference. If, as Johnson (1956, p. 23) commented, "we come in time to realize that every speaker is his own most captive listener," the teacher probably learned more about how he felt about the child than the parents learned about how they felt about the child. Basically, the teacher spent little time in listening to the parents and allowing them to listen to themselves discuss their child. Teachers do need to "listen to themselves" by talking about a child at times, but this is best done by talking to a listener other than the parent. The above-mentioned conference was probably more therapeutic for the teacher than for the parents.

The Surroundings

The physical surroundings can have an effect on listening. With a great deal of distraction, attending to another person—either visually or auditorially—becomes difficult.

And a parent's physical comfort can have an effect on the interaction. A businessman once tried an experiment. He placed two chairs in his office for people who came to see him. On one chair he cut 2 inches off the front legs, and on the other chair he cut 2 inches off the back legs. If he wanted the interview to be short, he had the visitor sit in the chair with the front legs shortened. If he was in no hurry, he seated the visitor in the chair with the short back legs. Merely controlling the seating arrangement seemed to have the desired effect (from Edge, 1993).

Taking Notes

Whether the teacher should take notes during a parent–teacher conference is debatable. With some parents, the teacher's taking notes seems to inhibit the flow of conversation. With other parents, the teacher's note-taking seems to increase the conversational flow. In any case, note taking is standard procedure for many professionals (e.g., doctors, lawyers).

In addition to generating a written record for later reference or review, something about the act of taking notes seems to help the note-taker focus on what is being relayed. Students sometimes say that taking notes during a boring lecture keeps their attention focused on the subject, especially when they are tired.

Note-taking is usually more effective than tape-recording a parent–teacher conference. Although tape-recording does capture the entire spoken message, it may give parents the false impression that they have a complete picture, when the tape does not convey the total picture of body language (e.g., fidgeting), setting, and other facets of the conference.

In short, many factors can affect listening in parent–teacher interactions. By becoming aware of the detractors to listening, teachers can improve their listening skills. The activities at the end of the chapter are intended to foster your listening skills.

PARENTS' ASSESSMENTS: ARE TEACHERS LISTENING?

Pruitt, Wandry, and Hollums (1998) conducted a study of 78 families of children or young adults with disabilities who were receiving special education services, seeking their suggestions. Their data revealed eight common themes, the number-one item of which pertained to listening:

1. Listen to us. Accept our input.
2. Improve the quantity and quality of communication between parents and professionals.
3. Increase our knowledge about various disabilities by making available current information.
4. Teach us how to react to an emergency situation arising with a child with special needs.
5. Demonstrate sensitivity to family needs.
6. Demonstrate respect for my child and meet his or her individual needs. Accommodate his or her academic, social, or physical needs.

7. Improve the IEP process.
8. Advocate for our children.

Summary

Listeners in a communication interaction can be classified according to four types:

A. Passive listener—attends to the speaker primarily on a nonverbal level

B. Active listener—works at helping the speaker clarify his or her thoughts, attitudes, and feelings about the subject being discussed

C. Passive nonlistener—does not attend to messages on a feeling level, although he or she may be able to repeat the speaker's words

D. Active nonlistener—takes equal time in any conversation, but it's usually not related to the topic of discussion. On another level, the active nonlistener may pick at the threads of a conversation and seemingly avoid the central issue being discussed.

Teachers should be aware of possible detractors to listening:

➤ Fatigue on the listener's part
➤ Either the parents' or the teacher's strong feelings
➤ Words themselves, if they are emotionally laden
➤ Excessive talk by the teacher
➤ The physical surroundings
➤ Note-taking

Listening is a skill that can be improved with practice. The activities at the end of this chapter may be helpful to the educator who is interested in learning new listening skills.

ACTIVITIES

1. Role-play a parent–teacher conference, with one participant being the teacher and the other the parent. Have someone videotape or

audiotape the interview. Play back the tape, and, using a stopwatch, record how many minutes the teacher talked. Time the total conference, then divide the number of minutes the interview took into the number of minutes you talked, to find the percentage of "teacher talk time."

2. In groups of three:
   a. One member in each group thinks of something exciting to relate; the second is the designated active nonlistener; and the third is an observer. Members 1 and 2 role-play for 3 minutes and then spend 2 minutes discussing their feelings with the third member (the observer).
   b. Then member 2 tells something exciting. Member 3 takes the role of an active listener and member 1 the observer. Members 2 and 3 role-play for 3 minutes. Member 1 then provides observer input in a 2-minute discussion of the listening behavior.
   c. The small groups assemble for a class follow-up discussion of the different listening styles demonstrated and the nonverbal signs of communication.

Note: Be sure to give each participant the opportunity to take the roles of speaker, listener, and observer.

REFERENCES

Barmor, C. (1991). *Improving the listening skills of fourth-grade students through a multifaceted guidance approach and active listening* (Ed.D. practicum). Ft. Lauderdale, FL: Nova University.

Edge, D. (1993). *Techniques for listening to parents* [video]. Greensboro, NC: National Training Network.

Johnson, W. (1956). *Your most enchanted listener*. New York: Harper & Brothers.

Maring, G. H., & Magelky, J. (1990). Effective communication: Key to parent/community involvement. *Reading Teacher, 43*(8), 606–607.

McDevitt, T. M. (1990). Encouraging young children's listening. *Academic Therapy, 25*(5), 569–577.

Pruitt, P., Wandry, D., & Hollums, D. (1998). Listen to us! Parents speak out about their interactions with special educators. *Preventing School Failure, 42*(4). Retrieved April 30, 2003, from University of Louisville's Academic Search Premier Database http://www.echo.louisville.edu/

Warner, I. (1991). Parents in Touch: District leadership for parent involvement. *Phi Delta Kappan, 72*(5), 372–375.

6

Parent-Teacher Conferences

During the formative years, a child's parents and teachers are the most significant adults in the child's life. Separately and together they provide the care and support, opportunities to learn, and skills the child needs to become a successful, productive adult (Benard, 1991). With the typical child, these significant adults should meet occasionally to exchange information about the child's progress. With children who have disabilities, more frequent meetings are essential for the child's welfare. In fact, federal law mandates parent–professional meetings at specific points related to the child's placement and educational programming.

One of the reasons for the frequently suggested reduction in class size is to give parents and teachers more of a chance to work together. This is especially important with parents of children who have disabilities, to ensure that their children receive the proper individual educational programming. Small-group meetings and individual conferences are more feasible when the teacher is able to relate to 15 sets of parents instead of 30 sets of parents. Frequent interactions allow parents to share information with the teacher, receive information from the teacher, and work with the teacher in preventing and solving problems that involve their children.

Conferences held before school starts in fall or early in the school year can get the child off to the best possible start. Holding conferences early has been demonstrated to result in improved grades and attendance and fewer disciplinary contacts. Holding conferences early gives the teacher and parent alike an opportunity to get acquainted and exchange pertinent information when both are fresh and do not bring existing problems to the exchange.

CUMULATIVE RECORDS

In preparing for this first conference, the teacher should review the available information about the child and family. Many times, any difficulties the child has had in school can be identified early, and the teacher can provide assistance before the child gets off to a poor start. The records also may contain a number of inconsistencies that can be cleared up in an early conference with the parents. Another good reason for reviewing the school records is to be able to answer parents' questions about information the school has about their child. Parents have a legal right to know what is in their child's school records.

A cumulative record folder is available to teachers on children who have been in school somewhere else, too. The four categories of information to which the teacher should pay particular attention pertain to the child's social, academic, intellectual, and physical growth and development.

Social History

From a careful reading of the records, the teacher may be able to determine some things about the family constellation and dynamics. For instance, the teacher might be able to determine whether the child is living with both parents, if both work outside of the home, and whether the family includes older children. This type of information can help the teacher arrange conferences so the parents can attend and might indicate whether older children are available to babysit and perhaps help tutor their sibling. Depending on the primary language spoken at home, communication may be enhanced by having a bilingual friend accompany the parent to a conference, or making available a translator if necessary. If both parents work outside the home, arranging conferences may be more difficult and require flexibility on the teacher' part.

The cumulative record may contain some information on the child's social life—any groups the child belongs to, churches attended, and interactions with other children in the past. If the record points out any problems with other youngsters, the teacher may want to gently explore this with the parents at their first meeting. The teacher should be looking for techniques to help the child have some positive early experiences in the new school year, and the parents, in turn, may be able to provide information that will be useful to the teacher.

At this point, the teacher is seeking to understand the child in his or her environment and is looking for areas to discuss further with the parents. The teacher is not trying to draw conclusions as to why the child behaves as he or she does socially but, rather, to determine whether the child's social behavior seems to carry over to different environments. The teacher also is trying to find out how to best conduct the forthcoming conference.

Academic Achievement

The child's cumulative record includes information such as standardized achievement test scores, report cards, written reports from previous conferences, and samples of the child's work.

The parents probably received this information in the past, but the teacher should not assume that the parents always fully understood or remember all the information they received. Analysis of the data may raise some questions the teacher will want to discuss with the parents. For instance, in preparing for a conference about Susie's growth in reading as measured by the results of achievement tests (see Figure 6.1), the teacher, Ms. Skinner, noticed that in the first and second grades, Susie was achieving in reading on grade level, but she leveled off in grades 3 and 4. Ms. Skinner may decide to show the chart to the parent(s) and ask for their input. The teacher also may notice a rather large discrepancy between her reading scores and math scores, which could be another point to discuss. Does Susie show any evidence of the same achievement patterns at home?

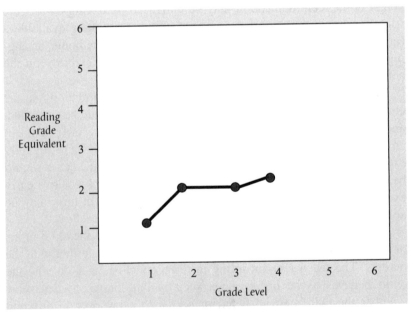

FIGURE 6.1
Susie's Rate of Reading Achievement

The teacher may want to ask the parents how they feel about the reporting system that has been used in the past. Parents often do not realize that teachers can give them information about their child's progress in ways other than, or in addition to, the quarterly report card system the school uses. In reviewing Susie's achievement data, Ms. Skinner might think that more frequent reporting to the parents would benefit the family and Susie alike.

Susie's parents may have samples of her work at home that would be useful to Ms. Skinner. Children sometimes do school-related tasks—such as writing poetry, keeping track of money they earn from an allowance or a job, drawing pictures, or demonstrating computer skills—that can help the teacher understand the child's skills and interests.

Intellectual Level

Intelligence quotients (IQs) are numbers laden with emotion. Teachers and parents often attach a great deal of significance to these scores and develop certain expectations that may or may not be warranted. Children with hearing loss, motor dysfunction, emotional disturbance, and those for whom English is not the primary language may have lower scores that do not accurately reflect their intellectual level.

The special educator should be aware of the conditions influencing the various intelligence measures, such as lack of motivation, that might yield a lower reading. The parents may be able to provide additional information about the child that will help the teacher better understand the test scores.

Physical Growth and Development

The cumulative record may contain information on the child's physical development that will help the teacher answer some of the following questions prior to the child's entering class for the new school year.

> ➣ How does the child compare in size to the other children who will be in the same room? Will the chair and desk be the right size for him? Will anything about his disability lead to teasing or hurt feelings? Is the child overweight? If so, will this limit his participation in recess activities? Are any physical accommodations required?

➤ Does the child have any sensorial defects? Routine testing by school health personnel may have disclosed that she has 20/200 vision. She may show up in class without glasses, perhaps because she simply doesn't like to wear them, or possibly the family has limited financial resources, in which case the teacher might be able to refer the family to an appropriate resource for help. Or a student's hearing test may reveal that she has a mild hearing loss. This should alert the teacher to provide special seating in the classroom.

➤ How does the child's past attendance record look? Did he miss Mondays most frequently? Attention to these and other questions about the child's attendance at school is often helpful in heading off potential problems in school. Obviously, if a child doesn't attend school regularly, the teacher's job becomes more difficult. Small gains may be lost because of irregular attendance.

In short, the teacher can pick up helpful bits of information from a child's cumulative record, and this information can lead to smoother sailing at the beginning of the year. The first meeting with a parent can give rise to many questions from parent and teacher alike. If the teacher is skillful in asking questions, parents' responses can yield valuable information without the teacher's being considered "snoopy." Both the teacher and the parents are interested in the child's welfare, and most parents appreciate that the teacher has taken the time to study the child's records before meeting with them.

THE INITIAL PARENT–TEACHER CONFERENCE

Some school districts and day-care centers permit and even encourage the teacher to have a conference with the parents before the child is accepted into a special education program. The teacher should prepare for this conference so it will run smoothly and be meaningful to both parties. Many professionals utilize some sort of outline in their initial interviews (Maring & Magelky, 1990).

Educators, too, should have an outline of the information they would like to obtain in an interview. The outline provided in Figure 6.2 is concerned with the child's growth and development, particularly as

Child's name _____

A. Present status

   1. Child's age
   2. Sex
   3. Grade/class/last year's teacher's name

B. Physical appearance and history

   1. General impression the child makes
   2. Obvious physical strengths and limitations
   3. General mannerisms, appearance, etc.

C. Educational status

   1. Present school achievement and samples of work
   2. Promotions, accelerations, lack of progress and causes
   3. Relations with individual teachers, present and past
   4. Books and materials used in the last educational setting
   5. Tests, individual or group, and types of measures used

D. Personal traits

   1. Personality—general statement
   2. Attitudes toward home, friends, self, family, other students, school
   3. Hobbies, play life, leisure-time activities
   4. Educational and vocational goals
   5. Likes and dislikes—foods, toys, TV programs, etc.

E. Home and family

   1. Individuals in the home
   2. Socioeconomic level
   3. Relations with home—brothers/sisters, parents, other relative
   4. Regular chores, pets, etc.
   5. Cooperation from home
   6. Record at social agencies

F. Child's work experience (if applicable)

   1. Part-time jobs (summer, after school)
   2. Attitude toward work, etc.

G. Additional information

   1. Sending school (if different from this one)
   2. Outside agencies
   3. Private sources: doctor, mental health center, etc. (need release forms)
   4. Health information

FIGURE 6.2
Initial Interview Guide

it relates to the child's educational life. Although many of the categories are self-evident, occasionally teachers forget one or another. Hence the importance of having an outline or checklist. Activity 11 in Appendix B illustrates how this outline is applied to four case histories.

Present Status

If the teacher has little or no prior knowledge of the child, or there are gaps in the record, the first order of business is usually to find out the name the child likes to be called, age, present status in school, and similar information of a friendly nature. This is a nonthreatening way to begin an interview. Even if the teacher has this information, it's a good idea to verify its accuracy.

Physical Appearance

A brief observation of the child will quickly clue the teacher as to any obvious disabilities, and subtle questioning may bring out some less obvious characteristics (e.g., fine-motor control, mild vision and hearing problems). In addition, many children with disabilities have a higher-than-average incidence of poor health in general, which could affect their attendance at school. Knowledge that a child has a pending operation or is highly susceptible to colds is helpful. If the child is taking medication, arrangements will have to be made and handled according to school policy.

Educational Status

To supplement the cumulative record, parents should be invited to bring samples of their child's work that was sent home during the preceding year. And parents can relate some of their child's feelings about, and experiences with, the previous educational setting. From this input, the teacher should be able to ascertain the parents' general attitudes toward school.

Personal Traits

Exploring the child's hobbies, free-time activities, and likes and dislikes can yield useful information for the first days of school. For example, books with themes of the children's favorite activities may give them an incentive to read. Their preferred activities can be incorporated into assignments. The child's hobbies can be topics for "show and tell" and are helpful in establishing rapport with the child.

Home and Family

Sometimes the first conference is held in the home. If this is the case, the observant teacher may detect many characteristics of the family's life that will be useful. Pictures, books, magazines, and newspapers reflect the family's socioeconomic status. The home environment also indicates what references and resources (including a computer) the child has available for homework activities.

Determining the predominant language spoken in the home and whether more than one language is used in the home is important, as this will influence home–school programs the teacher may want to set up. Parents may not understand written communications to the home. Daily report cards may not be productive or may require more careful explanation when there are language or cultural differences. What may seem to be a lack of cooperation from the home may actually be a problem in communication.

Work Experience

With an older child, information to be elicited may include any jobs the child has had and whether the child is currently working. After-school jobs may affect the child's performance at school.

Additional Information

Parents of exceptional children often have been contacted by agencies in addition to school contacts. This information does not always appear in the school records but nevertheless is important to the teacher. For instance, the parents may be involved in conferences held regularly with physical therapists, occupational therapists, psychologists, social workers, and others. These professional specialties each have their own philosophical bases and terminology, which understandably can be confusing to parents.

How the parent perceives the involvement with these agencies and professionals may shed light on why some parents are hesitant to attend parent–teacher conferences. It also may explain parents' desire, or lack of desire, to carry out certain home–school programs. If the various professionals involved with the child unknowingly are making inordinate time and energy demands on parents, the cumulative effect on the parents can be overwhelming. Thus, the teacher can benefit from knowing who is working with the family.

Most parents, in our experience, want to cooperate. They are willing to work within their limits to facilitate their children's growth. The teacher has an obligation to explore the parents' and child's limits by carefully studying the cumulative records and skillfully conducting interviews. By understanding the demands on parents by a child with a disability, the other individuals who live in the house, and the other professionals working with the parents, the teacher can plan more realistically for the child and have more appropriate expectations for parental cooperation.

REGULARLY SCHEDULED CONFERENCES

Regularly scheduled conferences are the primary basis of parent–teacher interactions. They are identified as a Level 2 need in the mirror model (see chapter 2). State and federal laws require parent–teacher conferences, and they may be written into local school policy. Educators who are skilled in conferencing take advantage of these meetings to provide parents with information and also to elicit from parents information that will further the child's education program.

The outline in Figure 6.3 may help you prepare for conferences. Having someone videotape you in an actual or role-played conference and reviewing the tape also can be helpful.

Preconference

Taking the four preconference steps listed in Figure 6.3 will help the conference go smoothly. First, the teacher should prepare some type of notification to be sent home. Although the school may have a form letter, the teacher is responsible for notifying the parents and following up in making the appointment. Appendix A contains tips for parents that can be sent home to help them prepare for this important meeting. Most parents appreciate receiving suggestions.

In preparing for the conference, the teacher should consult the child's cumulative record, as discussed earlier, then develop a plan or agenda. This agenda, of course, should be flexible, with the recognition that it may change after the conference starts.

PRECONFERENCE

_____ 1. Notify the attendees of the following:
  ➤ Purpose
  ➤ Place
  ➤ Time
  ➤ Length of time allotted

_____ 2. Prepare by doing the following:
  ➤ Review child's folder
  ➤ Gather examples of work
  ➤ Prepare materials

_____ 3. Plan agenda.

_____ 4. Arrange environment:
  ➤ Comfortable seating
  ➤ Eliminate distractions

CONFERENCE

_____ 1. Welcome and establish rapport.

_____ 2. State the following to the attendees:
  ➤ Purpose
  ➤ Time limitations
  ➤ Note-taking
  ➤ Options for follow-up

_____ 3. Encourage the following:
  ➤ Information-sharing
  ➤ Comments
  ➤ Questions

_____ 4. Listen:
  ➤ Pause once in a while.
  ➤ Look for verbal and nonverbal cues.
  ➤ Ask and answer questions.

_____ 5. Summarize (end on a positive note).

POSTCONFERENCE

_____ 1. Review conference with child, if appropriate.

_____ 2. Share information with other school personnel. if needed.

_____ 3. Mark calendar for planned follow-up.

FIGURE 6.3
Conference Checklist

So much has been written on the effects of the environment on interaction that this may seem like common knowledge, but horror stories are still cited. Parents have reported being seated on little chairs while the teacher sits in a regular-size chair. Or parents have been seated facing a light or a window. Sometimes privacy is lacking to talk over personal matters. And the teacher and parent may be separated from each other by a big table—or have no table at all to use for taking notes. Careful planning can avert these situations.

Conference

Establishing rapport in a 15-minute conference is a real challenge, but it is important. Getting up and meeting the parent at the door with a handshake will help get things off to a good start (Edge, 1993). And the teacher might relate a positive anecdote or mention something special the child did that day. The teacher should do something to break the ice—not just sit there. It is said that the success of a parent–teacher conference is determined in the first few minutes of the meeting.

Guidelines for the conference should be established at the onset. Parents should be informed of the time allotted for the meeting. Some research on time-limited therapies suggests that people will use the time allotted to them. The information exchange tends to be most lively as the deadline for termination approaches. If parents do not know how much time they have, they may not raise their questions or offer comments before it is time to leave. Important things can take place in a short time if the participants know what has to be accomplished and how much time they have.

The teacher should ask the parents what they think about the teacher's taking notes during the conference. Some like the idea and some don't. Sometimes, if the teacher wants to take notes and lets the parents know he or she will give them a copy of the notes at the end of the meeting, they are willing to go along with it. Or the conference can be tape-recorded, but that has its own limitations, as discussed previously.

Parents often have to be encouraged to share information. Many parents have a mindset that they are going to a meeting to hear about their child—not to give the teacher information about their child. The tip sheets in Appendix A can be a boon here.

Listening is the topic of chapter 5. It is not as easy as it may seem because, by nature or training, educators are highly verbal. We abhor silence and tend to speak up to fill the vacuum. By watching parents' body language and eye movements, we should be able to determine whether parents want to say something or are waiting for us to proceed.

The teacher is responsible for summarizing the conference, although he or she might want to ask the parents to recount the most important points to check how well they understood what was discussed. Also, the teacher may want to schedule a follow-up conference and delineate individual responsibilities.

Postconference

The child often attends the conferences along with the parents. To maximize the child's role, teachers are planning student-led conferences in which the student explains the goals and objectives of his or her program. Often, students participate in planning the goals for the next grading period.

If the student was not at the conference, the major points should be shared with him or her. The teacher often writes up the content of the conference, with an indication of what is to transpire before the next conference.

Dealing With Aggression

Occasionally teachers get involved in a hostile or aggressive interaction (Brooks-Bonner, 1994). Success in meeting with hostile parents can result from careful planning, an understanding of human behavior, and experience. Prior to the conference, teachers should ask themselves five basic questions:

1. Do I have confidence in my ability to conduct the conference?
2. Do I know enough about the conference participants?
3. Do I clearly understand the problem?
4. Have I scheduled sufficient time for the conference?
5. Have I developed a plan of action?

Establishing some ground rules can reduce the emotional stress of dealing with angry parties. These rules include the following:

1. Focus on the issues, not the people.
2. Allow anyone to speak for a given time without interruption.
3. Dismiss a question only when everyone present agrees that further discussion is not necessary.

4. Record the important points.
5. Include all participants in the proposed solutions.
6. Ask for the parents' response at appropriate times, but do not allow interruptions.

Parents and teachers must try to reach agreement in outlining the three steps: defining the problem, analyzing the problem, and generating and selecting solutions.

A counselor was asked to conduct a parent group consisting of parents of children with behavior disorders. The parents came to the meeting hostile about a number of events that had occurred. In opening the meeting, the counselor asked for their concerns, and the parents were eager to have their say: Their children didn't like the food. They were having to ride the bus too long. There were fights on the playground.

"Wait a minute. I'm not sure I can remember all of this," the counselor said. "Let me write down what you're saying." He picked up a piece of chalk and went to the board. Immediately the parents quieted

---

Tips for Dealing With Aggressive Parents

DO:

- Listen.
- Write down what parents say.
- When they pause, ask what else is bothering them.
- Exhaust their list of complaints.
- Ask them to clarify any specific complaints that are too general.
- Show them the list and ask whether it is accurate and complete.
- Ask for their suggestions for solving any of the problems listed.
- Write down their suggestions.
- As much as possible, mirror their behaviors, verbal and nonverbal. For example, if they speak louder, speak softer.

DON'T:

- Argue.
- Become defensive.
- Promise things you can't produce.
- Own problems that belong to others.
- Raise your voice.
- Belittle or minimize the problem.

Source: Developed by the Parent Center, Albuquerque, NM.

as he began to list their concerns one by one. He did not stop to discuss, argue, or defend any item as he recorded them. Then the parents clarified the concerns that seemed vague.

Going down the list, the counselor elicited suggestions for solving the problems, and the group generated a list of things to do. The counselor tried not to own any of the problems himself but left them to the parents to resolve. In essence, he taught them how to approach the solutions to their own problems. He kept his voice low and calm and didn't promise anything he couldn't produce.

When a professional comes on strong, the tendency for parents is to get defensive. By listening nonjudgmentally, the counselor or teacher gives parents an opportunity to purge their feelings. And writing down the concerns slows the tempo and assures parents that their concerns are being taken seriously.

CROSS-CULTURAL CONSIDERATIONS FOR IMPROVING PARENT–TEACHER CONFERENCES

Parents of children with special needs are particularly sensitive about discussing their families' and their children's educational needs. This anxiety may be exacerbated if cultural differences come into play.

> Teachers face the challenge of becoming aware of the personal beliefs, values, and expectations that guide their interactions with others.... If the proper groundwork is laid to create a welcoming environment for parents and students, and if appropriate interaction practices are used, educators can encourage a level of parental involvement that will benefit students academically and socially. (Jordan, Reyes-Blanes, Peel, Peel, & Lane, 1998)

They offer the following five guidelines:

1. Determine whether the conference is casual or purposeful (casual conferences are chatty, unscheduled, and informal; purposeful conferences focus on a particular topic).
2. Prepare for the conference by finding out about family roles and expectations for the child's behavior and academic performance.
3. Become culturally competent.
4. Plan the physical setting and make sure it is comfortable, private, and barrier-free.

5. Deliver information clearly, constructively, and completely so the parents will understand it. Avoid jargon, and be sensitive to the family's cultural reaction to a child's disability.

In addition, the teacher should:

6. Assess the family's cultural background. Do family members speak, read, and write English? If so, how well?
7. Make written reports simple, and explain anything verbally that the parents don't understand in writing.
8. Enlist the services of a translator if needed.
9. Develop a "survival vocabulary" list in the family's native language for use with parents and school personnel.
10. To ensure understanding, ask the parents to "echo" what you have communicated to them.
11. Encourage recent immigrants to relate previous educational experiences (their own and their children's) from their native country.
12. Welcome parents warmly into the school and the classroom.
13. Let the parents know their rights and responsibilities regarding their children's education.
14. Provide parents with sufficient information about the referral process, legal matters, and financial issues (adapted from Al-Hassan & Gardner, 2002).

SUMMARY

Early individual meetings with parents prevent or reduce potential problems of attendance, discipline, and dropout, have been shown to improve grades, and foster better home–school contacts. Proper preparation for an initial conference requires research on the part of teachers into the information available. A study of the student's cumulative records may help in the teacher's developing an agenda and may raise questions for the teacher to explore with the parents.

The first aim of the initial interview is to establish rapport with the parents. Then the teacher should proceed with the prepared agenda, with a willingness to be flexible. Regularly scheduled conferences require preparation in the same way that the initial conference does. Most school districts place time restrictions on conferences, so to get the most out of the limited time for meetings, teachers might send home in advance some suggestions and tips on things parents can do to prepare for the meeting.

At the conference, the teacher should have on hand all materials needed for the meeting. Teachers should take enough time to listen to the parents and encourage them to bring up questions and comments. After the conference, the teacher should pass along the major points to the child (if the child was not present) and to other school personnel, if needed.

Occasionally a teacher faces a hostile parent. Some responses to aggression include keeping cool, listening, writing down what the other person says, eliciting suggestions to resolve the concerns, not promising things they can't produce, not owning other people's problems, and not becoming defensive. An old adage is, "If you argue with a fool, it makes two fools."

ACTIVITIES

1. Using the four fictitious case studies from Activity 11 in Appendix B, engage in the role-playing activities and take the short self-test accompanying each case.

   a. In pairs, one person assumes the role of teacher and the other the role of parent.
   b. The "parent" spends about 5 minutes reviewing the information in Case History #1.
   c. The "teacher" does not look at the case but reviews the Initial Interview Guide (see Figure 6.2).
   d. The "teacher" conducts an interview of about 20 to 30 minutes.
   e. The "teacher" takes the test for Case History #1.
   f. The pair discusses the interview.
   g. The roles then are reversed for Case History #2.
   h. All four cases may be used, depending on allotted time.

2. Discuss with the class the feelings associated with interviewing and being interviewed.

   a. Did the conference feel natural?
   b. How did the participant feel in the role of the parent?

c. Was the "parent" allowed to talk, or was it just a question-and-answer session?

3. Discuss the reasons parents may feel fearful and defensive in their meetings with school personnel. What can be done to relieve these feelings?

4. After reviewing the legal information provided by a school, talk about the issues of confidentiality, privileged communication, and lounge-talk as it relates to parent–teacher conferences.

5. Review a child's cumulative record. Discuss what questions might be generated for the parent–teacher conference.

6. View a videotape such as "Preparing for the Parent–Teacher Conference" or "Conducting a Parent–Teacher Conference" (Edge, 1995a, 1995b). Discuss the issues related to the conferences.

7. Videotape a real or simulated conference, discuss the teacher's role, and offer constructive criticism.

REFERENCES

Al-Hassan, S., & Gardner, R. (2002). Involving immigrant parents of students with disabilities in the educational process. *Teaching Exceptional Children, 34*(5), 52–58.

Benard, B. (1991). *Fostering resiliency in kids: Protective factors in the family, school, and community.* Portland, OR: Western Center for Drug-Free Schools and Communities. (ERIC Document Reproduction Service No. ED 335 781).

Brooks-Bonner, L., (1994). When parents get aggressive. *Education Digest, 59*(6), 33.

Edge, D. (1993). *Techniques for conducting a parent conference* [videotape]. Louisville, KY: University of Louisville.

Edge, D. (1995a). *Conducting parent–teacher conferences* [videotape]. Louisville, KY: University of Louisville.

Edge D. (1995b). *Preparing for parent–teacher conferences* [videotape]. Louisville, KY: University of Louisville.

Jordan, L., Reyes-Blanes, M., Peel, B. B., Peel, H. A., & Lane, H. B. (1998). Developing teacher-parent partnerships across cultures: Effective parent conferences. *Intervention in School and Clinic, 33*(3), 141–147.

Maring, G.H., & Magelky, J., (1990). Effective communication: Key to parent/community involvement. *Reading Teacher, 43*(8), 606–607.

7

Informational Formats for Parents

Dad:	"What's your counselor's name?"
Marcus:	"I don't know."
Dad:	"Well, who's the principal?"
Marcus:	"I don't know."
Dad:	"What days do you have vacation?"
Marcus:	"I don't know."

Most parents are interested in their children's school life and their educational programs. In response to this need, many school districts are developing classroom and school handbooks, brochures, policies and procedure manuals, class and program schedules, calendars, computer information networks, videotapes, and other products to assist parents with the wide range of information needed to facilitate the education of their children (Edge, 1993, 1995; Harry, Allen, & McLaughlin, 1995). And to comply with state and federal legislation, local school districts must inform them of their rights and the rights of their children.

Some of the literature sent home does not take into account the parents' reading levels, and some materials are written as high as college level. The following selection is an example from an actual school handout:

> The educational diagnostician is a specialist knowledgeable in diagnostic and prescriptive intervention procedures. The diagnostician participates in the identification, planning, and referral of children needing special education and related services and provides consultative assistance to school personnel and parents.

Clearly, this passage is on a higher reading level than the Dear Abby column, which is a fairly good indicator of the reading level that most parents understand.

In addition to descriptions of districtwide services, special classes have policies and procedures specific to this population of children. The class day may be shorter, teachers may use different techniques to help children control their behavior, and they may schedule extra meetings.

Parents of children with disabilities are interested in the specifics of the educational program in which their child is enrolled. Therefore, providing the parents with more than a general handbook is helpful. Parents of children with disabilities may desire information that is specific to a situation or disability. For instance, they may want to read books about families that have children with the same disabling condition their child has, or they may want to know what agencies in the community provide services they can use (see Appendix D for a listing of national service organizations and technology centers). Because not all parents need the same specialized information, specialized information can be made available through handouts tailored to various issues. Teachers can provide a real service by preparing specific handouts for parents of children in their classrooms. Also, teachers may want to encourage their school districts or individual schools to publish things such as a tutor directory and a community guide for families with exceptional children. First, we will offer some suggestions for preparing a specialized handbook.

PREPARING A HANDBOOK

Handbooks for specific classes should be short, attractive, inclusive, and written at a level the parents can understand. In general, these handbooks should not duplicate information in the general school handbook, except the basic information that all students and parents must have. Other topics are those that warrant emphasis. The following is a suggested outline of contents.

1. *Special personnel.* At the beginning, information should include the names and phone numbers of school personnel the parents may need to contact during the year: principal, teacher(s), counselor, nurse, school psychologist, bus driver. This information might include office hours or preferred times to call and indicate how to make an appointment.

2. *Classroom procedures.* Any technique, method, or other information unique to that classroom should be pointed out—the use of material rewards, study carrels, time-outs, early dismissal time, and the like. Usually, the fewer surprises the parents face, the smoother the year will be. If any special testing or field trip request forms are different from the general school forms, these should be included.

3. *Classroom materials and supplies.* Special education teachers often have to call upon parents to supply special materials. A list of supplies the parents are to provide at the beginning and throughout the year should be brought to their attention.

4. *Transportation.* Children with disabilities often are transported to school in buses outfitted with special equipment. Parents should be informed of the bus schedule and special rules and regulations required for transportation.

5. *Conference and reporting system.* The schedule should indicate times of regular parent–teacher conferences and information on how parents can arrange for special meetings. This is a good

place to include some of the tip sheets from Appendix A, such as "Preparing for a Parent–Teacher Conference" and "Questions to Consider Before a Parent–Teacher Conference." If report cards are used, parents should be informed of the type of card and when they can expect to receive it.

6. *Additional information.* Other helpful information depends upon the child's age and specific program. For instance, if the program is for secondary-age children, the parents may need to know about work-study arrangements and how their children will receive high school credit. If the program is for younger children, tips for parents on managing their child's behavior might be useful. And the handbook could include a list of agencies that parents can contact for special services or books they might want to consult for additional information. If the children use the cafeteria, the handbook might include the prices of lunch programs and provisions for children who bring their own lunches.

As one of the most important communication tools for teachers, handbooks should be developed with the parents' needs in mind. They can be surveyed to determine what they would like to see in a handbook. Also, special attention should be given to any unique circumstances. For instance, in Albuquerque, some of the special education teachers have developed handbooks in both Spanish and English, in keeping with the parents' linguistic backgrounds.

Teachers should take care to spell and punctuate accurately. Teachers and school systems should set an example of proper grammar.

With the availability of computers, classroom or school handbooks can be stored on the school's computer for rapid review and revision. Individual copies can be printed for parents who want extra copies and for new transfers. This handbook, too, should be brief—a few pages highlighting the special information that parents need in addition to the general information. Parents will appreciate this concise, specialized handbook more than a long, in-depth document.

DEVELOPING HANDOUTS FOR SPECIFIC SITUATIONS

Developing handouts represents an effort to individualize programs for parents. The handouts can be area specific, age specific, or theme specific. They usually are best developed in small groups, which tend to generate more ideas. In general, handouts should not be too lengthy, they should be clear, and they should include all pertinent information.

The variety of handouts that could be developed for parents of children with disabilities is limited only by your time and imagination. Parents often want to know what books they can read that pertain to their child's disability. Others ask what games they can play with their children at home; where they can take their children on field trips; what book, tape/CD, or magazine clubs they can subscribe to; and what activities are available for their children in the summer and during trips.

Other topics that parents bring up include which pets are suitable for children with disabilities, suggestions for helping the exceptional child with homework, where secondary-level exceptional children can find part-time work, cookbooks for exceptional children to use, restaurants that are "friendly" to children with disabilities, and hobbies for people with disabilities.

The information in a handbook might be organized by type of disability, chronological age of the child, level or difficulty of the concept presented, or readability level or predominant language of the parents. The following are possible topics for handbooks and handouts.

Games to Play at Home

When parents and children sit down together in the evening, they can do many things besides watching television, playing computer games, or laboriously sharing a homework assignment. Many suitable, fun games are available commercially or homemade. Educational games have the advantage of reinforcing a specific skill or concept. Sometimes a game reinforces more than one skill. An example is the game Anagrams, which has a primary purpose of promoting spelling and at the same time calls upon math skills and abstract reasoning.

In a university course on counseling and consulting with parents of children with disabilities, a small group of graduate students decided to prepare a handout describing games in which parents and children could participate together. Rather than undertaking the formidable task of listing handmade and commercial games, they decided to first give parents some general guidelines, as follows:

1. Select games that give children needed practice and also are of interest to them.

2. Keep in mind that each child is an individual with unique needs and preferences.
3. Use simple games with young children and slow learners. Games utilizing concrete materials (beanbags, balls, cards) are easier for children to learn than games requiring only mental processes.
4. Demonstrate the game as necessary.
5. To include language practice, have children occasionally give the directions for games orally.
6. Protect children's feelings in games as in other activities. Don't force timid children to play a game against their will. Perhaps giving them a game to play individually will help them feel accepted until they feel secure enough to take part willingly in a game involving more participants.
7. Insist on playing games according to the rules. If children want to change the directions, tell them you will try their suggestions the next time you play the game. Emphasize the importance of following the rules to make the game meaningful and enjoyable.
8. Discuss and agree upon who is to take responsibility for putting away the game in good order.

Next, the graduate students organized the games according to the three basic headings of mathematics, reading, and spelling. They further divided these categories into homemade and commercial games progressing from simple to difficult.

Homemade Games

For the homemade games, they used the following as an example of the format:

Name: "If I Had $10"
Purpose: To reinforce monetary concepts
Materials: A sheet of paper, the daily newspaper or a catalog, and paste or paper glue
Procedure: Give the child a piece of paper and the newspaper or a catalog. Have the child cut or tear out advertised items. As they select each item, they are to write down its name and how much it costs. With each additional item, the child totals the prices to see

whether he or she has spent the allotted $10. If the child spent more than $10, he or she must remove an item until the total spent is $10 or just under $10.

Variations: Vary the amount the child can spend, higher or lower.

The format of the games was kept simple, and the materials were those that would be readily available. Variations usually were added to make a game more complex for students at higher levels.

Teachers have the advantage of knowing the concepts and skills in which the student needs more work. Many times, the teacher can adapt games used in the classroom for use by parents.

Commercial Games

For commercial games, the graduate students used the same format to describe the game, but they kept instructions for playing the game to a minimum. Instead, they included the company that produced the game and the cost of the game. Also listed on the handout were names of the stores in their area where parents could purchase the games.

Make-and-Take Workshops

Some schools have found the make-and-take workshop to be well received by children, parents, and teachers alike. In this workshop, parents are taught how to make games, nutritious snacks, presents, or other things to bring home after the meeting. Developing a handout on games (as described above) is one of the most popular themes for these workshops.

Checkout Systems

Most teachers of exceptional children use a checkout system. Checkout systems need not be limited to books. Innovative teachers have set up checkout systems for audio recordings, CDs, and pictures. Games are a natural for checkout systems because teachers usually have a number of commercial games in their rooms to be used for various projects, learning experiences, or free-time activities. These might be available for students to check out for a weekend or overnight. The child could earn the privilege of being able to check out a game by demonstrating appropriate use of the game or by other contingencies.

Roosevelt–Perry School in Louisville, Kentucky (Jefferson County Public Schools, 1995), is known for unique educational programs. In one of these, the school made available about 65 computers for parents and children to check out. According to Jay Back, the school's principal, not one computer was lost, and the computer skills of the families and the children increased tremendously. In addition, a number of the children and their family members were invited to local businesses to show off their computer skills and networking capabilities.

Parent Corner

An innovative teacher of gifted children at Eugene Field Elementary School in Albuquerque developed a "parent corner" in her classroom. This was a place where parents could read and look at materials while waiting for their children in a nonthreatening environment and didn't have to go to the city library to get the same books. Often, children and parents who didn't have much reading material at home spent time together selecting books and games they could enjoy with one another. A checkout system could be created for the parent corner as well.

Summer Programs for Children With Disabilities

A common question parents ask special education teachers is, "What programs are available for my child during the summer?" Therefore, a handout listing summer programs is desirable. The teacher may want to recommend some specific programs to meet the educational or social needs of individual students. To individualize a prepared list, place the child's name at the top and place a star beside or circle the activities most relevant to the child.

After compiling the master list, the teacher can readily update it from year to year. The advent of computers has simplified this task. The office secretary or director of special education may be willing to update the list by making the necessary phone calls in early spring.

Guidelines for preparing a list of summer programs are as follows:

1. List the questions parents will want to have answered. For instance:

   ➤ For whom is the program intended?
   ➤ What will be the age range of the children for whom the program is intended?

➤ What is the location of the program?

➤ What is the duration of the program? When will it start and finish?

➤ Is this a morning, an afternoon, or an all-day program?

➤ Does the program have a fee? If so, how much?

➤ Does the program have any provision for transportation?

➤ When and where is registration?

➤ Who is the person in charge, or who is the phone contact for further information?

2. List places to contact for information about programs:

➤ *Public schools.* Someone in the administration office probably has a brochure from which programs applicable to exceptional children can be derived.

➤ *City parks and recreation office.* A call to this office may elicit the information needed and also may provide an impetus for offering new programs for exceptional children.

➤ *City library.* Most libraries offer a variety of programs for children with disabilities.

➤ *Community centers.* Many cities have community centers that operate year-round, most of which have provisions for children with disabilities.

➤ *Private schools.* The yellow pages of the phone book list schools that parents may check for possible programs.

➤ *Universities and colleges.* To have practicum experiences for their students, universities sometimes set up summer school programs through their special education departments, reading departments, or physical education departments.

➤ *YMCA and YWCA.* These organizations usually offer sports programs, arts and crafts, and similar programs for all children.

➤ *Mental health centers.* Some mental health centers provide educational programs and play activities, as well as therapy sessions.

➤ *Art galleries.* Some art galleries announce classes or special events for children during the summer.

➤ *Associations.* Associations with local offices include those for children with special needs—mental retardation, behavior disorders, cerebral palsy, cystic fibrosis, epilepsy, multiple sclerosis, muscular dystrophy, and so on. Many of these associations collect the appropriate information, and some sponsor programs for children.

➤ *Camps.* Some day camps are offered especially for children with disabilities. Sponsors have included the Boy Scouts, Easter Seals, Campfire Girls, and local churches, in addition to the local YWCA or YMCA.

➤ *Riding academies.* Horseback riding academies sometimes have special programs for children with physical disabilities, as well as other exceptionalities. Horseback riding has been known to help children with behavior disorders.

3. Decide on a format for the handout. Because many summer programs apply to a range of disabilities, categorizing the information by exceptionality probably would be redundant. Organizing the handout by activity (educational, recreational, camping, special interests, and so on) usually is more functional. Whenever possible, the information should provide responses to the questions posed in the first guideline. The information can be presented in a number of different ways, two of which are as follows:

➤ A single booklet covering all the information. This may give a parent more information than necessary, though.

➤ A computer database developed according to subject, place, program, and date. The information could be easily customized and updated because only specific pieces of the database, rather than the entire handbook, have to be changed. Microsoft Excel is an excellent program to categorize the information.

A number of teachers working cooperatively to gather data on summer programs could accomplish the task in a relatively short time. Or summer programs might be the theme of a workshop or an in-service project.

COMMUNITY SERVICES

Parents are continually searching for new information, and professionals often have a list of local resources available for them. As an informal network of parents and teachers evolves, a telephone call may be all that is needed to obtain the names of people who can provide specific assistance.

In rural areas, one of the important networks is the county extension service. County extension agents are excellent resources for parents of children with disabilities. Many materials have been developed and are available in county extension offices throughout the United States.

At the most basic level, the parents could be given a telephone number to call in an emergency. This might be, for example, the number for the local chapter of the Arc (formerly the Association for Retarded Citizens) or the number of the state director of special education. For more detailed information, parents may be given a directory of community services compiled by the city or by interested teachers. If parents want to participate and be involved, they might be involved in developing handouts along with the teachers. A sample handout is shown in Figure 7.1.

Field Trips

Many exceptional children have been limited in experiential learning because of their physical disabilities or parents' reticence to take their children with behavior disorders to a movie or the mall. Recognizing this need, many teachers expose children to new opportunities in the community. They arrange field trips to the fire station, dairy, bakery, and grocery store, for example (Larry E. Decker & Associates, 1990).

In compiling a handout for field trips, the following steps are suggested.

1. *Brainstorm with experienced teachers.* Other teachers may be the richest source of information. Someone will know of a nature trail for the blind, a guitar maker, an auto mechanic who enjoys children, or an animal shelter that children can visit with adult supervision. The suggestions should include information on whom to contact for the necessary arrangements or for additional information.

2. *Develop a list of questions.* As in summer programs, questions should be prepared in advance. In addition to the name of the place, the person to contact, and the telephone number, needed information includes:

   a. *Times open:* When is the facility open for visitors? Saturdays and Sundays? Do the hours change during the summer?

**IN ORDER TO GET THE MOST OF YOUR COMMUNITY SERVICES,
CONSIDER THE FOLLOWING RESOURCES:**

Associations
➤ Associations have handouts, and they know people.
➤ The yellow pages have a listing of "Associations."
➤ Associations may be similar in nature and subject matter even if not
  exactly the same.

Schools
➤ Administrators in the public school system usually know about services
  available in the community.

County
➤ The county public health nurse or the county mental health office is
  available for help.

Politicians
➤ Voters put and keep representatives in office. Make them work for your
  vote.

State
➤ Every state has a state department of special education.

Church
➤ Most clergy are aware of community services and are glad to help.

Legal Services
➤ The yellow pages list free referral services if you need help.

City
➤ Most large cities have community resource directories.
➤ The United Way or the mayor's office will give referrals.

**FOLLOW THESE TIPS IN ORDER TO BENEFIT THE MOST FROM
THE SERVICES IN YOUR COMMUNITY:**
➤ Keep cool.
➤ Be patient.
➤ Don't worry about hurting someone's feelings.
➤ Be optimistic. Most people want to do the right thing.

FIGURE 7.1
Sample Handout: A Parent's Guide to Community Services

    b. *Tours:* Some places conduct tours at specified times. They might prefer that parents and their children come at the beginning of the tour time.

    c. *Groups or individuals:* Should parents bring their children individually, or will they have to round up neighborhood children to have enough visitors to warrant the organization's time?

    d. *Disabilities:* Does the organization accommodate and welcome children with disabilities? Some places that parents may want to take their children have dangerous or delicate operations. The contact may ask for specific information about the type and severity of disability before agreeing to the visit.

    e. *Cost:* Is there a fee? This should be checked out ahead of time to avoid any misunderstandings.

    f. What might the children expect to see or do while there?

3. *Decide on a format.* The information should be arranged in a precise format. For example:

    a. Name:

    b. Location:

    c. Person to contact:

    d. Phone:

    e. Hours:

    f. Days:

    g. Age requirements:

    h. Purpose:

    i. Cost:

    j. Comments:

After the information is compiled, it can be entered on the computer and stored for later reference. The information can be organized into usable categories in a number of different ways: cost, ages, times open, or purpose.

Taking children to new places is exciting for everyone—children, their parents, and teachers. Collecting information in advance and preparing the children for the experiences is a necessary prerequisite.

Subscription Services and Clubs

Who doesn't like to receive something through the mail—unless it's a bill? Exceptional children are no exception. Children can receive things by mail periodically at a nominal cost. A number of magazine, tape/CD, and book clubs are geared especially for children. Public libraries subscribe to a number of publications that may help parents select materials and activities for their children. Parents' Choice Foundation publishes a monthly e-mail newsletter that shares articles and provides information on its award-winning books, videos, audios, computer software, and toys (see www.parents-choice.org). The foundation is also a regular contributor to *Reader's Digest,* giving tips about games, toys, activities, travel, and its products. Using such publications, teachers can compile a handout appropriate for parents of children in a given classroom.

Modern technology has provided media for learning and entertainment that reach far beyond the printed word. Of course, the family must have access to the equipment necessary to use these media. Parents who are interested in subscribing to a tape/CD club or a computer software club can benefit from the teacher's advice. For example, if given a choice of free-time activities, does the child gravitate to the CD player, the tape recorder, or the computer? Second, can the child manipulate the equipment adequately, or can he or she learn to use it easily?

If these two prerequisites are met, perhaps the parents could benefit from a handout giving some information about clubs and subscriptions specifically for children. Information in the handout should include the name of the club or subscription service, its address, and a description of the type of records/tapes/CDs/books the club offers. Sometimes, local music stores provide a specialized subscription service. Before investing in any club or subscription, parents should, of course, read the contract carefully.

Many children have started reading or have been encouraged to read more by being on the receiving end of book clubs. Something about receiving one's own books through the mail and starting a miniature library is gratifying. Some exceptional children who have severe reading problems or who cannot read at all will derive their greatest pleasure from receiving books their parents read to them.

Handouts on media clubs and services can be compiled in workshops or as an in-service project. In preparing the handouts, teachers may want to send for the literature the subscription services supply and read it carefully. And reviewing magazines that are candidates for the handouts is desirable so adults can determine for whom the activities and articles are most appropriate. The format, size, and quality of content all should be considered in the teachers' evaluation.

Educators also might consider compiling a list of free and inexpensive things children can send for through the mail. Some of these sources could be included in the handout to parents, and others might be used in special projects for children in class.

Travel Tips

Traveling with children, exceptional or not, can be a pleasure or an ordeal, depending in some part on planning and preparation. Parents usually appreciate receiving a handout on travel tips, which often can be used for many years because much of the information is timeless. The handout might utilize a checklist format, covering the following major points:

1. *Easy access items.* Parents will want to keep some things handy, perhaps in a small box in the front seat. These items might include a first-aid kit, snacks, a litter bag, pencils, notebooks, car games or toys, and a camera. The first-aid kit can be either homemade or commercial. A first-aid manual that is easy to read is also a good idea.

2. *Safety tips.* Parents can discuss safety tips with their children before the trip. Sometimes a list of safety suggestions from the child's teacher can reinforce the parents' rules ("Miss Mendez says we shouldn't throw things out of the window").

3. *Games to play.* Over the years, parents traveling with children have invented car games that make the miles fly and keep the children occupied. These games often require the child to be able to count or know the alphabet. Even if the child is unable to do this, he or she could be a member of a team with Mom or Dad.

4. *Helpful hints.* Teachers may want to brainstorm a number of ideas to facilitate the trip: how the children can be included in planning for the trip, where and when to stop, how to pack suitcases, and what the child can take along to play with. Some oft-forgotten items for parents to bring along include pillows and plastic bags for dirty clothes.

Car games should be simple to explain. Giving the game a name, and maybe writing a simple explanation of how it is played, may be helpful. Some games might be played simultaneously. For instance, parents and children may decide to make a list of license plates they see from different states. Because this game may not be concluded during the trip, License Poker or the Alphabet Game could be played at the same time.

As a result of his or her experience with the child, the teacher might indicate (with checkmarks, gold stars, highlighter, or other indicator) which of the items on the handout are the most appealing and appropriate for that individual child. Parents appreciate individualization of information. Because travel tips are valuable only when the family is going on a trip, this information is not necessarily included in a handbook for all parents. It is most useful as a special-purpose handout.

Other Parent Packets

A number of other situational handouts might be developed. For example, a group of teachers might cooperatively develop a handout on holiday suggestions for children with disabilities. This could include items from some of the other handouts, such as subscriptions and commercial games, as well as toys for specific needs. The information would be disseminated in advance of the holiday or provided at a parent–teacher conference.

Some parents appreciate information on how to host a party for a child with a disability. This handout might include what type of refreshments to serve and when, how many children to invite or how many adults to have per number of children, what games allow a child in a wheelchair to participate (if applicable), how long the party should last, what the best time of day and week is, what information parents of the invited children might need, and so on.

Some additional handouts are found in the way of the tip sheets in Appendix A. These constitute a way of providing information for parents on an individualized basis. These tip sheets can be duplicated and sent home, passed out to parents at an open house or parent–teacher conference, included in newsletters, or made available through school, community, and business organizations.

SUMMARY

Parents need information so they can boost their children's opportunities for success in school. Because special education programs utilize special techniques and procedures, the general handbook the public school provides to parents may not include the specific information that the parents of exceptional children want. Also, parents of exceptional children can benefit from handouts covering specific situations and information directly relevant to parents in these circumstances.

Handbooks should be brief, attractive, and written at the parents' reading level. These handbooks should contain key names and phone numbers, any unique procedures and techniques, information on transportation, a list of special materials for special children, and additional information germane to the child.

Situational handouts can be beneficial to parents if they are available when parents need them. Suggestions for homemade or commercial games that parents and children can play together are welcomed. The games may be used to teach academic skills or to develop cooperative social behaviors. And parents often are interested in a compilation of programs available for their children during the summer. To broaden their child's experiential environment, many parents are willing to take their children on field trips if they know where to go and whom to contact. Also, many magazine, tape/CD, computer, and book clubs are available to give children hours of enjoyment. Subscriptions make good gifts. Finally, travel tips may be useful to parents.

ACTIVITIES

1. Prepare a brief handbook for the parents of the children in your classroom.
2. Prepare a handout for a specific situation. Use the tip sheets in Appendix A as examples if you wish.
3. Generate new ideas for information sheets or handouts that might be developed for parents.
4. Using a commercial readability analysis program, analyze the passage about the diagnostician found at the beginning of this chapter.
5. With other teachers, prepare a handbook of community services in your area.

6. Visit your county extension service and gather materials that would be useful for parents.
7. Visit some of the community services in your area, and interview a staff member.
8. With a group of teachers, develop a directory of tutors.
9. Visit the public library and generate a list of books appropriate for parents of exceptional children. Enlist the help of a librarian to develop this as a handout.
10. With a group of teachers, identify a list of books and resources on the Internet for parents of children with disabilities.

REFERENCES

Edge, D. (1993). *Understanding the principles of the changing family structure* [videotape]. Greensboro, NC: National Training Center.

Edge, D. (1995). *Parents and families: Research on involving parents in the educational process.* Louisville, KY: University of Louisville.

Harry, B., Allen, N., & McLaughlin, M. (1995). Communication versus compliance: African-American parents' involvement in special education. *Exceptional Children, 61*(4).

Jefferson County Public Schools. (1995). *Best practices for parent involvement: A resource for the school staff.* Louisville, KY: Author.

Larry E. Decker & Associates. (1990). *Community education: Building learning communities.* Alexandria, VA: National Community Education Association.

8

Reporting
Progress

Mom: The school called today.

Dad: What did he do this time?

Mom: He tore up his math paper and said he wasn't going to do it.

Dad: Why don't they ever call when he does his math instead of just when he doesn't?

Mom: They want us to come to school tomorrow morning.

elephone calls and letters from school personnel usually strike fear in the hearts of parents. This is because the messages are almost always associated with something negative about their children. A mother whose child had been having problems at school once said, "I shake every time the phone rings during the day." Many parents wonder (as the father does in the opening example) why they don't get called when their child does something positive (Newman, 1995).

Traditionally, reports to parents have consisted of a parent–teacher conference and quarterly report cards. Departures from this routine occur when the child misbehaves or is failing in school. Therefore, parents tend to have negative feelings about their communications from the school (Markoff, 1992; Merina, 1991).

Astute observers of students' behavior often notice an increase in their academic production just before and immediately after the date when report cards go home. At the same time, these students' socially unacceptable behavior decreases. This is consistent with the learning theory approach (Webber & Scheuerman, 1991). According to the learning theory approach, when a specified behavior is rewarded it will be maintained or accelerated. If a specified behavior is punished, the behavior will decline or be eliminated. Action tends to surge around deadline times (Long & Edwards, 1994). Behaviors can change around the date when report cards are issued, but because report cards are sent home once every 9 weeks, the effect is minimal (Simmons, 1990). Daily report cards will allow the teacher or parent to modify a specific behavior, and they will allow the significant others in a child's life to keep a visual record to see if what they are doing is having the desired effect. Various behavior-monitoring systems are discussed in the following sections.

REPORTING SYSTEMS

To counteract the effects of infrequent reporting, some teachers and schools have instituted more frequent reporting systems and other means of communication, especially for children with special needs. The most intensive of these are daily reporting systems.

Daily Reporting Systems

To improve student production may mean reporting to parents more frequently about their child's school performance and also encouraging parents' responses to this information. Essentially, all these systems operate in a similar manner. Daily reporting systems use the same format as the less frequent report card. Parents receive results of the day's production at the end of every day, which gives them an opportunity to reward their children for accomplishments immediately. Children with disabilities often benefit from this frequent feedback and monitoring of progress, which also allows for any needed changes in programming.

Weekly Awards

As the end of the school year approached, Sharon Schmitz decided to enlist parental support to help maintain good social behavior in her third-grade class. She decided to try a weekly report and in early March sent home the letter shown in Figure 8.1.

For each child, Mrs. Schmitz reproduced a form like the example in Figure 8.1. She placed a form inside a piece of construction paper folded in half and gave this folder to each child to keep at his or her desk. During the last 4 or 5 minutes of each day, she went from child to child and asked each child to "grade" his or her behavior by placing a star, a smiling face, or a frowning face on the report. At the end of the week, the children took their records home.

The results of the program seemed to justify the extra teacher time, and the teacher was pleased to agree that the children usually assessed their behavior fairly accurately. She said, "This report was intended to reward good behavior and to alert the parents to any current behavioral problems. The response by parents and children was favorable. Parental support, recognition from the teacher, and personal satisfaction worked in concert to reinforce positive behavior."

This program had several positive features:

➤ The end-of-the day assessment settled down the class. They all sat quietly in their seats for this final activity of the school day.

➤ Each child in essence had a mini-conference with the teacher every day—which meant that each child had some individual attention from the teacher daily.

➤ The parents were involved in the program. They were alerted to their child's daily activity and were invited to provide feedback.

Dear _____

This note is to inform you of a new behavior report we have introduced in our class. Each Friday, your child will bring home a report concerning his/her behavior in school during the week. This is a sample of what the report looks like:

BEHAVIOR REPORT

Name _____

Monday 3/5	Tuesday 3/6	Wednesday 3/7	Thursday 3/8	Friday 3/9

A record of my behavior this week: ✱   ☺   ☹

           Very Good   OK   Bad

Each day, I will speak to your child about his/her behavior and mark the chart. When your child brings home this report on Friday, I would like your support in *praising good behavior.* If your child neglects to bring home the form, please ask about it. If you have any questions concerning your child's behavior, please let me know. Your part in following up on this is important!

Thank you for your help.

Sincerely,

Please sign this part and send it back to school with your child Monday to let me know you have received this report and will support us in this effort.

Child _____

Parent _____

Date: _____

FIGURE 8.1
Behavior Report Letter to Parents

Merit Achievement Award System

Another reporting technique that Mrs. Schmitz used effectively was the merit achievement award system. In this program, every time the child accomplished a designated behavioral objective, the teacher designed and filled out a certificate like the one in Figure 8.2 and sent it home. According to her, "The children valued and respected these awards. The first certificate was used to stimulate children as they acquired the skill of cursive writing. Later they helped decide which other skills were important enough to be rewarded with a certificate."

The merit achievement award system offered a means to recognize the academic performance of every child in the class. This system was based on the behavioral objectives the teacher had established for each child in her class. It also enabled parents to see how their children were progressing, which reinforced the school as a positive learning environment.

Self-Reporting Reward System

Sharon Vaughn, a teacher in the New Albany school system, used self-reporting systems for students with behavioral problems who were

---

CERTIFICATE

This will certify that _____

has learned to _____.

This skill is a valuable tool for good communication.

Teacher's Name _____

Date_____

Class _____

FIGURE 8.2
Merit Achievement Award System: Certificate

included in general education classes. Contingent on the students' performances, they could earn free time, supplies, and pizza parties (for the entire class). The teacher recorded and signed each self-report daily and sent home a record of the students' records weekly.

The teacher and parents reviewed these reports during parent–teacher conferences. Ms. Vaughn reported a significant change in the children's behavior, which she credited to her use of the daily/weekly reporting systems.

Teacher–Parent Communication Program

The Special Education Instructional Materials Center at Lawrence, Kansas, developed a teacher–parent communication system to teach parents and teachers how to effectively maintain a reporting system. Since its inception, this system has been used with numerous groups of teachers and parents. The teacher–parent communication program usually is used with a single child in a general education class who has been identified as needing special attention. The procedure is as follows:

1. When a child has been identified as having a social or academic problem in the classroom and has not responded to typical behavior modification programs or remedial techniques, the teacher initiates a conference with the parents and the child.
2. In the conference, the teacher delineates the problem behavior and develops a worksheet that is in essence a behavioral contract.
3. The teacher explains the program, based on cards stating "acceptable" or "unacceptable" (these can be index cards with the word written on them and perhaps laminated for multiple reuse). The worksheet specifies the academic or social performance required to receive an "acceptable" card. The contract indicates the number of cards to be given out daily (usually 10 cards, one every 40 minutes). The teacher, parents, and student together agree upon the number of "acceptable" cards that will entitle the child to a daily reward, as well as the possibility of a weekly reward.
4. The parents and child agree upon the rewards to be earned. The daily rewards are usually simple—such as "stay up an extra 15 minutes" or "watch a favorite TV program."

This program is commendable in that the child is involved in the conference and he or she has a say in what the rewards are to be. Also, the child is able to listen to the explanation, to avoid misunderstandings.

The benefits of the program are many. As social and academic behaviors change, parents are kept informed and their input is solicited as well. The parents are encouraged to give their child positive reinforcement frequently, and the children are able to see the relationship between their behavior and its consequences. This program was found to be successful, and the investigators stressed the importance of consistency and realistic expectations—the student should not be expected to behave better than other children in the same class.

MicroSociety Program

The original MicroSociety Program was developed by Dr. George Richmond, Lowell, Massachusetts (Bronger, Chastain, Meurer, Oakes, & Sanford, 1994; Richmond, 1989, 1990). The Johnstown Road MicroSociety School in the Jefferson County School System in Louisville, Kentucky, represents an adaptation that transformed a general elementary school into a thriving mega-operation of a minisociety supervised by John Waldrop (principal), Pat Meurer, Andy Bronger, and Lisa Oakes (teachers), and the rest of the staff. This program was designed to involve each student and his or her parents in performance activities related to the functioning of a normal society.

The Johnstown Road MicroSociety School consists of a bank under the supervision of the Bank of Louisville (now BB&T), a clothing store, a number of manufacturing businesses, a candy store, post office, town government, police department, and a number of other ventures. The students operate the school and monitor their own performance. For example, if a student has a problem with another student during the day, the students are taken to court. Elected conflict resolution experts (students) on the town board listen to the case and decide how to resolve the problem. The school maintains a record of each issue and its resolution. Every student has a job to perform in the minisociety, and everyone earns J-Bucks they can spend in the various stores operated by the MicroSociety School.

Daily and weekly progress is maintained on a bank of computers operated by the students. They present performance and progress reports regularly to the school-based decision-making team and the parents. Parents have reported significant improvement in their children's managing their school and home chores.

Kroth, Whelan, and Stables's Project

Kroth, Whelan, and Stables (1970) were pioneers of a project that included parents in a reinforcement program for their children with emotional disturbance. These students were in a structured educational environment that utilized behavioral principles, and the parents were asked to become involved in a reinforcement program for their children. They helped to develop a simple daily report card, listing the subjects in which the child was enrolled, as well as social behavior (see Figure 8.3). The scores were recorded on the card as the percentage of problems or exercises worked correctly, and the social behavior was reported. The percentages were added and divided by the number of subjects being measured to obtain a daily average. Each child filled in his or her own report card. Then the teacher checked, dated, and signed it.

DAILY REPORT CARD

Name _____

     Language Arts   _____
     Mathematics   _____
     Science   _____
     Literature or Reading   _____
     Spelling   _____
     Typing   _____
     Social Behavior   _____

Total Points _____ Daily _____

Date _____

Teacher's Signature_____

FIGURE 8.3
Kroth, Whelan, & Stables's Project

The system was introduced in a parent group meeting. The parents were instructed in graphing procedures and in methods for conferring rewards. They were encouraged to utilize rewards that were within their individual value systems. The emphasis was on reward rather than punishment. The project directors also reinforced the parents with praise when merited.

To test the effects of the program, the parents were encouraged to select two or three specific areas on the report card on which to concentrate their reinforcement efforts and to withhold knowledge of those areas from the staff for a few months. It was found that in the areas the parents chose to reinforce selectively, the children grew more than they did in the areas that the parents did not reinforce. This outcome suggests that the program is viable for changing the behavior of children with behavioral or emotional disorders. Parents can greatly influence what happens in the classroom if they are invited to participate.

OTHER REPORTING PROGRAMS

Many teachers have phoned parents or sent letters home when their children have performed well in school, but they probably have not systematized their efforts in quite the same ways as the programs outlined previously. Teachers continue to experiment with a number of ideas that seem like potent ways of sharing information with parents. Some of these ideas show promise.

One example of a teacher catching a child being good and reporting the child's progress is that of Judy Zimmer, Minot, North Dakota. She took a camera to school to "catch children being good" and then showed the pictures to the parents. The parents were pleased to see these snapshots of their happy children, smiling and cooperating. A natural outcome is that the parents become more accepting and willing to participate in the educational program for their children.

Just before their scheduled parent–teacher conferences, Jeanne Marie Stables asked her junior high children to write notes to their parents reporting their academic progress. She showed these notes to the parents at the conference, along with examples of the child's work. The parents were asked to respond to their child's letter with one of their own to the child, reinforcing the child's growth.

Ann Tice, of Shawnee Mission, Kansas, brought a tape-recorder to the parent–teacher conference. After looking over their child's work, the parents recorded a message to their children. They were asked to be positive in their comments. The following morning the children listened to their parents' taped messages. These recordings were saved as a permanent record for future reference.

Carol Bartlett, of Louisville, Kentucky, similarly reported to parents through videotaped messages. The parents could observe their children participating in educational activities and listen to their children read and perform other educational tasks. The videotapes became a permanent record that enabled teachers to review the tapes for later programming decisions.

Based on a school survey, Jan Lowe, of Louisville, Kentucky, discovered that about 55% of all students enrolled at Roosevelt–Perry School had cable television. She worked with the University of Louisville Television Services, TKR Cable Television, and the students at Roosevelt–Perry to develop and present half-hour programs about the school to the parents via television. The parents and children were encouraged to call the studio for more information about the school's activities.

In the early days of e-mail, Jan Cerrito, a parent at Pitt Academy in Louisville, Kentucky—a school for children with severe learning disabilities and developmental problems—taught parents and teachers to use e-mail to communicate with each other. The messages involved daily school events, lessons plans, homework assignments, and the general curriculum. The parents were able to access the Internet to download math and reading programs. The system was expanded to enable children to communicate with other children from around the country—and the world.

Modern technology and media offer expanded ways for schools to report to parents. Videotapes, digital cameras, movies, and computers, along with traditional verbal and written records, have vastly widened the avenues for reporting to parents. A good rule in using alternative reporting systems is to show examples of what children *can* do rather than to point out their deficits. This is particularly true with children who have been classified in some way as exceptional. All too often their weaknesses have been highlighted, and reinforcement of their successes has been shown to be much more effective.

SUMMARY

Traditionally, public school systems have delivered report cards and held parent–teacher conferences infrequently. The report usually consists of a summary of the child's work for a 9-week period. Children, particularly those with special needs, require much more reinforcement for their optimum academic and social growth. To involve parents in reinforcing their children's efforts, the parents must receive information from the school more often. This chapter has presented daily and weekly reporting systems and other ways to report and reinforce the students' academic and social growth. Follow-up studies have verified the viability of these programs.

Among the reporting systems teachers have developed are to take pictures of children at work and play and show them to the parents; have children write notes to their parents and have the parents respond; tape-record messages between parents and children; videotape children in productive activities; and utilize e-mail and other technology in reporting to parents.

ACTIVITIES

1. Develop the framework for a daily or weekly reporting system for the parents.
2. Organize a parent team to write and distribute a newsletter for your class.
3. Set up a program for a child or a few children using special reporting techniques so parents can see their child's changes in either academic or social behavior.
4. Call a different parent every school day for a month, or until you have called them all, and tell them something good their child did that day.
5. Take a picture of a child in your class working on something (and looking like he/she enjoys it) and send it home to his/her parents.
6. Devise a certificate or award to send home when a child accomplishes a behavioral objective.
7. As a group project, develop a brief video for the parents, explaining and showing classroom activities. Involve the children in the video.

8. Explore how you might use computer and/or other technology in the school as a means to communicate with parents.

REFERENCES

Bronger, A., Chastain, K., Meurer, P., Oakes, L., & Sanford, H. (1994). *Micro-society: A strategy for whole school and classroom management*. Unpublished manuscript, University of Louisville, KY.

Kroth, R. L., Whelan, R. J., & Stables, J. M. (1970). Teacher application of behavioral principles in home and classroom environments. *Focus on Exceptional Children, 2*(3).

Long, N., & Edwards, M. (1994). The use of a daily report card to address children's school behavior problems. *Contemporary Education, 65*(3), 152–155.

Markoff, A. M. (1992). *Within reach: Academic achievement through parent–teacher communication*. Novato, CA: Academic Therapy Publications.

Merina, A. (1991). School comes to parents at their work. *NEA Today, 9*(6), 27.

Newman, R. (1995). The home-school connection. *Childhood Education, 71*(5), 296.

Richmond, G. (1989, Nov.). The future school: Is Lowell pointing us toward another revolution? *Kappan.*

Richmond, G. (1990, Nov. 28). Micro-society: Restructuring schools to restructure society. *Education Week.*

Simmons, B. J. (1990). The home-school connection: Let's get serious about it. *Clearing House, 63*(5), 223.

Webber, J., & Scheuermann, B. (1991). Managing behavior problems: Accentuate the positive...Eliminate the negative! *Teaching Exceptional Children, 24*(1), 13–19.

9

Parent Group Meetings

One of the quickest and most effective ways of presenting information of widespread parent interest is the small-group meeting (Seifert, 1992). Some topics are not of interest or relevance to all parents attending whole-school meetings. The small-group format should not be confused with small-group sessions designed to train parents in specific child-rearing techniques or meetings whose goal is a therapeutic outcome. The major purpose of the parent group meeting discussed in this chapter is to relay information to parents effectively and efficiently and elicit their participation.

Parents are more satisfied when they have opportunities to talk and share information with one another (Karasik & Samels, 1990). Further, they can pass along what was discussed to parents who cannot attend. The parent group is one way to bridge the information gap concerning issues of child rearing.

PLANNING FOR THE PARENT GROUP MEETING

Effective planning increases the teacher's chances of being successful in developing parent groups (Davies, 1990; Edge & Franken, 1996). Before the school year begins, teachers should generally assess classroom needs and decide what group meetings may be helpful during the year, what purposes they are to fulfill, and when these meetings should be held to have the most meaning for parents. The teacher has to decide who will be involved and the best format by which to relay the information. Each special education program will dictate the content and type of meeting.

Suggested Topics

The following topics are some of the many possibilities.

➤ *Classroom policies, procedures, and techniques.* Early in the school year, the teacher meets with the parents to explain his or her classroom policies and procedures. Additional participants in this group meeting might be the counselor, social worker, principal, and bus driver. The latter is particularly important, as transportation is often worrisome, and the sooner parents understand how it works, the better.

Some teachers use special techniques in their classrooms, such as reward systems and time-outs. The teacher should explain the how and why of these techniques. If children are in special classes for part of the day and included in the general education classes for part of the day, this configuration should be explained.

The parent group meeting might be held in the teacher's classroom so the parents can see—and perhaps use—the special equipment the teacher has available. The parents should be encouraged to ask questions, and parents and teachers should discuss their expectations and clarify them. Name tags will help parents and teachers alike begin to identify each other by name early in the year.

➤ *Grading procedures.* Before the first grading period, the teacher should explain the method he or she will be using to evaluate children and report to the parents. Parents will be interested in any differences from the normal reporting procedures and how these differences will affect the child if he or she is returned full time to the general classroom.

➤ *Parent–teacher conferences.* Parents can be informed of what to expect in the parent–teacher conference, as mandated by IDEA, and how they can prepare for the conference to facilitate a smoother relationship between parent and teacher. Some of the tip sheets in Appendix A can be helpful in preparing the parent for the parent–teacher conference.

In September 1994, the Jefferson County Public Schools in Louisville, Kentucky, mailed a tip sheet outlining things parents could do to prepare for their scheduled parent–teacher conferences. As a result, 98% of the parents reported that they felt prepared for the parent–teacher conference and were pleased with the parent–teacher interactions. Freda Merriweather and Sandy Poe (personal communication, June 1995) reported that the parents enjoyed the parent–teacher conferences more than they did the open-house activities. As a result of careful preparation and communication, the parents and teachers learned a lot about working with each other.

➤ *Introduction of specialists.* The teacher may want to introduce to the parents the specialists who will be involved in some way with their children in the coming year. These specialists may include the school counselor, school psychologist, speech therapist, physical therapist, school nurse, and others. Each could briefly explain what he or she does, followed by a time for questions and discussion.

Because of the sheer amount of information, the teacher may want to have two or three parent group meetings instead of just one. One meeting might feature the speech therapist, nurse, counselor, occupational therapist, assistive technology specialist, and school psychologist. These specialists often do intelligence and achievement testing, hearing and vision screening, speech assessment, evaluation of physical development, and review of technology utilization. They can explain their tests or assessment tools and how the results will be used.

Another meeting might introduce the physical education teacher, librarian, and cafeteria personnel, who would lead the parents on a tour of the area of which they are in charge and explain their role in the child's education.

➤ *Related outside agencies.* Some special education students are heavily reliant on outside agencies. Personnel from agencies such as guidance centers, mental health centers, and family service centers that provide direct support to children and their families might introduce themselves and lead a discussion on how they assist the children.

➤ *The business community.* Businesspeople in the community who are working with the schools are good prospects for speaking to parent groups. If they are involved in hiring students, for example, the prospective employers could explain their criteria in selecting applicants to work for them, and they can suggest ways by which parents can improve their child's chances for employment.

➤ Parents as *active participants.* Parents are encouraged to play an active role in their child's education. Some parent group meetings have this specific goal.

➤ *Seminars.* Over the years, the Parent Involvement Center in Albuquerque, New Mexico, and the Parent Education Resource Center, Louisville, Kentucky, experimented with a variety of parent seminars in a number of different settings. They found that parents like to interact with guest speakers on topics such as discipline, adolescence, drugs, divorce, communication skills, leadership, curriculum, community resources, library access, trusts and wills, assessment, assistive technology, and understanding children with special needs.

Television and Radio

Public-access channels represent a vehicle for presenting information to parents who cannot attend group meetings in person. Some TV stations feature public information programs, including ideas from educators, in their formats. Jan Lowe, at Roosevelt–Perry Elementary School in Louisville, utilized broadcast television programs via cable to inform and educate parents. This program was a half-hour interactive program through which parents could see the children and the school and could interact though live telephone call-ins.

The award-winning "PEP Talks for Parents" radio program developed by the Parent Education and Resource Center offered 1-minute informational radio spots on many topics of interest to parents. Many communities have adopted this format.

PARENT INVOLVEMENT IN PLANNING

Teachers should invite parents to participate in planning the parent group meetings, as they will more likely attend the meetings if they are involved in the planning. And they often come up with good ideas to contribute that teachers would not have thought of. The teacher might establish a small advisory committee of parents to help plan some meetings. In selecting members for this advisory group, the teacher should look for enthusiastic parents who are willing to serve for a year. They should be representative of the total group, if possible. Activities and responsibilities of the advisory group might include:

1. *Surveying the group.* Either by questionnaire or by personal contact, the advisory group should survey the other parents to find out what topics they would like to see covered. The questionnaire may be open-ended, or it may consist of a list of topics from which to choose. Examples of surveys are given in Appendix C.
2. *Arranging for participants.* If the parents have decided they would like to hear from a state legislator or the school superintendent, for example, members of the advisory group

should initiate the contact, agree on a date, and complete other details.

3. *Conducting the meeting.* The advisory group should choose a spokesperson to introduce the speaker and to make necessary arrangements for any special equipment or materials.

4. *Refreshments.* Even minimal refreshments are appreciated.

In the meetings that parents plan and conduct, the teacher should stay in the background. The teacher may be asked for advice and help with arrangements, but he or she should keep a low profile and give the parents the credit for the meeting.

SUGGESTIONS FOR IMPROVING MEETINGS

To enhance the probability of successful parent group meetings:

1. Initiate a parent telephone-calling tree, in which parents phone other parents to remind them of the upcoming meeting.

2. Keep the business part of the meeting short.

3. Don't overtalk or line up more presenters than can be accommodated comfortably in the amount of time allocated for the meeting.

4. Start on time. This sets a good example.

5. End on time. Let the parents know ahead of time when the meeting will conclude, and stick to it. Many parents have to line up babysitters or have other commitments after the meeting.

6. Provide an activity room or area for children, with supervision provided by volunteer parents or school personnel. Parents are more apt to come to a meeting if they are able to bring their younger children along. Set up television or cartoon movies and maybe provide healthy snacks for the children.

7. Also provide refreshments for the parents—a proven enticement to meetings.

8. Occasionally have the students perform. A variety show, a demonstration of physical education activities, a song or two, a display of artwork, or a videotape of a classroom activity provides added incentive for parents to come to a meeting.

9. Allow enough time for a question-and-answer period.

10. Provide paper and pencils for the parents so they can take notes on important ideas.
11. Take some pictures of the parents. Show the children these pictures so they can see that their parents come to school, too.
12. Jot a note to parents thanking them for coming to the meeting.

FORMATS FOR SPECIAL EDUCATION MEETINGS

Parent group meetings should be developed around a specific purpose and designed for a specific audience. If parents have a common bond—band members' parents, athletes' parents, parents of children with disabilities—attendance is likely to increase.

Special educators in Odessa, Texas, developed two different means of presenting information to parents—the video presentation and the dialogue technique.

Video Presentation

For the video presentation, the special educators developed a narrative on the Odessa work–study program in conjunction with a videotape. They took still pictures to accompany the video. These were used together in meetings with parents whose children were eligible for the program. This program turned out to be a good public relations venture because many businesspeople in the community were involved, and showing pictures of children at work in different businesses was a way of rewarding those who had participated.

Dialogue Technique

The dialogue technique is self-descriptive: It is based on a dialogue between an adult and a child that demonstrates some concept or principle. The dialogue is audio- or videotaped, and parents claim that they often relate to the characters in the dialogue. One videotaped dialogue was between a mother and her child after school. It gave the professionals in Odessa a vehicle for explaining what a child in a special program meant when he said he had been playing games all day in school. The dialogue raised a number of questions in the mother's mind as to what was going on in the special class, and the answers helped explain some of the games—which were demonstrated during the meeting. Then the child stated what he did at school—and now the mother understood: "That must be to develop eye–hand coordination or to encourage cooperative play behavior."

The dialogue technique is a unique way to communicate with a group of parents. It is a good instructional device, and it is fun besides.

SUMMARY

One efficient and effective way of providing a number of parents with information is through one or more parent group meetings. These meetings should be well thought-out and planned carefully. A number of topics—classroom policies, grading procedures, and the introduction of supporting personnel—are relevant to most parents of children with special needs.

A parent advisory committee is suggested as one way to give parents an opportunity to plan a meeting or two a year around topics in which they are interested. The parents should survey the group for topics of interest, make arrangements for speakers, rooms, and refreshments, and conduct the meeting.

Teachers and parents can do a number of things to improve the chances for the success of parent group meetings. Parents appreciate meetings that are brief and on target, starting and ending on time, and having some provisions for children during the meeting.

ACTIVITIES

1. Invite a small group of parents to participate in a planning meeting for a parent group meeting in your classroom. Rather than set out the agenda, listen to the parents and record their ideas.
2. Survey parents to find out topics on which they would like to have information, using one of the interest surveys from Appendix C. Or develop your own questionnaire or interest inventory as a source for good topics to be explored at a parent group meeting.
3. Select the topics and potential presenters for a series of short informational meetings for parents. Record the purpose of each

meeting, who would present the information, and when the meetings would be held during the year.

4. Develop a video presentation or an audiotaped dialogue to be used in a parent group meeting.
5. Invite a group of parents of exceptional children to discuss their ideas on parent meetings—the importance of these meetings, times and length, possible hardships on the parents to attend, and suggestions for improving meetings.
6. Contact the local cable station about working with the schools and parents to develop a "spot" or half-hour program.

REFERENCES

Davies, D. (1990). Success for all children through school-family-community partnerships. *Equity and Choice*, pp. 21–25.

Edge, D., & Franken, M. D. (1996). *Planning effective parent involvement and public engagement programs at schools* [interactive television series]. Lexington, KY: Kentucky Educational Television.

Karasik, J., & Samels, M. (1990). Banding together: Speaking with one voice. *Preventing School Failure, 34*(3), 11–13.

Seifert, K. L. (1992). *Parents and teachers: Can they learn from each other?* Winnipeg, Manitoba, Canada: University of Manitoba, Faculty of Education, Educators' Notebook.

Part Three

Resolving Problems With Parents

10

Defining the Problem

"Mrs. Sandhu?"

"Yes."

"This is Ms. Rogers, Delmar's teacher.
I'm having a little problem getting
Delmar to work on his spelling.
Do you suppose you could help me?"

"I don't know much about teaching
spelling..."

"But you do know Delmar, and I could
use your help if you could spare
a little time."

"I'll stop in after school when I come
to pick up the kids."

Problem solving requires delicate listening and reflective skills. The opening scenario provides some insight into the issue at hand and the listening that will be required to solve the problem. The techniques and examples presented in Part One and Part Two are primarily means for sharing information between parents and teachers. Utilizing these practices can prevent problems from arising or make problem solving easier (Flood, Lapp, Tinajero, & Nagel, 1995; Swick, 1992). And some of the techniques discussed in chapter 5, "The Art of Listening," and chapter 8, "Reporting Progress," could be considered as problem-solving techniques. If parents and teachers have established a good working relationship, problem solving becomes a cooperative venture (Israeloff, 1992).

In the conversation at the beginning of this chapter, Ms. Rogers and Mrs. Sandhu are setting the stage for a problem-solving conference. Ms. Rogers is having trouble getting Delmar to work on his spelling. She is soliciting help from Mrs. Sandhu, Delmar's mother. She is not blaming Delmar for not doing his spelling, nor is she blaming his mother. She is accepting responsibility for the problem. She has made an initial attempt to define the problem as "working on spelling."

Problem solving has two important initial steps:

1. Determine ownership of the problem. Though the answer to the question of "who has the problem" would seem likely to be self-evident, it is not always that apparent (Council for Learning Disabilities, 1991). A problem is often like the proverbial "hot potato." Nobody wants to take hold of it. In the example, if Ms. Rogers were less self-confident in her role as teacher, she might have claimed that Delmar had a problem or that Mrs. Sandhu had a problem rather than take the responsibility herself. So a first step is to analyze where the problem lies and who will take the major responsibility for its solution.

2. Define the problem in operational terms, and identify the situations in which the problematic behavior occurs. Initially, problems are often stated in general, global, nondefinitive terms. For instance, if Mrs. Sandhu had said that Delmar was irresponsible, the label "irresponsible" would have to be redefined in more definitive terms.

The listening techniques described in chapter 5 are particularly helpful in accomplishing these first steps. The person using the listening techniques, however, must realize what he or she is trying to accomplish: determining ownership of the problem and coming up with an operational definition of the behavior that is considered to be a problem.

Boutte, Keepler, Tyler, and Terry (1992) discussed the six types of parent behavior that annoy the teacher the most:

1. Antagonistic
2. Know-it-all
3. Complaining
4. Negative
5. Shy/unresponsive
6. Illiterate

The teacher first has to understand the type of behavior he or she is dealing with (Boutte et al., 1992). Regardless of the behavior that parents demonstrate, though, good communication skills will help the teacher communicate effectively.

WHOSE PROBLEM IS IT?

Often we look at how a problem is presented rather than who presents it. Analyze the following statements:

Mother: Your son didn't get in until 12 o'clock last night.

First, the mother is trying to push ownership of the problem onto the father by saying "your son." Second, the implication is that the son has a problem of not getting home on time. In reality, the mother is the one who is concerned, and she has the problem of dealing with the son who comes home late. The boy probably was enjoying himself immensely; therefore, he does not view his behavior as a problem. The father may not have considered it as a problem until the mother said "your son." The mother and father could well end up arguing about whose problem it is, and little will be done to improve the mother's ability to solve her problem of dealing with a son coming home late.

Teacher: Your son would rather draw than do his math.

Does the boy have a problem? No, he is probably quite content while he is drawing, and he prefers this activity to math—except when the teacher yells at him or tears up his drawings. Does the mother have a problem? No, the behavior occurs in the teacher's environment. The parent may be made to feel guilty and, therefore, decide to "own" the problem by saying she will talk to the boy. In this case, though, the teacher owns the problem and feels frustrated at not being able to solve it.

Mother: Victor never brings any papers home.

This is the mother's problem. *She* wants Victor to bring the papers home. The teacher may agree that this should happen and may be willing to help Victor's mother solve the problem, but it remains Victor's mother's problem.

Cathy: You never let me be first to get a drink.

Cathy has expressed *her* problem of not being first to get a drink. The teacher may be able to help Cathy resolve the problem, but Cathy still owns it.

Phil: The kids on the playground knocked me down.

The teacher may be inclined to accept ownership of this problem and intervene, but it is still Phil's problem. The above solution does not help Phil analyze (a) what he does before he is knocked down—the stimulus condition—or (b) what he does after he has been knocked down—the consequence condition.

The most successful resolution of problems requires participants to come to grips with who owns the problem. Outside agents—the federal government, the courts, the school administration, or the power of parents—may resolve the problem, but the individual who owns the problem will not likely learn to be a successful problem solver until he or she acknowledges ownership.

Teachers must recognize which problems are theirs, which ones are the child's, and which ones are the parents'. Through active listening, teachers often can determine who has the problem. Confronting a parent or child by saying, "That's your problem" is seldom useful, but by not assuming ownership of the problem, teachers often can help a parent or a child realize that this problem is his or hers to solve.

IDENTIFYING THE PROBLEM

Many special education terms are so global that they do not lend themselves to modification, although to say that a child is "gifted" or "hyperactive" is not particularly descriptive of the child's behaviors. When a parent or a teacher uses a term such as "irresponsible" in describing a child, he or she usually has in mind one or two specific behaviors that prompted use of the label. Perhaps the child who is labeled irresponsible has left her bicycle at school, or another child did not take a pencil to class, or another did not feed his dog. Some observable behaviors do not occur often enough to satisfy the observer, or—in the case of children who are labeled "hyperactive"—they occur too often.

The first step is to help the owner of the problem reduce the problem to behaviors that can be observed and measured. This usually can be done by listening to the person who has the problem and by listing the behaviors used to describe the problem. Returning to the example of Ms. Rogers' concern with Delmar's spelling performance—she might think that Delmar does not study his spelling words long enough, or does not write them legibly, or gets only half of his words correct on a spelling test. Each of these behaviors is observable and measurable. She could keep records on how long Delmar attends to his spelling words when the children are assigned study time, or the number of words he writes legibly, or the percentage of words on the spelling test he spells correctly. Any of these measures can tell Ms. Rogers whether she is making progress in solving her problem of getting Delmar to work on his spelling. If the problem is reduced to measurable terms, the observer should be able to collect data in one of the following ways:

1. *Number of occurrences.* How many pages did Bella read? How many problems did Andrew work correctly? How many times did Tonya hit her brother? These are all examples that allow data to be collected in terms of number of occurrences.

2. *Duration.* How long did Delmar work on the assignment? How long did he take to arrive at the breakfast table after he was called in the morning?

3. *Percent.* What percent of the problems were correct? What percentage of times when Cathy was asked a question in arithmetic did she answer correctly?

4. *Rate.* How many times was Victor out of his seat without permission in an hour? How many words did Erik read per minute?

A good test of whether the problem has been reduced to a *solvable* problem is whether it can be measured in one of these four ways. If the problem cannot be put into measurable terms, a person will have difficulty determining if and when the problem has been solved.

In helping a parent define a problem, the teacher usually goes through a number of steps. These are not necessarily followed sequentially, but the teacher may use them as a guide.

1. Reduce a global problem into measurable problems.
2. Check your listening by restating the measurable problem to make sure it is what the parent intends.
3. List the "new problems" on a sheet of paper.
4. Ask the parent to establish a priority list of the problems he or she would like to work on.
5. With the parent, determine how that specific behavior might be measured.

Perhaps the following example will help clarify the procedure.

Mother: Angela makes me so mad. She never remembers to bring things home. She keeps me in the dark.

Teacher: She never brings things home?

Mother: I haven't seen any of her school papers or PTA notices. If you hadn't called me, I wouldn't have known about this meeting.

Teacher: Anything else that she doesn't bring home?

Mother: She left her bike someplace yesterday, and I don't know where her coat is.

Teacher: Let's see. You said she doesn't bring home her papers, PTA notices, bike, or coat. Is that about it?

Mother: That's mainly it.

Teacher: Let me write them down.
a. school papers
b. notices from school
c. bike
d. coat

	Now, which of those things would you like to work on first?
Mother:	The school papers. Really, the bike and the coat are not big problems because she usually brings them home. She just forgets them once in a while. I guess all together they just seemed like an overwhelming problem.
Teacher:	But they aren't so big when we break them down?
Mother:	No, but I would like to do something about the school papers so I could see what she's doing at school.
Teacher:	I usually send papers home on Monday, Wednesday, and Friday. For the next two weeks, why don't you keep track on your calendar at home on those days? After you have an accurate record of what she's doing, we'll see if we can't set up a program to help get those papers home.

In this instance, the mother was able, with the teacher's help, to break the problem down to a manageable size. The teacher checked her perceptions with the mother and found them to be accurate. They listed the problems and established a priority. The teacher then set up a procedure for the mother to start recording the behavior in a simple way.

Being a good listener is often not enough. Parents often need help in specifying their problems and establishing strategies to deal with those problems (Bunting, 1990). Some problems may not be appropriate for the teacher to deal with in that they are not school related or they are so deep-seated that other professionals would be better qualified to help solve them. As the problems begin to unfold, the teacher may recognize that the parent should be referred to outside agencies. Wise teachers work on problems they can help identify and help solve and are willing to turn over to others the problems that are not in their own area of expertise.

OBSTACLES TO PROBLEM IDENTIFICATION

Problem identification faces a number of obstacles. Some have already been identified and are reiterated. Others may be less easily recognizable.

➤ Unwillingness to accept or allow ownership of a problem is a major barrier to identifying problems. Rather than acknowledging that they have a problem, some parents say, "I have a friend whose son still wets the bed." The teacher may decide not to push the parents for ownership at this time but, rather, proceed through the steps of problem identification, which makes the process a bit more difficult.

➤ Equally difficult is the situation in which the teacher decides to take over a problem that should be the parents' to solve. When the parents might need to learn how to identify a problem and how to apply reinforcement techniques to solve the problem, sometimes the teacher steps in and ensures that the problem is resolved. In the earlier case of Angela, the teacher might have said, "I'll just not send home any papers, and you won't have to worry about it. I'll keep them until the next conference or send them in the mail." This is not conducive to real problem solving.

➤ The tendency to use labels to describe a child is not productive. Using labels for children in special education has become so common that labeling has lost its original purpose—as being *descriptive* of behavior—and instead is viewed as being a *cause* of behavior. In so doing, many problems that could be reduced to measurable terms are ignored because they are considered to be part of the larger syndrome and are "caused" by the label. For instance, a teacher may say, "Most brain-damaged children are hyperactive." Following this line of thought, the teacher feels no need to try to break the word "hyperactive" into measurable entities. Categorical labeling, then, can hinder problem identification.

➤ At times, heredity is used as an excuse not to identify a behavior for problem solving. Problems sometimes are thought to be inherited. If a child fights on the playground, the teacher or the parents may say, "It's in his blood." A person might say the same of poor math performance or discourteous behavior. If the behavior is explained away by heredity, chances are that no further attempt will be made to define the problem in behavioral terms. The problem has been "solved" by relegating it to an accident of birth.

➤ Sometimes parents or teachers simply do not see a problem, or if they do, they refuse to admit it. In the course of a conference, a parent might say that he has to keep his child away from matches continually. In the next sentence, the parent may say that this is not really a problem because all children like to play with fire. In this case, the teacher does not own the problem because it does not occur in the teacher's environment. The child enjoys lighting fires, and the parent refuses to admit that a problem exists.

Identifying a problem can be an uphill battle with many obstacles. Teachers need a great deal of patience and willingness to listen reflectively, help the parent identify who owns the problem, and work together to figure out how to solve it.

SUMMARY

The first consideration in problem solving is to establish ownership of the problem. This step may seem clear-cut, but parents and teachers tend to place the problem in the other's domain. Second, problem-solving capabilities are enhanced if broad problems can be reduced to measurable and observable entities. Defining behaviors in measurable terms helps place the problem in perspective, removes the subjectivity surrounding the problem, and enables the person to more readily determine when the problem has been solved.

Problem identification is not easy. Unwillingness to accept ownership of the problem impedes problem solving. Using labels as excuses for behavior or explaining the behavior as inherited often prevents the teacher and the parent from coming to grips with problem-solving techniques.

Teachers who serve as the catalyst in the problem solving (a) reduce the problems to measurable terms, (b) restate the problems to verify their perceptions, (c) list the problems, (d) ask that the problems be prioritized, and (e) set up a procedure for measuring the behavior.

ACTIVITIES

1. Listen to statements made in the teachers' lounge or another group of adults and see whether you can determine who has a problem that is being discussed and how it is being handled.

2. Divide into pairs for role playing. One person is to be the parent, and one is the teacher. One or more of the following problems is voiced. How does the problem-solving sequence unfold?

    a. The irresponsible child
    b. The hyperactive boy
    c. The lazy girl
    d. The mean boy
    e. The immature child
    f. The anxious child
    g. The nervous child
    h. The shy girl
    i. The girl with learning disabilities
    j. The stupid kid

3. Divide into groups of three. Two members of the group participate in the discussion, and the third member observes, listens, and identifies the problems of getting parents involved in the school.

REFERENCES

Boutte, G. S., Keepler, D. L., Tyler, V. S., & Terry, B. Z. (1992). Effective techniques for involving "difficult" parents. *Young Children, 47*(3), 19–22.

Bunting, C. (1990). Schools and families: The tie that bonds. Should educators assume the childrearing roles abandoned by parents? *School Administrator, 47*(6), 16–18.

Council for Learning Disabilities. (1991). Retrieved June 1, 2003, from http://www.cldinternational.org/

Flood, J., Lapp, D., Tinajero, J. V., & Nagel, G. (1995). "I never knew I was needed until you called!": Promoting parent involvement in schools. *Reading Teacher, 48*(7), 614.

Israeloff, R. (1992). How to talk to your child's school. *Parent's Magazine, 67*(10), 115.

Swick, K. J. (1992). *Teacher–parent partnerships* (ERIC Digest). Urbana, IL: ERIC Clearinghouse on Elementary and Early Childhood Education.

11

Reinforcers and Reinforcement

Changing children's behavior requires careful analysis of the behavior and the conditions that maintain the behavior. After the teacher and parents agree on a strategy, a great deal of effort is required of the change agents—in this case, the parents—to maintain the consistency necessary to carry out the plan.

Teaching parents the ABCs—antecedents, behavior, and consequences—of behavior modification is a proven strategy. Parents learn, individually or in groups, how to select appropriate consequences or reinforcers for the child and how to use the reinforcers to shape the behavior change.

WHAT IS A REINFORCER?

The words *reinforcer, reward,* and *consequence* have been used interchangeably in the behavior modification literature. For something to be reinforcing, it has to follow a specific behavior and have some effect on that behavior—to decrease, increase, or maintain the behavior. Parents sometimes say, "Rewards don't work with my child," but, by definition, what they are calling a reward is not a reward. The parents may hand the child candy, allow additional TV watching, or give a lot of kisses and hugs for a certain behavior, but if the child's behavior does not change, whatever the parents are calling rewards are not viewed as rewards, consequences, or reinforcers by the child. In effect, the parent is saying, "I'm doing something that I think is rewarding," but the child does not see it the same way.

The following points attempt to define and explain reinforcement so it can be applied with more success.

1. A reinforcer is something that the recipient needs or values and the giver does not necessarily value. Parents may decide that Cassie has done her homework so faithfully that they will let her stay up an extra 15 minutes, as staying up an extra 15 minutes is often rewarding to young children who resist going to bed. In Cassie's case, she may not appreciate the extra 15 minutes that her parents think is rewarding. So, after staying up an extra 15 minutes to receive her "reward," she does not do her homework the next night and the parents think that rewards don't work with their daughter. For Cassie, being able to sleep

an extra 15 minutes in the morning or to sleep in on Saturday mornings may be more rewarding.

Parents often are surprised at holidays or on birthdays when a child opens several expensive presents and puts them aside to play with some inexpensive toy. And parents sometimes become disconcerted, after traveling hundreds of miles on a vacation trip to see some historical monument, to realize that the children are more enthusiastic about the swimming pool at the motel. A child may remember for years the time he got to sleep in a camper trailer and barely remember the magnificence of Niagara Falls viewed during the same trip.

Giving a rubber band to a girl who has just broken her hair cruncher is much more rewarding at that moment than giving her a $10 gift certificate to the local department store. Whose values or needs are being met or are being considered when giving a reward? Adults, parents, and teachers sometimes think in terms of what they consider reinforcing rather than what the child considers a treat. Before stating that rewards have no meaning to a child, adults should figure out what is rewarding to the child.

2. A reward must be timely. "Study hard in kindergarten and you can go to college" is a reward that does not have a reinforcing quality because of the long delay between the behavior desired and the consequence that is supposed to motivate it. The promise of rewards in heaven for good behavior on Earth clearly has not had a tremendous effect on humankind.

Parents sometimes select rewards that are truly reinforcing to children in that the child needs or values them, but by placing them so far in the future, they lose their motivating quality. Therefore, a parent who says that rewards don't work with his son because "even the promise of a motorcycle didn't result in better grades" shows a lack of knowledge about timing and the need for relating behavioral principles to his child.

Smaller rewards, timed closely after the behavior, may be much more reinforcing than larger rewards that are poorly timed. An ice cream cone immediately after the child rakes the lawn could have a much larger effect on raking behavior in the future than the promise of a quart of ice cream for maintaining the lawn all fall.

3. The applied consequence must be associated directly with the behavior to be changed. Some children have difficulty seeing a relationship between the behavior and its consequences. This may result when the consequences for a given behavior are sometimes positive and sometimes negative, or when the rewards are dispensed regardless of whether the desired behavior occurs.

As young children venture into their neighborhoods, they often get involved in minor scraps with other children. The incidents may relate to possession of toys, dissension about games to play, and so forth. In any event, a fight or quarrel ensues and the child goes home. On one occasion, the father may demonstrate pride: "That's my son—a chip off the old block." The child may receive a lot of social rewards for fighting with the neighbor boy. In a sense he is made to feel good, which reinforces the fighting. Under these conditions, the fights can be expected to continue. The next day, however, the other child's father may call and complain about the fighting. This time, the child is punished and sent to his room for fighting. The inconsistency of one day being rewarded and the next day being punished is confusing for the child and does not allow him to see the relationship between the behavior and its consequences.

Or a child may be told that she can watch a favorite TV program if she finishes her homework. If the program comes on and the child is not finished with her homework but the parent decides to let her watch the program anyway, the child sees no relationship between her studying and the reward of watching her TV program. The parents then may say that watching a favorite program does not seem to have any effect on their daughter's doing homework, and in this case they will be right: No relationship has been established.

Promises not kept seem to have a negative effect on children. Children are more affected by what we do than by what we say. Unenforced contracts are better left unstated. To say the child will not work for the reward of watching TV is unfair if the child has not had a chance to do so.

Reinforcers, rewards, or consequences live up to their name only if they change behavior. Events or things that the giver labels as rewards may have no reinforcing value to the child. For a reward to result in change, it must have value to, or be needed by, the recipient; it must be timely; and it must have an association with the desired behavior.

SELECTING REINFORCERS

Selecting things, events, or activities that have reinforcing qualities for someone else can present quite a challenge. Not all children like to be read to, stay up late, ride horses, bake cookies, or whatever. A child from a rural area may have different needs than a child from an inner-city area. Young children want rewards different from those older children want (Popkin, 1993).

Sometimes, rewards might be the lesser of two evils. A child might think that washing the car is more rewarding than washing the dishes. Likewise, getting out of some activity might be more rewarding than getting to do something special. For instance, Jill might be told that if she eats the food on her plate, she won't have to wash the dishes that day (a regularly assigned task). Just as children differ in so many of their behaviors, so do their rewards and reinforcers vary. Therefore, the bestower of rewards must study the child and his or her individual needs.

1. *Observe the child.* Although it may sound simplistic to suggest to parents that they go home and watch their child to see what he or she likes to do, this probably remains one of the best ways to determine a reward system. Watching the foods children select, the games or toys they play with most, the places they ask to go, TV programs they like to watch, computer games they ask for, the types of books they pick to read, and children they prefer to play with provide indications of what is rewarding to specific children.

   Parents might check out potential reinforcers by suggesting a trip to the store, walking through a toy department, or going for a ride, meanwhile observing the child's reaction to the various things around him or her. In this way, they can build up a reservoir of rewards to use in various circumstances. By observing the child in a number of different situations, parents can learn to understand their child better. And sometimes parents bring to the teacher new insights about themselves and their children. Occasionally, as they study their child, they find that the behavior under question is really not as important as they had originally thought.

2. *Ask the child.* Just as asking the child what behavior he or she would like to change may be a good idea, simply asking the child what reward he or she would like to receive for changing this behavior may be effective. Then the parents and the child can come to an agreement about what reinforcers to use for the child's improved school behavior.

The obvious advantage to asking the child is that it instills some commitment to change, in that the child puts his or her own price on the effort. The obvious disadvantage is that our rewards often are so much a part of our everyday living that we do not think about them. Using the form entitled "Reinforcement Questionnaire for Students" (see Appendix C) will give children an opportunity to think about various things that turn them on or off.

3. *Create reinforcers.* As the story goes, an American firm was producing a product in a developing nation. Employing local labor was necessary to make the product available. After a while, production began to lag, and one day very few workers showed up. The American supervisor asked the local foreman what the problem was. Wages seemed adequate, working conditions were good, most of the people seemed happy, but something was missing.

The foreman told the supervisor that his people were happy and did not want more money or shorter hours. It was just that most of them had earned all the money they needed to buy supplies and their needs were fulfilled. They would be back when they needed money, but in the meantime they were well satisfied. Although this was a happy state for the local workers, it was not doing anything for production. The American supervisor pondered the problem and finally came up with a solution: He had department store catalogs sent to every local household.

Quite often, things become *needs* only after they are placed before our eyes or are presented to us. We acquire many of our so-called needs over time. We find some new foods to be pleasurable, and activities take on a new meaning when we become skilled at these or when they are associated with friends.

Many times, a child has to be reinforced or rewarded to learn a new skill, but when the new skill is learned, it becomes a reward in itself. Consider, for example, a small boy learning to ride a bicycle. His father pushes him and runs along beside him shouting words of encouragement. Each new accomplishment receives a lot of social reinforcement. After the boy learns to ride without falling off, the riding itself becomes reinforcing and can be used as a reward for other behaviors. The mother might say, "When you finish feeding the dog, you may ride your bike." Many skills that children work hard to achieve—reading, driving, swimming, dancing, piano playing—become reinforcers later.

Sometimes, the way an activity is presented to a child helps to create its reinforcing value. A mother wanted her daughter to learn to play the piano. Because piano practice often becomes a hassle, the mother took a different tack. In the beginning, she told her daughter that if she finished her chores, she could practice the piano for 5 minutes. At the end of 5 minutes, the mother stopped the practice. The mother kept track in a little notebook of the number of minutes the girl practiced. Before long, the daughter was asking to practice more. The mother slowly increased the time to practice, usually stopping the practicing before the child was satiated and almost always using practice as a privilege for getting her daughter to do other things.

In this way, piano practice was created as a reward or reinforcer, whereas in many homes the reverse is true: The child has to be reinforced for practicing. Much more common is the enticement, "When you've finished your half hour of practice, you can go out to play."

How something is presented—whether it will be received as a positive or a negative event—is important. Note, for instance, in the adult world, when one is accorded a great deal of fanfare ("You've been selected to be chairperson of the fund-raising committee," a laborious task often accompanied by more criticism than praise), people accept the job because it is *presented* as a privilege or reward.

TYPES OF REINFORCERS

Some authors have made distinctions between tangible and social rewards.

Tangible Rewards

Tangible rewards consist of *things* a person receives for accomplishment. They may be learned or unlearned reinforcers, such as money (learned) and food (unlearned). Tangibles often are things the child can keep as reminders of specific achievements for some time to come.

Some parents and teachers criticize the use of tangible rewards with children because this type of reward may give the impression of "paying" children to do something they should want to do or should do anyway. It might be argued, however, that almost all behavior is learned and that few things are done without some type of reward—or from fear of punishment.

Consider for a moment the power of tangible rewards. Certificates, diplomas, and awards are examples of tangible rewards. Many businesspeople, doctors, and lawyers prominently display these symbols of achievement in their offices, along with trophies and plaques they have received. Many adults save and cherish medals, blood-donor pins, past-president pins, and the like. Scrapbooks, photo albums, newspaper clippings—all reflect the importance people place on tangible things they have received in the past. Children often have a special drawer where they keep trinkets, toys, ribbons, certificates, old report cards, and other symbols of achievement. Few mothers discard mementos received from their children for being a "Super Mom." Tangible rewards obviously are reinforcing for most people in our society, because we keep them.

Social Rewards

Social rewards are especially potent because the parent or teacher "carries them around," to be conferred immediately. And they can be changed on the spot. These rewards include verbal praise, touches, pats, hugs, kisses, playing games together, going for rides together, and many other things one person does for or with another. Some people seem to be natural social reinforcers. They are warm and sensitive and respond readily to others' accomplishments.

The power of social reward is well recognized. Teachers often comment about how some children will do anything for attention. The musical show *Applause* points out the importance of clapping. Social approval of the hometown crowd is a crucial factor in competitive athletic events.

At the end of this chapter are lists of rewards that parents have found to be effective. They are grouped for younger and older children here, but a parent may want to check both lists because of individual differences in children. Many of the items on the lists, you will note, are inexpensive or free.

SUMMARY

New patterns of behavior are learned through a process of reinforcement. This is sometimes known as the ABCs of behavior modification, consisting of antecedent–behavior–consequences. A reinforcer, reward, or consequence is something that follows a behavior in such a way that the recipient sees a relationship between the behavior and its consequences. Reinforcers are something the recipient values or needs and is given immediately after the desired behavior. The applied consequence can be considered a reinforcer only if it changes the behavior in some way.

Reinforcers that the child will find rewarding can be identified by observing the child to see what he or she prefers to do or to play with when given a free choice. Another way is to simply ask the child what he or she would like to have or to do. Sometimes reinforcers can be created by providing children with new experiences or things they have not experienced before.

Reinforcers often are classified as tangible or social. "Tangible" means *things*, whereas social reinforcers are kisses, hugs, words of praise, or similar encouragements, which have the advantage that they can be bestowed immediately and are directly related to the child's behaviors. If children have learned to value the social rewards of significant adults in their lives, these reinforcers can be applied immediately, and they can be related directly to the child's behavior.

ACTIVITIES

1. Observe a child with whom you have contact, and list the things he or she seems to like to do. Then ask the child to list the things he or she would like to have or do, and compare them with your observations. You may want to use the reinforcement questionnaire (see Appendix C) for this activity.

2. If you are a teacher, ask the children in your class to prepare a list of things they like to do or have at school or at home. From these lists, make a list of your own to have available to share with parents as ideas for reinforcers.
3. Develop certificates or awards that parents might use with their children at home for specific behaviors—helping clean the kitchen, washing dishes for a week, making the bed, etc.
4. Conduct a survey of the parents of the children in your classroom. Ask the parents to list the things the children like and don't like. Compare with your observations.

Some Reward Ideas for Younger Children

Being read to
Getting a bubble pipe
Helping make cookies
Playing tic-tac-toe with Mom or Dad
Listening to a favorite CD or tape
Playing a video game
Watching a favorite TV show
Staying up an extra 15 minutes
Going for ice cream in pajamas
Putting special papers on the wall or refrigerator
Getting a subscription to a magazine
Getting a dog, cat, fish, or gerbil
Choosing a new pair of tennis shoes
Visiting a fire station
Selecting something special at the grocery store
Calling Grandma long distance
Making popcorn
Getting to help wash dishes (very young!)
Getting out of washing dishes (older)
Getting stars, gummed stickers, etc.
Using some of Mom's makeup
Getting homemade certificates or awards for "Super Helper"
Getting pipe cleaners to make things
Having a big box to play in
Having overnight guests
Going to a movie

Using "grown-up" tools
Enjoying a specified (in writing) amount of Dad's or Mom's time
Playing games
Getting pats, hugs, kisses
Going to a friend's house
Buying comic books
Using a kitchen timer or a stopwatch
Having a chart with checkmarks for completing tasks
Getting balloons
Doing things first, such as reading the comics in the paper
Setting the table
Having free time
Getting a new bedspread or Snoopy blanket
Having a pint of ice cream of one's very own
Getting a library card
Responsibilities that may be considered rewards: feeding pet, taking
    out trash, turning out lights, safety inspection

Some Reward Ideas for Older Children

Attending a rock concert
Having a party
Staying up late on Friday or Saturday night
Using the car (contingent upon having a driver's license, of course!)
Having own set of car keys or house keys
Getting a favorite book
Taking driver's training
Buying new clothes
Having extra money
Buying posters
Rearranging furniture in room
Watching the *Tonight Show* or *Late Show with David Letterman*
Taking a friend out to dinner
Going to a movie, skating, or other event
Taking special lessons: dancing, skiing, scuba diving
Going on a picnic
Playing chess, cribbage, bridge, computer games
Having friends stay overnight
Getting a pet

Building something with a parent
Having a friend stay for the weekend
Getting a new tape, CD, or DVD
Getting out of specified chores
Physical contact, touches (often missing with older children)
Taking trips to special places
Getting flowers
Getting a magazine subscription
Getting materials for rebuilding a car, radio, TV, etc.
Going to camp
Enjoying special snacks
Having "goof off" time with no responsibilities
Getting one's picture taken
Getting breakfast in bed

REFERENCES

Popkin, M. H. (1993). *Active parenting today: For parents of 2 to 12 year olds* (Parent's guide). Marietta, GA: Active Parenting Publishers. (ERIC Document Reproduction Service No. ED 356 055)

12

The Reinforcement Menu

Parents who have participated in training programs understand the use of positive reinforcers and procedures for changing behavior (Brown, Ilderton, Taylor, & Lock, 2001; Cruz & Cullinan, 2001; Higgins, Williams, & McLaughlin, 2001; Newby, Fischer, & Roman, 1991). Having lived with their child for a number of years, they have observed how the child picks up toys so he or she can go someplace or vacuumed the carpet before being permitted to go to a movie. They've watched their child save pennies to buy a certain toy.

Effects of the reinforcement system are dramatic (Martens, Lochner, & Kelly, 1992). The most productive way to help parents understand how to use the reinforcing menu described in this chapter to effect behavior change of children is to present clear examples of the process and stay away from technical jargon.

Parents tend to carry out numerous "mini-mods" (miniature modifications). Vacuuming the carpet, washing the car, and cleaning the bedroom on Saturday illustrate on-the-spot behaviors that are dealt with at the time. "You may use the car tonight if you wash it this afternoon" is a mini-mod. Problems arise when an undesirable behavior, such as a tantrum behavior or not getting up in the morning when called, persists over time. Although the same principles used to get the carpet vacuumed are applicable to getting the child up in the morning, they must be applied consistently and over time to effect behavior change.

In chapter 11 you learned how to select and apply reinforcers. The identified reinforcers may be used for short-term projects and for some long-term problem solving. One strategy for dealing with persistent behaviors is to establish a reinforcement menu for the child. A reinforcement menu is simply a listing of reinforcers, along with a point value for each, from which the child can choose when he or she has earned the required number of points. The following procedure demonstrates how to set up and carry out a program for behavior change with a reinforcement menu.

DEFINING THE BEHAVIOR

During the parent–teacher conference, Mrs. Midkiff complained that her son, Allen, was so lazy that it was getting on her nerves. She was constantly yelling at him, and she had to tell him four or five times to do assigned chores. The teacher, Mr. Diaz, realized that "lazy" means many different things to different people and that getting a grasp on it is difficult unless it is defined in more behavioral terms. He asked Mrs. Midkiff what she meant by saying that Allen was lazy.

Mrs. Midkiff:	He won't get up when I call him in the morning, and I have to tell him again and again to take out the trash.
Mr. Diaz:	Anything else?
Mrs. Midkiff:	He wanted a dog so bad, and he got it, but now he forgets to feed the dog, and I have to remind him or do it myself.
Mr. Diaz:	Yes...
Mrs. Midkiff:	He won't make his bed without my nagging. I suppose he's just going through a stage, but I'm tired of it.
Mr. Diaz:	Even if it's a stage he's going through, I imagine you'd like to do something about it.
Mrs. Midkiff:	You bet! But what I'm doing now sure isn't working.
Mr. Diaz:	Let's see if I can help. This is a method that one of the mothers tried last year, and she said it worked for her.

Mr. Diaz listed the behaviors that Mrs. Midkiff had called "lazy."

1. Get up in the morning when called.
2. Take out the trash.
3. Feed the dog.
4. Make his bed.

Mr. Diaz then asked, "Are these the main things that are getting on your nerves?"

Mrs. Midkiff:	Well, there are a few others, but those are the most bothersome to me and his dad.
Mr. Diaz:	Do you want each of them to happen every day?
Mrs. Midkiff:	No. I don't care if he sleeps in on Saturday and Sunday, and the trash has to be taken out only on Tuesday and Friday, but I wish he'd do the others every day.

Mr. Diaz:	Let's make a chart that will help to remind him. (He then sketched out a work chart—see Figure 12.1.) Allen probably needs some help to remind him of what he should do and when he should do it. If we make a little chart like this and put it on the door of his room, he'll be able to see what he's supposed to do. Then you can check it off with the assigned number of points when he's done. You can make a task worth as many points as you want to, depending on how important the task is. For instance, if you really want him to make his bed, you might make that worth more points.
Mrs. Midkiff:	What if he doesn't make his bed until just before he gets back into bed that night?

Week _____ Supervisor _____

	Monday	Tuesday	Wednesday	Thursday	Friday	Saturday	Sunday
1. Gets up when called							
2. Takes out trash							
3. Feeds dog							
4. Makes bed							
5.							
6.							
7.							

Total Points

1. Gets up when called once	=	10 points
Gets up when called twice	=	5 points
Doesn't respond	=	0 points
2. Takes out trash	=	10 points
3. Feeds dog	=	10 points
4. Makes bed	=	10 points

Total Possible = _____ Total Earned = _____

FIGURE 12.1
Allen's Work Record

Mr. Diaz:	You'll have to decide with him what you consider to be a deadline time for the points to be earned and then stick to it.
Mrs. Midkiff:	I see. Is that all there is to it?
Mr. Diaz:	No. I think we need to make the points worth something, don't you?

PREPARING A POINT RECORD SHEET

The next step is to develop some type of "accounting system." Mrs. Midkiff and Mr. Diaz had developed a plan for Allen to earn points, and now they were going to develop a plan so Allen could keep track of and spend the points.

The parent can use any of a number of systems, depending on the child's age and what the parents want the child to do. One teacher, for instance, made individual "checkbooks" for her students. They deposited the points they earned into their "checking account." If a student wanted a certain item or event, he or she wrote a check for the required number of points and subtracted them from the balance. In this way, the students practiced handling a checking account and they used the arithmetic skills of adding and subtracting.

Allen's mother and Mr. Diaz decided on a rather simple record sheet to help Allen keep track of his points. As shown in Figure 12.2, it had five columns—one for the date, one for the points earned on that date, one for the points spent (if any), one for the balance of points, and one to note what Allen spent the points for. This notation would give Mrs. Midkiff an indication of what seemed to be strong reinforcers for Allen. By checking the dates on which he spent points, she could see if he was learning to save or whether he needed more immediate gratification.

PREPARING A REINFORCEMENT MENU

The next step is to prepare a reinforcement menu. One of the benefits of preparing a list from which Allen could select items was that Mrs. Midkiff did not have to try to determine the single most reinforcing event for him. She could put a number of items on the menu, each with its own price tag, and Allen could make up his own mind about

Date	Points Earned	Points Spent	Points on Hand	Points Spent For

FIGURE 12.2
Point Record

how he wanted to use his points. In addition, the list could be changed periodically just as a menu is changed at a restaurant. The "prices" also could be altered if deemed necessary.

Mrs. Midkiff and Mr. Diaz went through the process described in chapter 11 for selecting reinforcers. They relied on their observations of what Allen seemed to like to do or have, then asked Allen for his suggestions as to what he would like to work for, using some of the questions on the "Reinforcement Questionnaire for Students" (Appendix C). In addition, they looked through the list of possible reinforcers at the end of chapter 11 and came up with the following list of nine items:

1. Watch TV for 1 hour   5 points
   (maximum 3 hours of TV on weekday)
2. Go bowling on Saturday   160 points
3. Get an evening snack   5 points

4. Have a friend stay overnight   180 points
5. Get a new baseball glove   380 points
6. Go to Dad's office   70 points
7. Stay up an extra 15 minutes   Bonus for a perfect
       Tuesday or Friday
8. Play a computer game with Mom   25 points
9. Not have to do the dishes   40 points
     as usual on Friday

Mrs. Midkiff and Mr. Diaz came up with the various items and their respective point values for a number of reasons. Allen liked to watch TV and have an evening snack almost every day. The low point totals would not force him to use all his points on these items but would almost guarantee that he would change at least one of the behaviors that Mrs. Midkiff would like him to change. Tuesdays and Fridays were the biggest days in that Allen had to take out the trash, get up in the morning when called, feed the dog, and make his bed on these days, so a bonus of staying up 15 extra minutes at night was thrown in as an added incentive. Going bowling or having a friend stay overnight required him to have a good week. He could not get enough points in a week to do both, but he could do one of these if he wanted to save his points. The baseball glove was something the family probably would get him eventually, but Allen could earn the new glove in two or three good weeks by managing his points. If he showed no indication of working for it after a few weeks, this item could be replaced by some other big item.

Allen had been assigned of the task of helping with dishes on Friday night, which often ended in an argument. By placing a point value on getting out of doing the dishes, the arguing behavior might be reduced. He could buy his way out of the task by spending 40 points, or he could do the dishes. The visit to Dad's office was included to see whether it was a reinforcer for Allen.

The list was posted for Allen to see. If he had been younger, Mrs. Midkiff might have used pictures of reinforcers instead of the list of words.

The next step was to go over the procedure carefully with Allen so he would understand the whole process. This was presented not as a punishment for his not doing these things earlier but, instead, as an aid to help him remember. The reinforcement menu can be compared to a department store catalog in that they both state what is available and give the cost.

Things to Remember

In carrying out the reinforcement procedure, the following tips will help to ensure its success.

> ➤ *Make sure the process is clear to the child.* In the example, Allen should know what constitutes a "made bed" and when the deadline is for the bed to be made. He should know how and when he can spend his points.

> ➤ *Don't shift point values.* If Allen is working hard to save the 380 points for the baseball glove and the parents discover they have underpriced the item, they should not raise the price just before Allen achieves enough points to get it.

> ➤ *Don't offer a reinforcer that you are not willing to give.* Parents and teachers sometimes list on a menu an item that looks especially attractive but they cannot or will not deliver. For instance, the parents may list a trip to the zoo at 300 points and promise it for the first Saturday after the child has earned the points. The Saturday in question arrives, but Dad has a golf game scheduled and Mom has bridge. After working 3 weeks for the trip to the zoo, the child should not be denied, except under unquestionable circumstances. Otherwise, the reinforcer should not be listed, as you will lose the child's trust.

> ➤ *Be consistent.* If Pete has not earned the necessary points for TV watching, don't give in, even "just this once." Or if Annie has enough points for a friend to stay overnight, don't deny her because she spilled her soup. Being consistent is difficult, but lack of consistency is what often caused the problem in the first place.

> ➤ *Evaluate the program continually.* By analyzing the child's work record, the parent can see what is working and what is not working. For instance, Allen might be earning enough points to satisfy his immediate needs by doing some of the tasks on the list and not doing others. Maybe he still is not feeding the dog regularly but Mrs. Midkiff would like to see this happen. She

can do a number of different things: She might increase the amount of points that Allen can earn for this activity and thereby make it worth more. She might add another reinforcer that is especially desirable so Allen would have to earn more points to get it. She might eliminate one of the tasks on the list that seems to have become a habit and thus make it necessary for Allen to feed the dog to get enough points to live in the style to which he has become accustomed.

Kari's mother came to the clinic because of her daughter's "uncontrollable temper tantrums." Kari was of school age, and Mrs. Y was concerned because Kari persisted in getting her own way at the most inconvenient times—either by throwing a temper tantrum or by threatening to throw one. A graduate student was assigned to the case and worked closely with the mother throughout the project.

For a week, Mrs. Y was asked to keep track of the number of temper tantrums Kari threw each day. The first week, she averaged 3.42 tantrums a day (see Figure 12.3). The mother and the graduate student then developed a point system and a menu of reinforcers (see Figure 12.4). The point system was set up around a plan for losing 5 points for each temper tantrum and earning points for other behaviors.

The worksheet (see Figure 12.5) and the point system were explained to Kari. Her mother was encouraged not to react to a temper tantrum with anything other than the 5-point deduction. During the next 8 days, the average dropped to .5 times a day. At this point, the mother quit the point system for 9 days, and the tantrums increased to an average of 1.7 times a day. Reinstating the reinforcement system reduced the number of tantrums to only two for the next 7 days.

Concentrating on the positive aspects of the child's behavior and establishing a point system seemed to have positive effects on the child's behavior. It also was effective in getting Kari to do some other chores that the mother deemed important. The "uncontrollable temper tantrums" became controllable by instituting a positive, systematic approach.

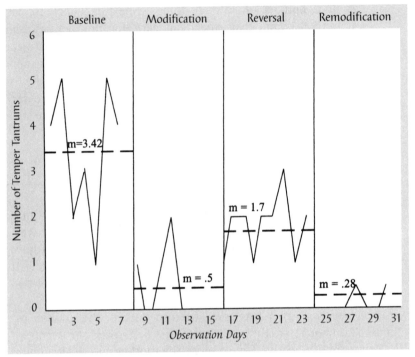

FIGURE 12.3
Graph of Kari's Temper Tantrums

Mrs. Midkiff should evaluate the effectiveness of the reinforcers on the menu. If Allen is not using some of them, she may either want to exchange them for new ones or decrease their point value.

➤ Involve the child in as much of the decision making as possible. It helps the child understand the process. The child's choice of reinforcers can help parents see what is important to him or her. If children believe they have some input as points are renegotiated for reinforcers, they will be more committed to producing the desired result. When they understand the process, they will learn new ways to order their own lives.

Tasha was being reinforced with gold stars for doing her homework. She told her mother that she wanted to teach her

To earn points, you may do the following:

Plus Points

1. Keep your room in order
bed made...5
dresser arranged neatly 5
clothes put away...5
toys put away 5

2. Do home chores
empty trash..5
do dishes 5

3. Practice the horn
each 10 minutes..5

4. Complete schoolwork...5

Minus Points
For each temper tantrum, you lose...................................5

You may spend points on the following privileges:

1. Bowling...500 points
2. $1.00 for shopping...400 points
3. Stay all night with a friend..........................300 points
4. Dad plays with you..200 points
5. Make goodies with mom...............................100 points

FIGURE 12.4
Point System and Menu of Reinforcers for Kari

dog to eat his food. Her mother thought that was a good idea and asked her how she was going to do it. "By giving Blackie a gold star every time he cleans up his dish," the girl replied. She understood the process. She just had the wrong reinforcer.

➤ Make the program positive. Programs have a much better chance of succeeding if they are based on a reward system rather than a punishment system. In Allen's case, if Mrs. Midkiff had chosen to look at the unmade bed as a target and

Points Earned Week of _____

	Sat.	Sun.	Mon.	Tues.	Wed.	Thur.	Fri
Bed							
Dresser							
Clothes							
Toys							
Trash							
Dishes							
Horn							
Homework							
Minus Points							
Sum							

Sum Carried Over _____

This Week's Sum _____

Cumulative Total _____

FIGURE 12.5
Worksheet for Kari

had set up a system in which a specified number of unmade beds led to his staying in his room or having no TV privileges, the stage would have been set for a power struggle and Allen would have viewed the whole project negatively. The reinforcement menu should be a tool to reduce conflict between the parent and the child through positive means rather than to increase hostility through punishment.

Setting up a program to change home behavior using a reinforcement menu can be exciting. Most parents are willing to try it if the teacher will take the time to help them set it up. The Work Record and Point Record forms are good templates to follow.

SUMMARY

This chapter has presented a plan for parents to promote better behavioral patterns in their children through a reinforcement menu. The procedure is as follows:

1. The parent identifies one or a small number of behaviors that he or she would like the child to change or do.
2. The parent, with the teacher's assistance, assigns each behavior a point value.
3. The teacher and the parent develop a system for keeping track of the points the child earns and spends.
4. The parent selects a number of items that seem to have reinforcing value to the child and assigns a point value to each. The points a child earns can be spent to obtain the reinforcers.

The list of reinforcers and their values comprise the reinforcement menu.

The child should clearly understand the process. After the point values have been established, they should not be altered arbitrarily. The reinforcers should be obtainable. The program should be administered consistently, and it should be evaluated continually to make sure it is accomplishing its objectives. Best results will be realized if the child is consulted about the total program and involved in its implementation. Above all, the program should be positive.

ACTIVITIES

1. Set up a reinforcement menu for a child, including a point system for the child to obtain the reinforcers.
2. Help a parent set up a reinforcement menu to use at home to change child behaviors that the parent would like to see modified. Assist the parent in monitoring the program over 8 to 10 weeks.
3. Conduct a case study on the use of a reinforcement menu with a child over a 3-month period. Measure baseline behavior and intervention strategies over 8 to 10 weeks.
4. Form a group with other teachers. View a commercial video pertaining to reinforcement and discuss it.

REFERENCES

Brown, M. S., Ilderton, P., Taylor, A., & Lock, R. H. (2001). Include a student with an attention problem in the general education classroom. *Intervention in School & Clinic, 37*(1). Retrieved June 3, 2003, from http://www.echo.louisville.edu/

Cruz, L., & Cullinan, D. (2001). Awarding points, using levels to help children improve behavior. *Teaching Exceptional Children, 33*(3). Retrieved June 3, 2003, from http://www.echo.louisville.edu/

Higgins, J. W., Williams, R. L., & McLaughlin, T. F. (2001). The effects of a token economy employing instructional consequences for a third-grade student with learning disabilities: A data-based case study (EJ635096). *Education and Treatment of Children, 24*(1). Retrieved June 3, 2003, from http://www.echo.louisville.edu/

Martens, B. K., Lochner, D. G., & Kelly, S. Q. (1992). The effects of variable-interval reinforcement on academic engagement: A demonstration of matching theory. *Journal of Applied Behavior Analysis, 25*(1), 143–151.

Newby, R. F., Fischer, M., & Roman, M. A. (1991). Parent training for families of children with ADHD. *School Psychology Review, 20*(2), 252–265.

13

Parent Training Groups

Groups are everywhere. Do you want to lose weight, learn to meditate, find romance, learn to square dance, grow better flowers, stop smoking, or stop drinking? Clubs, organizations, and groups are available to serve almost any special interest imaginable. Groups for parents of children with disabilities are no exception (Gibbs, Edge, & Petrosko, 1993).

In most large communities, parent groups have been organized to provide psychotherapy, teach behavior modification principles, teach parents how to listen to their children or how to play with them, explore their feelings and attitudes, or deal with single parenthood or children on drugs. These groups serve as a vehicle for problem solving, with nearly every philosophical position—psychoanalytical, behavioral, developmental, phenomenological, transactional analysis—represented (Kagan et al., 1992; Kagan, Neville, & Rustici, 1993).

The rationale for parent training groups is that, through planning and conducting effective, comprehensive parent education programs, educators and parents will become partners in educating children. Research indicates that parent training groups are highly effective in helping parents promote behavior change in their children in a positive direction.

Often, these groups are facilitated by a counselor or other professional, although some teachers lead parent training groups themselves. Andy Gill (1998) conducted an extensive study on using parent training groups to help parents develop effective strategies for coping and intervention. He concluded that training groups do have a positive impact on parent effectiveness in managing children's behavior. If programs are organized systematically and provide complete, factual information about the intent of the program, the attending parents seem to be successful in carrying out the required program of activities.

If one holds the view that differential diagnosis should lead to differential treatment, different types of programs for parents are needed to provide a variety of choices. Most of these groups report that they are effective. That they remain in existence indicates that parents find them satisfying.

DIRECTIVE VERSUS NONDIRECTIVE GROUPS

Groups often are differentiated by the amount of direction the leaders provide, by the underlying assumptions about human behavior, and whether the targets of the group are behavioral or attitudinal. Table 13.1 summarizes these distinctions, which may be somewhat artificial when considering what actually takes place in a group. The leader may choose to provide a great deal of direction or relinquish the leadership to group members in a nondirective way in which parents may feel more comfortable verbalizing their needs. For the group to be effective, a skillful leader often employs techniques derived from various philosophical models.

Because of the many types of groups, we cannot review them all here. We have chosen to highlight certain programs in some detail because of their potential for use with parents of exceptional children (Edge, Veasey, Chittick, & Mullins, 1993).

EDUCATIONAL MODULATION CENTER

The Educational Modulation Center (EMC), founded in Olathe, Kansas, in the late 1960s, was established to investigate procedures for providing special educational services for children with disabilities in a

---

TABLE 13.1
Continuum of Structure in a Parent Group

	Structured by Group's Participants	Structured by Group Leader
Degree of Leadership	Group leader sets the stage—provides minimal control, accepting-type atmosphere.	Strong leadership—often almost an instructional model
Assumptions	Given a warm, accepting atmosphere, parents will make appropriate decisions.	Parents have not been able to make appropriate decisions; therefore, they need specific guidance.
	Individuals are capable and have free choices.	Behavior is learned and, therefore, can be taught.
Targets	Feelings and attitudes of participants	Specific behaviors

---

rural area where few, if any, special classes existed. The concepts developed by the EMC still hold true today. A significant part of the total program was a strategy to involve parents in the education of their own children. When general classroom teachers in the service area believed that a child demonstrated a discrepancy between ability and performance, he or she was referred to the EMC for further evaluation. If the teacher's referral was deemed appropriate for the EMC program, the teacher and the child's parents were asked to attend a workshop consisting of four meetings. Figure 13.1 is a diagram of the workshop's organization.

The EMC program was based on behavioral principles of learning theory. The strategy was to teach the participants—parents and teachers—how to modify children's behavior (specifically, academic behavior) by using the consequences available to them. The parents met separately for the first three meetings, and the parents and teachers came together for the final meeting to share the results of their work. Following is a brief summary of the content of the four parent meetings:

1. The parent group consisted of about 25 to 30 parents whose children had been referred for services, along with 6 to 10 methods and materials consultants (M & Ms). The leader presented a brief overview of behavior modification, emphasizing that behavior is learned and that parents are influential teachers. The M & Ms also stressed that most parents following the planned program would be successful, setting a high level of expectancy for success.

   The parents then were instructed in the importance of selecting measurable and observable targets. They were shown how to proceed from a global label of "laziness," for example, to a more specific target of "not getting up in the morning when called." The leader distributed forms for the parents to prioritize the behaviors they would like to see changed. The leader also provided forms for collecting and recording data.

   A brief question-and-answer session followed the general presentation. Then the parents met in small groups with the M & Ms to make sure they had selected measurable targets and that they understood how to collect data. The parents went home with the assignment to collect one week of baseline data.

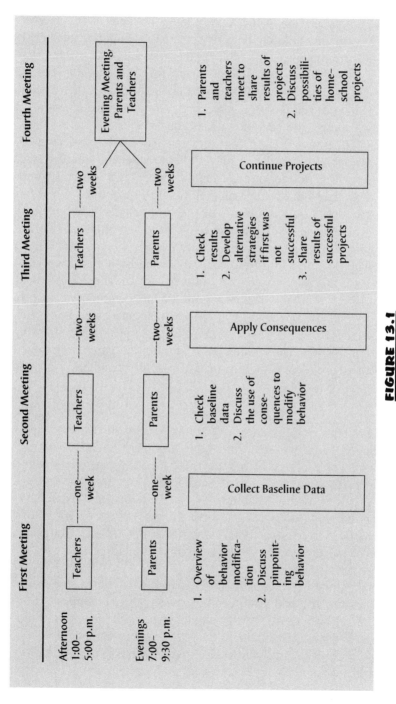

FIGURE 13.1
EMC Parent–Teacher Workshop Structure

2. The parents met again a week later. The aim of this meeting was mainly to teach the parents the ABCs (antecedents, behavior, consequences) of behavior modification. The parents were encouraged to think of the many rewarding conditions and events they already had available in the home (the graphic behavior chart, visual checklists, kitchen timers, extra TV watching, later bedtime, special snacks, etc.).

   If graphs derived from previous successful projects were available, the leader displayed them. A general question-and-answer period followed. Then the parents met in small groups with the M & Ms to graph their baseline data, select a new target if the first was found to be inappropriate, and choose a consequence or develop a plan to alter the antecedent events that might be affecting the child's behavior.

3. The third meeting followed the second by about 2 weeks to give the parents enough time to notice changes in their child's behavior. The major aim of this meeting was to give parents an opportunity to share their successes with each other. The M & Ms reviewed the basic principles, stressing consistency. During much of the time, the parents presented their projects to the group. This usually resulted in a great deal of peer reinforcement.

Dee, a fifth-grade teacher with about 40 years of teaching experience, had discovered during the first week of class that year that David couldn't read fifth-grade material and seemed to have little interest in learning. She tried third-grade, then first-grade materials with him, without success. She was one of those exemplary teachers who are willing to put forth the extra effort to bring students along. She referred David's parents to the EMC and targeted for David the academic goal of "being able to identify the letters of the alphabet."

At the fourth EMC session, Dee joined the parents in expressing their pleasure at David's improved behavior, both academically and in attitude. David had met the goal of identifying all the letters of the alphabet and was even looking forward to going to school. His father beamed with pride and said to Dee, "My boy has been looking for you for 5 years."

Parents who still were not successful in getting their child to change his or her behavior or who wanted to work on extra projects met briefly with the M & Ms. They received praise for their efforts and were given tips and encouraged to keep trying. The total group was reminded that the next meeting would be a joint meeting with the teachers to share the results of their work.

4. The teachers were invited to attend the fourth meeting along with the parents, a week or two later. After a brief general session in which both groups were praised for their diligence in the program and the success many of them were able to attain, parents and teachers met in small groups with the M & Ms to discuss the results of their work. These sessions tended to be beneficial because the teachers and parents often found common reinforcers to be effective with the children.

Although parent training programs are regarded as a Level 3 Needs activity in the mirror model, these programs sometimes become a Level 4 Strengths activity if they lead to parents' later conducting workshops like those in which they have participated.

Shirley was a parent as well as a grandparent of a child with mental disabilities. She enrolled in a parent program on behavior management, sponsored by the Parent Involvement Center for Rehabilitation. She was highly successful with her own two charges and caught on immediately to the ideas the program conveyed. At the conclusion of the training, she asked if any more sessions were planned.

"Yes, but instead of attending more yourself, how would you like to help us run some other sessions?" we asked.

"I'd love to!" she replied.

She started helping us run programs, and the next thing we knew, *we* were helping *her*. She began to help other teachers in the school system develop and conduct behavior management programs. This is a glittering example of the actions of which parents are capable.

FILIAL THERAPY

Filial therapy, a parent training program developed by Guerney (1969) to teach parents the principles of play therapy, is still going strong today. Although the philosophical base and the underlying assumptions of play therapy are different from those of the EMC behavior modification program, the structure of the program has a number of similarities, such as the use of small parent groups, the sharing of results with the group, and the goal of behavior change—with the obvious difference that the filial therapy program uses play as the medium of behavior change.

1. In the first stage, parents are instructed in the purpose, value, and techniques of play therapy. The leader demonstrates play sessions and introduces some role-playing techniques. The parents are encouraged to discuss their feelings about their interactions with their children in light of the techniques they observe.
2. The parents then attempt play therapy with another child, or their own child, under supervision. This is followed by a discussion of what they observe so they can learn from it and work on their techniques.
3. When the group leader and the parents feel ready, the parents begin the play therapy at home with their own children. They take notes and bring them to the next session to discuss with the other parents.
4. In the final stage, the group leader and the parents begin to disengage from the program structure and share what they have gained.

The filial therapy program usually runs from 12 to 16 sessions. Teaching parents to be play therapists with their own children, it is hoped, will open lines of communication between parents and their children.

PARENT COUNSELING GROUPS

The emphasis of parent counseling groups usually is on the affective domain, and nondirective counseling techniques are employed.

The content of the meetings is the responsibility of group members, and the group leader tries to reflect the feelings expressed by the participants.

PARENT EFFECTIVENESS TRAINING

The parent effectiveness training (PET) program, conceived by Gordon (1970), along with filial therapy and many of the behavior modification parent programs, attempts to teach parents to become therapists for their own children. In this 8-week course, parents are instructed in the techniques of active listening and problem solving. Parents are taught how to analyze their communication transactions with their children.

The groups are composed of 10 to 12 parents plus the group leader. The participants sit in a circle and are encouraged to express their agreement or disagreement with the ideas of the leader or other members. The group offers ample opportunity for demonstrations and role playing. Parents are coached in how to encourage their children to express their feelings, and are taught how to express their own feelings in an open, honest way with their children.

An emphasis is placed on encouraging children to accept ownership for their problems. In being active listeners, parents can help their children arrive at solutions to their own problems. PET provides methods for mutual problem solving and agreement when parents and children come into conflict over an issue. Solutions arrived at jointly have a higher success rate than solutions either party arrives at independently. In this way, neither party loses.

THE PARENT "C" GROUP

Another type of parent group, the "C" group, was popularized by Dinkmeyer and Carlson (1973). The premise was that the most successful programs are those directed at practical problems. It is called a "C" group because of the components of collaboration, consultation, clarification, confrontation, concern and caring, confidentiality, and commitment to change.

The group is kept small—usually 6 to 10 members plus the group leader. The leader sets the stage with a brief discussion of the theoretical position and then encourages one of the members to present a practical problem. With a small group, the leader tries to get all the members involved in suggesting ideas for solving each others' problems. During a session, each member is supposed to present a problem, develop a hypothesis about the problem, and propose a tentative solution to take home and apply in trying to solve the problem. A public declaration of commitment to change is thought to be important to the program's effectiveness.

In all of the groups discussed, one of the group leader's goals is to enlist new leaders who can conduct groups. Many professionals recognize that they cannot serve all parents' needs by themselves. Therefore, training others in their skills is important.

ADVANTAGES OF PARENT GROUPS

The popularity of parent groups is still on the rise. Working with a group of parents who have something in common—either the child's age or a specific disability—has obvious advantages, some of which are the following:

➤ Parents realize that they are not the only ones with a specific problem. Often, a parent with a child who has been classified as having a disability feels alone in this circumstance.

➤ Parents can share their strong emotions with others who understand. They often are relieved to find that guilt or anger regarding a child with a disability is frequently expressed in a group meeting. The realization that other members of the group have similar feelings has a therapeutic effect.

➤ Parents can share solutions, too. They are more likely to accept ideas from other members of the group than they will from an outside authority. Knowing that other parents have been confronted with a situation similar to their own and have resolved it makes the proposed solution much more palatable.

➤ More parents can be reached in a group than individually. The group represents an efficient use of the leader's time.

GROUP SIZE

As much interaction as possible within parent groups is desired. The possibility for interaction increases rapidly as the number of individuals increases. For instance, if a group has two people, it allows two interactions, but in a group of 7 people, 42 interactions are possible if everyone initiates an interaction with everyone else in the group. With 10 people in a group, 90 different interactions are possible if everyone interacts with everyone else. The optimum size of a parent group such as the ones considered here is thought to be 10 or fewer participants.

The parent group does not offer a panacea for all parents' concerns. Some parents benefit most from one-to-one contact with the teacher or counselor to talk over an issue. Also, some teachers do not feel comfortable leading a group of parents. They prefer that the leader be someone other than themselves because they think parents would not be at ease in a session conducted by their child's teacher. This is a legitimate concern. Parent group meetings are presented as an option for consideration, but not as one that all teachers should feel compelled to lead for parents in their classrooms.

PARENT EDUCATION MATERIALS

Parent education programs and materials have been developed to assist parents with the many facets of their large task at hand. These resources can also be used by professionals in planning their parent education groups. A few of these programs are listed here:

The STEP Program: Systematic Training for Effective Parenting
http://www.agsnet.com/group.asp?nGroupInfoID=a16200

The Practical Parenting Video Series
http://www.practicalparentseries.com/

Active Parenting Now AudioBook
http://www.activeparenting.com/xapnab.htm

SUMMARY

Parent training groups have become a popular means of working with parents of exceptional children. Strategies for training parents to become therapists for their own children are formulated around all the major theoretical positions, and they all report successful results. Those described here include the EMC parent–teacher workshop, filial therapy, parent effectiveness training, and the parent "C" group.

These workshops and sessions usually have been conducted by leaders other than the teacher, such as the school counselor, but teachers are welcome to consider this role if they are comfortable in serving as both teacher and group leader to parents of children in their classrooms. Further, parents with the time, strength, energy, ability, and desire may be trained to learn to conduct these groups. They can be a definite asset to a comprehensive parent involvement program.

An advantage of parent training groups is that they make efficient use of the leader's time. Also, parents in groups discover that they are not alone in their feelings, and they realize that they can learn from each other.

ACTIVITIES

1. Role-play a group meeting using one of the programs outlined in this chapter.
2. Develop a handout explaining a parent training group. Share it with classmates for review.
3. Interview a group of parents about their interests and concerns for developing and operating a parent training group.
4. Read more extensively about one of the types of groups reported in this chapter, and explain it to the class.
5. Discuss the pros and cons of the teacher being the leader of a parent group.
6. Design a parent group. Implement it if you have the means.

REFERENCES

Dinkmeyer, D., & Carlson, J. (Eds.). (1973). *Consulting: Facilitating human potential and change processes.* Columbus, OH: Charles E. Merrill.

Edge, D., Veasey, M., Chittick, G., & Mullins, J. (1993). *Evaluation report.* Louisville, KY: Jefferson County Public Schools.

Gibbs, C., Edge, D., & Petrosko, J. (1993). *Evaluation report of Even Start.* Louisville, KY: Ohio Valley Educational Cooperative.

Gill, A. (1998). *What makes parent training groups effective. Promoting positive parenting through collaboration.* Retrieved in 1998 from http://www.practical parent.org.uk/page2.html

Gordon, T. (1970). *P.E.T. Parent effectiveness training: The tested new way to raise responsible children.* New York: Peter H. Wyden.

Guerney, B. R., Jr. (Ed.). (1969). *Psychotherapeutic agents: New roles for nonprofessionals.* New York: Holt, Rinehart & Winston.

Kagan, S. L., Costley, J., Landesman, L., Marx, R., Neville, P., Parker, S., et al. (1992). *Family education and training: Obstacles, opportunities, and outcomes for low-income mothers* (Rep. No. 4). Baltimore: Johns Hopkins University, Center of Families, Communities, Schools, and Children's Learning. (ERIC Doc. Rep. Service No. ED 345 869)

Kagan, S. L., Neville, P., & Rustici, J. (1993). *Family education and training from research to practice: Implementation plan* (Rep. No. 14). Baltimore: Johns Hopkins University, Center of Families, Communities, Schools and Children's Learning. (ERIC Doc. Rep. Serv. No. ED 360 044)

Part Four

Technology and the Future of Parent Involvement

14

Assistive Technology and Devices

DEA 2004 aligns closely with the No Child Left Behind Act of 2001, helping to ensure equity, accountability, and excellence in education for children with disabilities. While regulations implementing IDEA 2004 are being prepared (at press time), the regulations implementing the 1997 reauthorization remain in effect, to the extent that they are consistent with the IDEA 2004 statute. Under IDEA, the Office of Special Education Programs (OSEP) within the Office of Special Education and Rehabilitative Services (OSERS) supports a technical assistance and dissemination network designed to improve results for children with disabilities.

The Technology-Related Assistance for Individuals with Disabilities Act of 1988 (Tech Act, PL 100-407) and the Individuals with Disabilities Education Act of 1990 (IDEA, PL 101-476) defined assistive technology (AT) as "any item, piece of equipment, or product system, whether acquired commercially off the shelf, modified, or customized, that is used to increase, maintain, or improve the functional capabilities of a child with a disability." Technology falls into three categories (Behrmann & Jerome, 2002):

1. No tech (e.g., a nonelectronic device such as a study carrel, a piece of foam glued to the corner of a page to make turning easier)
2. Low tech (e.g., an electronic but unsophisticated device such as a tape recorder)
3. High tech (e.g., computers, synthesizers, and other highly complex devices)

AT requires accompanying support and follow-up services. This support is defined in IDEA as "a service that directly assists a child with a disability in the selection, acquisition, or use of an assistive technology device." According to the National Information Center for Children and Youth with Disabilities (cited in Parette & Brotherson, 1996), AT also may include occupational therapy, physical therapy, speech therapy, and evaluations. AT services also may include "such supportive activities as purchasing and leasing devices and equipment; customizing and adapting devices; repairing devices; training in the use of devices; and coordinating therapies, interventions, and services."

Both pieces of federal legislation mandate that AT be considered in developing individualized education plans (IEPs) for students with disabilities, who must be guaranteed access to the general education curriculum. IDEA requires that schools provide "AT services and equipment for a student with a disability if the services and/or equipment are required to ensure a free and appropriate education [FAPE]" (Merbler, Hadadian, & Ulman, 1999). The Tech Act marked the beginning of a discretionary grant program that is available to all states to assist them in developing AT equipment and services for individuals with disabilities, regardless of age.

FAMILY-CENTERED AT EARLY ASSESSMENT AND INTERVENTION

If AT is to be used effectively to enable young children with special needs to be active participants in life and school, families must be involved in the entire assessment and intervention process. AT gives infants and young children the ability to "move around their environments, speak and communicate with others, and participate in developmentally appropriate activities that might not be possible [otherwise]" (Judge, 2002). The 1997 reauthorization of IDEA also "mandates that [AT] devices and services be among the early intervention services that can be included in the Individual Family Service Plan (IFSP)," which dictates services for children with disabilities who range in age from birth to 3 years.

IEPs AND IFSPs

IEPs are prepared for school-age children. IFSPs are prepared for children birth to age 3. Although the role of parents in developing and implementing both plans is important, it is even more crucial in the latter. Families that "maintain or acquire a sense of control over their family life . . . attribute positive changes resulting from early intervention to their own strengths, abilities, and actions" (Dunst, Rivette, & Deal, as cited in Parette & Brotherson, 1996). Family members must be the ones to decide what the intervention and implementation goals should be. Family values, routines, and resources must be considered because family members are the ones who ultimately must endure the demands that AT may require. Lifestyle modifications to accommodate the use of AT in the home can affect the entire family dynamic.

Family-centered assistive-technology decision making should be framed against the background of cultural and family considerations (Parette & Botherson, 1996; Parette & McMahan, 2002). According to Parette and Brotherson, a culturally sensitive approach to an AT assessment incorporates five domains:

1. Child
2. Technology
3. Service system
4. Family
5. Culture

Culture refers to "the customs, values, and beliefs that are unique to family members and children from a specific cultural group" (Parette & Botherson, 1996).

In the past, traditional assessments of the efficacy of AT for young children provided limited opportunities for parental involvement. According to Judge (2002), "The results . . . [often led] to the recommendation of a device geared toward specific tasks as opposed to a tool to facilitate independent functioning of a child in multiple environments." One direct consequence of this lack of parental input is that AT sometimes has been abandoned.

AT ABANDONMENT

The large room was packed with people for an IEP. In the middle of the room was Ernest, in a motorized wheelchair. Surrounding him were his grandmother, an occupational therapist, a physical therapist, a speech therapist, his teacher, an assistive technologist, the director of special education, and a few others. Ernest had been the victim of a drive-by shooting, and most of the team members were new to this recent case. Also present was a TV cameraman, to capture the highlights for the local news.

After introductions, the team launched into a discussion of goals for Ernest. Some of the more obvious goals included mobility, communications, and assistance in the classroom. It was decided that he could use his computer for e-mail and lessons, he could practice mobility in his wheelchair, and the teacher's aide would be available for assistance. Ernest had never been much of a student, and he didn't seem to have a great deal of stick-to-itiveness. He had acquired his wheelchair through a financial settlement and the federal requirements. The suggestions ranged from his using eye-movement software to voice-recognition software for communicating with his computer. One attendee commented on how well the brilliant scientist Steven Hawkins was able to communicate through AT.

But Ernest just sat there. Some attendees attempted to get him to try the various AT devices presented to him, but it became obvious that he wasn't catching on, and he quit trying fairly soon. The teacher, aide, and counselor huddled and began discussing how to motivate Ernest. The local TV cameraman took some final footage and packed up to leave so he could make the 6 o'clock news.

The participants filed out, leaving Ernest, the grandmother, the teacher, and the aide to finish up. And another meeting came to a close.

$$***$$

Depending on the type of device, the rate of AT abandonment ranges between 8% and 75% (Scherer, as cited in Judge, 2002). The reasons given for this non-use include the following (Phillips & Zao, cited in Judge, 2002):

1. The child having outgrown the device
2. Professionals *not listening* [italics ours] to preferences expressed by the child and family
3. Lack of training for family members in how to use the device
4. Lack of ongoing team support
5. Oversophistication of the device—confusing to the child and family members
6. Lack of information about repairing and maintaining the device
7. Lack of motivation on the part of the child to use the device for its intended purpose

Parents usually know what's best for their children. They are competent and capable of making the most appropriate decisions about the selection and provision of AT for their youngsters. According to Judge

(2002), professionals need to reassess their roles and responsibilities and develop effective help-giving behaviors and attitudes for parents. Functional use of AT in the child's natural environment increases when parents are totally involved in the AT assessment and intervention process. Parents should have the final say in deciding what devices appropriately match the child's needs, what goals and interests should be pursued, and what courses of action will be taken to attain the stated intentions. Keeping all these considerations in mind will reduce the frequency of AT abandonment.

AT Partnerships

To act in the best interests of the child, professionals and family members must develop a collaborative partnership, based on "mutual trust, honesty, respect, open communication, and respect for cultural diversity" (Judge, 2002). Professionals must

> provide families with relevant and accurate information,
> use effective communication skills,
> confer responsibility to the family to make informed decisions, and
> protect the family's privacy.

Further, Judge suggests, professionals and families must

> agree to pool their resources (knowledge, skills, and past experiences);
> work toward a mutually acceptable AT goal or interest;
> define their roles based upon the family's needs, resources, routines, and values; and
> be willing to renegotiate roles and goals as the assessment and intervention process evolves.

In her article, Judge also provides a list of timely and pertinent questions, ranging from asking parents what level of involvement they want at all stages of the AT assessment process to informing families that they, and they alone, have to make the final decision regarding their acceptance or rejection of professional advice.

AT Practices

Family-centered AT assessment and intervention plans should include three phases (Judge, 2002):

1. Setting the stage
2. Activity-based assessment
3. Ongoing intervention and evaluation

Teamwork is the key to the successful provision of AT devices and systems. One model that has proven to be effective in delivering AT services to families and children is the *transdisciplinary team model* (Judge & Parette, as cited in Judge, 2002). This team approach differs from other team models in that

> it attempts to overcome the confines of individual disciplines to form a team that crosses and re-crosses disciplinary boundaries and, therefore, maximizes communication, interaction, and cooperation among team members . . . and work[s] together to make programmatic decisions and accomplish a common set of service goals for a child and his or her family. (Bruder & Boologna, as cited in Judge, 2002)

Although all the team members develop the intervention plan, the parents, along with one designated team member, are responsible for making sure it is carried out.

Setting the Stage

When families first express an interest in AT assessment and intervention services for children with disabilities, they receive information covering everything from the philosophy of a given program, to the background of the professionals who will be involved in the process, to the designation of roles on the team. At this initial meeting, family members are encouraged to express their concerns, relate past experiences with AT devices and systems, and explain their goals for themselves and their children. This meeting also gives family members an opportunity to see and touch AT devices. They can ask questions and become more familiar with the devices to help them to decide what devices are best suited to their children's daily routines and activities.

Activity-Based Assessment

At this stage, the families and children meet with other team members to conduct an activity-based AT assessment in a natural setting (usually home or child-care facility).

> If family members are willing to play an active role in the assessment, play situations are arranged that allow them to interact with their child while other team members observe the interaction and responses of the child. (Judge, 2002)

Ongoing discussions and feedback determine whether extra time or activities are needed. Near the end of this stage, the team members meet to discuss their observations, share information, and decide on the next steps. If families decide at this juncture to borrow AT devices to test their effectiveness, professionals can offer training and suggestions for optimal use.

Ongoing Intervention and Evaluation

At this stage, home or child-care visits continue. The families prepare goals for each of these visits, and information or skills required for them to meet these goals are identified and reflected in the IFSPs. This stage is dynamic and ongoing. Changes are made to address the family's concerns and priorities and to accommodate the children's needs. This evaluative assessment of the efficiency and appropriateness of AT devices should be "an integral component of the [AT] assessment processes" (Judge, 2002).

AT IN THE CLASSROOM

> AT, including adaptive or alternative input devices, voice synthesis and recognition technologies, and specialized software, can facilitate inclusion of students with disabilities [into the classroom] by making previously difficult or impossible tasks feasible. (Merbler et al., 1999)

Technology in general also can lessen teachers' responsibilities to prepare and keep records and reports. AT can assist students with learning disabilities in six areas of instruction (Lahm & Morissette, as cited in Behrmann & Jerome, 2002):

1. Organization
2. Note-taking
3. Writing
4. Academic productivity
5. Access to educational materials
6. Cognitive assistance

Care must be taken that AT equipment chosen for use in the classroom setting meets the children's needs and abilities. Factors to consider include (Merbler et al., 1999)

➤ ease of use,
➤ learning required for student to become proficient,
➤ appearance of device (noisy? large? strange looking?),
➤ potential danger to user or bystanders, and
➤ maintenance (does it require constant teacher attention?).

Merbler et al. (1999) also made several recommendations that teachers might consider when adapting the computer technology already present in their classrooms to meet the needs of children with disabilities:

➤ Choose alternative keyboards (e.g., overlays, chording, miniatures, and on-screen) that make inputting information easier.
➤ Choose alternative input devices (e.g., blow tube switches, trackballs, and large push buttons).
➤ Use touch screens.
➤ Use speech-input and -recognition software.
➤ Encourage the use of hardware and software in writing lessons: spell/grammar checkers, word processors, word-prediction programs, and scanners.

The potential for computers and related technologies to facilitate instruction in inclusive classrooms is great. The following recommendations (arranged in no particular order or priority) compiled by Merbler et al. (1999) can help teachers maximize this potential in their classrooms:

➤ Use open-ended devices that permit customizing for the user and/or task.

➤ Try to find the lowest-technology solution that can provide the desired level of performance or function, rather than a complex, high-technology device or system. For example, simply changing a student's angle of view of a computer monitor (e.g., placing the monitor at eye level rather than hairline level or above) could improve the student's performance substantially.

➤ Collaborate with other teachers. Technologies are developing too quickly for one teacher to monitor them all. Sharing expertise can help.

➤ Work with parents to ensure that AT devices that go home are properly used and maintained. Parents also can be an excellent source of evaluative information on how effectively a device or piece of software is working.

➤ Don't believe that you have to master a device or software application completely before you begin using it. Many times an application can be used successfully early in the learning curve, and learning by doing can promote eventual mastery.

➤ Match AT devices to the user's age, gender, and preferences to promote acceptance and use.

➤ Ensure that the arrangement and operation of controls are predictable and natural. Feedback to the user must be meaningful.

➤ Be sure that your school or school system has a comprehensive policy covering AT, including the protection of student and teacher privacy, repair and maintenance of equipment, and the home use of school-purchased equipment. Be sure also that the policy states the AT resource for IEP teams.

➤ Allocate funds to ensure that teachers and other potential AT service providers receive training in how to use the equipment. Simply purchasing AT equipment does not ensure its use.

➤ Don't be afraid to experiment. AT is a relatively young field, and everybody is learning.

Table 14.1 gives examples of AT devices and adaptations to consider for use with children in various learning tasks.

IEPs, Assessment, and the IEP Team

AT devices can nourish the academic success and independence of students with disabilities. They can help the child focus on his or her

TABLE 14.1
Examples of Assistive Technology Devices and Adaptations

Academic Area/Task	AT Devices/Adaptations
Listening	Assistive listening device Variable speech-control tape recorder/player Conventional tape recorder/player
Writing	Word processor Spell-checker Proofreading programs Outlining/brainstorming programs Abbreviation expanders Speech synthesis/screen-reading programs Word-prediction programs
Reading	Optical character recognition/speech synthesis Speech synthesis for "books on disk" Variable speech-control tape recorders Audiotaped books
Organization/memory	Personal data managers (stand-alone) Personal data organization software Free-form database Calendar programs Tape recorder/player
Mathematics	Talking calculators Conventional calculator On-screen (computer-based) calculator

Source: From *Functional Evaluation for Assistive Technology,* by M. R. Raskind and B. R. Bryant, 1999. Austin, TX: Psycho-Educational Services.

strengths, interests, and experiences rather than on weaknesses and limitations. But not all AT devices are appropriate for every child in every circumstance. IEP teams are responsible for determining whether children with disabilities require AT devices and services and, if so, which are the most appropriate. The fundamental question to ask is: Will AT adaptations help this special-needs child be successful academically?

An IEP team might be composed of an occupational therapist, a speech pathologist, a physical therapist, an AT specialist, and educational professionals. They all play a role in the assessment process. It's their job to determine whether AT devices and services will guarantee a free appropriate public education to a child with special needs. A list of questions to ask in that regard is as follows (Chambers, 1997):

➤ Is the provision of an AT device or service essential for the student to receive FAPE?
➤ Is an AT device or service necessary for the child to be educated within the least restrictive environment?
➤ Are the AT devices and/or services a necessary related service?
➤ Given AT services and/or devices, will the person with disabilities have access to school programs and activities?

INTEGRATING AT INTO THE STANDARD CURRICULUM

Technology that supports students in accessing the curriculum does not have to be expensive or complicated to make a difference in learning. Both low-tech and high-tech applications have been used successfully to ensure students' success in the general education curriculum. . . . Educators must start with the curriculum and then ask how tools [AT] might assist students in achieving outcomes [identified in the students' IEPs]. (Warger, 1998)

The education TECH point system was developed by Gayl Bowser and Penny Reed to help educators deliver effective AT delivery systems (Warger, 1998). It is a strategy for identifying the following specific points in the planning process where AT should be considered:

➤ Initial referral question
➤ Evaluation questions
➤ Extended assessment questions
➤ Planning of development questions
➤ Implementation questions
➤ Periodic review questions

State policies and practices can go a long way in supporting local school districts as they attempt to meet the federally mandated requirements of IDEA '97. These include

➤ a statement of AT outcomes;
➤ policies for delivering AT services;

➤ staff development and technical assistance;
➤ evidence of research-based practices to support the use of AT;
➤ mechanisms for interdisciplinary involvement;
➤ policies for purchasing, using, and managing equipment;
➤ strategies for obtaining adequate funding; and
➤ strategies for communicating these policies.

When implementing AT into the classroom setting, the following are some considerations:

➤ Locate equipment where instruction and learning are taking place.
➤ Place AT in the classroom where it is accessible to the child.
➤ Select low-tech applications wherever possible.
➤ Integrate the use of technology into lessons in a purposeful and meaningful way.
➤ Have the same equipment used in the classroom available in the child's home, if possible, to promote continuity of learning.
➤ Offer training and technical support to classroom teachers initially.
➤ When the technology is available in the home, provide training to family members.
➤ View the initial fiscal and human resources as an investment that the child will continue to benefit from in subsequent years.
➤ When possible, use AT that is already in place.

AT IN TEACHER PREPARATION PROGRAMS

When teachers graduate from teacher preparation programs, they often are unprepared and ill-equipped to discuss AT services available to students with exceptional needs. Their knowledge of AT and services is limited and, consequently, they may have difficulty explaining the various options to the students' parents and families. Bryant, Erin, Lock, Allan, and Resta (1998) have written an informative article dealing with this very issue. Of particular interest is the inclusion of extensive and detailed tables that list the competencies, objectives, and strategies that should comprise a preservice AT curriculum.

SUMMARY

Federal legislation has mandated that AT and the accompanying services and support must be included in the development of IEPs for children with disabilities so they are ensured a free and appropriate public education. IDEA '97 instituted the same for development of IFSPs for children ages birth to 3 years. To use AT successfully, professionals must keep the family at the center of any intervention plan. Families and professionals must work collaboratively in the best interests of the child with special needs to avoid abandonment of AT.

Family-centered assessment and intervention plans include setting the stage for the process to begin, conducting an activity-based assessment, and maintaining ongoing intervention and evaluation. IEP assessment teams also can help teachers utilize AT optimally in the classroom setting and determine which AT devices and services are most appropriate for helping children with special needs achieve academic success. One of the best ways to help teachers become more aware of and more comfortable with AT is for them to be introduced to it while attending teacher preparation programs.

ACTIVITIES

1. Reread the scenario presented in the discussion of AT abandonment. Divide into small groups of three or four to discuss the procedures and expected outcomes.
2. Describe in no more than two pages a personal experience you have encountered with an AT device and (a) learning to use it for yourself or a family member, (b) teaching someone else how to use it, or (c) obstacles to using it in your home or classroom.
3. Prepare a portfolio containing descriptions of three or four AT devices. Describe them, and explain how they can be used to the most benefit.
4. Suppose a child in your classroom is having difficulty using an AT device. Describe the process you might follow to ensure that this child continues to use the AT device.

References

Behrmann, M., & Jerome, M. K. (2002). *Assistive technology for students with mild disabilities.* (ERIC Digest #E623). Retrieved February 10, 2003, from http://www.echo.louisville.edu/

Bryant, D. P., Erin, J., Lock, R., Allan, J. M., & Resta, P. E. (1998). Infusing a teacher preparation program in learning disabilities with assistive technology. *Journal of Learning Disabilities, 31*(1). Retrieved February 19, 2003, from http://www.echo.louisville.edu/

Chambers, A. C. (1997). *Has technology been considered? A guide for IEP teams* (p. 5). Reston, VA: Council of Administrators of Special Education and Council for Exceptional Children, Technology and Media Division.

Judge, S. (2002). The need for and challenges of assistive technology. *Infants and Young Children, 15*(1). Retrieved February 15, 2003, from http://www.echo.louisville.edu/

Merbler, J. B., Hadadian, A., & Ulman, J. (1999). Using assistive technology in the inclusive classroom. *Preventing School Failure, 43*(3). Retrieved February 19, 2003, from http://www.echo.louisville.edu/

Parette, H. P., & Brotherson, M. J. (1996). Family-centered assistive technology assessment. *Intervention in School & Clinic, 32*(2). Retrieved February 27, 2003, from http://www.echo.louisville.edu/

Parette, H. P., & McMahan, G. A. (2002). What should we expect of assistive technology? Being sensitive to family goals. *Teaching Exceptional Children, 35*(1). Retrieved February 27, 2003, from http://www.echo.louisville.edu/

Raskind, M. R., & Bryant, B. R. (1999). *Functional Evaluation for Assistive Technology.* Austin, TX: Psycho-Educational Services.

Warger, C. (1998). Integrating assistive technology into the standard curriculum. *ERIC/OSEP Digest E568.* Retrieved February 19, 2003, from http://www.echo.louisville.edu/

Wrapping Up and Looking Ahead

Parent involvement can transform the culture of a school and change the structure of a community (Rouse, 1994). It can change attitudes and increase student achievement. It can increase attendance and reduce tardiness. It can make schools better. Most parents want information about their children's academic performance but also about how they as parents can contribute to the educational process. To build a home–school connection, educators must consider ways of involving parents. The Southwest Educational Development Laboratory, through its research on parent involvement, has identified seven common elements in a comprehensive parent-involvement program (cited in Schurr, 1992):

1. A written policy that legitimizes the importance of parent involvement
2. Administrative support that is represented by allocation of dollars, space, and people power
3. Training that focuses on communication and partnering skills for parents and staff members
4. Emphasis on a partnership philosophy that creates a feeling of mutual ownership in the education of students
5. A two-way communication structure that occurs regularly and consistently
6. Networking that facilitates the sharing of information, resources, and technical expertise
7. Regular evaluation activities that attempt to modify or revise program components as needed

Such overwhelming evidence exists in support of school–parent partnerships (Schurr, 1992) that school leaders must take the initiative to create an environment that invites rather than discourages families of all configurations and socioeconomic levels into the school. Educators must open the doors of their minds to the endless possibilities for increasing student academic and social behavior performance through parent involvement.

Research has clearly shown that parent involvement improves children's academic performance. Clark (1995) chronicled the following parent-involvement activities of the 1990s that demonstrated a significant shift toward parent support:

1990   Individuals with Disabilities Education Act was amended to define parents' rights.

1991   National PTA passed resolution on parents' rights and responsibilities.

1992   National PTA sponsored national summit on parent involvement.

1993   National PTA endorsed requirement for teacher preparation in parent/family involvement.

1994   Goals 2000 was passed with parental involvement as one goal.

1994   Elementary and Secondary Education Act was reauthorized with parent involvement requirements. The secretary of education at that time, Richard W. Riley, unveiled a national family-involvement school initiative.

1994   International conference on parent involvement was initiated.

Since then, there have been two reauthorizations of IDEA (in 1997 and 2004), along with the passage of the No Child Left Behind Act (NCLB) of 2001, all of which emphasize parent involvement in the schools.

TEACHER PREPARATION IN WORKING WITH PARENTS

The importance of effective parent–teacher relationships cannot be overemphasized. Teachers who understand the child in his or her home environment can make appropriate educational plans in the classroom. Clearly, teachers represent the greatest potential link between home and school.

Parents who are provided with information about the school setting and their child's progress can be strong supporters and assistants in the child's educational growth and development. Parents and teachers who recognize each other's capabilities can join together in successful problem solving, enabling students to make significant gains both academically and socially.

The teacher qualification statute in No Child Left Behind is clear. It specifies degrees, competencies, and training requirements for established teachers as well as those who enter through alternative certification programs. NCLB specifically discusses rigorous tests to measure students' knowledge of content. This is the most crucial part of the law and at the same time the most difficult for the states. A strong relationship between school and home can facilitate the children's best efforts in meeting the NCLB standards.

Parent involvement ranges from being active in parent–teacher organizations, to helping children with homework, to taking an active role in school governance, as in the recent trend toward school-based councils in schools. Efforts to boost parent involvement range from rewording a school's visitor sign (to something such as VIPS—VERY IMPORTANT PARENTS—AND VISITORS PLEASE CHECK IN AT THE OFFICE) to active community outreach including visits to parents at home.

CLAIMING THE CHILD

A wise teacher once said that when teachers "claim" a child as their own responsibility or the parents "claim" the child as a part of their life, the child's chances for optimum growth are elevated. In doing this, teachers must go beyond the brief interactions with students in presenting subject matter. It doesn't mean that teachers should try to "own" a child and the child's problems but, rather, that they feel strongly enough about the child's welfare to provide many opportunities for children to grow and encourage them to accept responsibility for their own behavior.

By their verbal and nonverbal interactions, teachers can show that they care. They can do this in their classroom by sharing in the joys and important events in each child's life. Some teachers send their pupils birthday, holiday, and valentine cards. A personally addressed card from the teacher is especially appreciated. Some teachers phone the child when they see something they think the child would be interested in, or they call the parents when something positive has happened to the child that day. These little touches help the child know that the teacher has "claimed" him or her and the child has entered into the teacher's world.

Much of what the teacher does to care and support the child helps that child build a positive self-image. The child's resiliency is strengthened through receiving care and support, high expectations, and meaningful opportunities for participation (Benard, 1993). Teachers are charged with these daily tasks of caring for and supporting children. Children come to school daily needing nourishment in terms of both food and psychological support. They grow and develop through an array of experiences undergirded by the support of adults.

More and more schools are redefining themselves as community institutions, collaborating with community agencies to address the multiple needs of children and families. The emphasis is on the whole child, and the community education movement designates the school as the hub of learning and support for the child and family.

REINFORCING THE PARENTS

In entering into the child's world, teachers realize that the other significant adults in the child's life need reinforcement for their good work. When parents are asked to alter their daily lives by listening to their child read, play games with him or her, or help make class projects, parents will fulfill these tasks more readily if the teacher reinforces them with praise, notes, letters, and telephone calls. The more positive the interaction between parents and teachers, the greater is the probability that parents and teachers together will work in the best interests of the child.

DEMONSTRATING TO PARENTS

Many group parent programs (see chapter 9) include demonstrations among their teaching techniques. If the clarity of the procedure or whether the parent can carry out the technique is questionable, demonstrating it for the parents may be a good idea. Many times we learn best by imitation or by modeling after a master teacher. Teachers should not hesitate to *show* parents the techniques they believe may be effective.

Many professionals have come to realize that they cannot do the entire job alone, that parents are teachers, too, and that sharing their techniques with parents is to the child's benefit. After all, dentists teach parents and children how to take care of their teeth; physical therapists show parents how to exercise their children; and psychologists teach parents to be therapists for their own children. Actually, nearly every helping profession has ways of involving parents in the practice of their skills.

Preschool programs for children with auditory, visual, or physical disabilities have strong parent components. This has not been by chance. The importance of parents as teachers of their own child should not be underestimated.

Something about a relationship between a parent and teacher that is built on respect makes both more capable of serving children in their own best interests. Many teachers lack the confidence to take the first step, but the rewards of linking the school and the home are well worth the extra effort.

One significant person can have a profound positive effect on a child's life (Benard, 1993). That significant person must reach out and claim the child. Pick up the phone or a pad of paper. Call or write to someone else who cares as much as you do and who will be equally excited about your message—the child's parents.

WHAT'S AHEAD?

A lot has changed over the years in terms of parent involvement in the schools. Before, parents' opinions weren't asked for and appeared not to be valued as highly. Now, as we expect parents to take an active role in their child's education, we value their opinions and look to them for some answers. We want to work together.

As our society shifts and changes, and as responsibilities delineate, we will continue to rely on parents and their involvement in the schools to help all of our students succeed. We not only call on parents to be proactive for their own children, but we can ask them to be advocates for the school in general and all of its students. Parent volunteers in the classroom, chaperones for field trips, and special lecturers can make a difference in any child's life, not just his or her own offspring. As budget cuts in public schools increase and important parts of the curriculum are eliminated, parents can come into the classroom and teach what they know. Often those kinds of programs, such as music and art, speak to children with exceptional needs in unique ways.

Technology continues to develop at a rapid pace, and often we have no choice but to embrace it and use it to our advantage. Most schools have their own websites, and many communicate with their students and families via e-mail and/or Web pages. School newsletters, memos, and handbooks can be published and sent electronically (reducing the risk that they will be lost in a child's backpack), which makes for faster and more efficient communication. Although it is still important to communicate personally with parents and families (through phone calls and face-to-face conferences), these technological advances can help to keep parents informed.

Parents can use technology to help their children make the most of their education. Books on tape and/or CD are becoming more and more popular, and some libraries and websites now allow patrons to download books in order to listen to them on their MP3 players. For students with reading problems, listening to stories can be a great way to get into storytelling. Cable television went from having a few extra channels to having hundreds of channels (and probably still growing), and there are some stations out there, such as Animal Planet, that can teach children and allow them to have fun while learning. Parents can be encouraged to get involved with technology's progressions. Using a search engine to read up on telecommunications skills, online courses, and current research in the field can be invaluable for both parents and professionals. We can all work together to stay informed and stay involved.

The future of our schools is limitless, and it is impossible for teachers to anticipate all that might happen in the upcoming years. However, it is clear that parent involvement will always be a priority for schools and students. We must strive to keep expanding the lines of communication and keep developing strategies for creating new methods. Our exceptional children need us, and we—both teachers and parents—owe it to them to be there.

ACTIVITIES

1. Have someone take a picture of you and a parent and a child with whom you have worked successfully. Place the picture on the bulletin board.
2. Call a parent with good news about a child.
3. Write an article for the school newsletter on parent-involvement activities.
4. Organize a potluck dinner to celebrate parents and children.
5. Find out a personal interest of at least five of your parents. Arrange for class visits so they can share their hobby or pursuit with your students.
6. Practice with a search engine and look up prominent people in your field.

REFERENCES

Benard, B. (1993). Fostering resiliency in kids. *Educational Leadership, 51*(3), 44–48.

Clark, C. S. (1995, January 20). Parents and schools. *CQ Researcher, 5*(3), 1.

Rouse, J. M. (1994, Fall). Parents as teachers: Investing in good beginnings for children. *Spectrum*, 25–30.

Schurr, S. L. (1992). Fine tuning your parent power increases student achievement. *Schools in the Middle, 2*(2), 3–9.

Tip Sheets
for Parents

WORDS OF ADVICE IF YOU HAVE A CHILD WITH A LEARNING DISABILITY

1. Identify how your child's learning disability will affect him / her daily.
2. Ask for help from people who know your child's problem:
   - Teacher
   - Counselor
   - Doctor
   - Other specialist
3. Decide on the behavioral expectations you have for your child.
4. Discuss with your child the consequences for noncompliant behavior.
5. Be firm and consistent in meting out the consequences related to the child's behavior.
6. Administer consequences without long lectures.
7. Really listen to your child. When the child misbehaves, he/she often is saying "help me."
8. Accept your child as he/she is:
   - Don't try to "fix" your child.
   - Love your child, but not the misbehavior.
   - When trying to teach concepts, present one-step directions.
   - Use concrete examples when you teach the child.
   - Ask the child to repeat the directions you give.
   - Ask the child to look at you when you are giving oral directions.
   - Assign the child short-term tasks.
   - Praise the child's efforts.
9. Spend quality time with your child.
10. Praise the child's smallest accomplishments.
11. Encourage all family members to accept the child, disability and all.
12. Anticipate your child's needs.

(continued)

13. Place your child in groups that would encourage good work and effort.
14. Be honest with your child.
    ➤ Don't say, "There's nothing wrong with you." The child knows that he / she is "different."
    ➤ Discuss ways of coping with the problem.
    ➤ Don't promise things you can't deliver.
    ➤ Take a positive approach.
15. Develop faith and trust in the people who are sincerely trying to help your child.
16. Keep communication lines open between yourself, your child, and your child's teacher.
17. Talk with other parents who have children in learning disability classes.

Source: Adapted from *Counseling Parents of Exceptional Children* by J. C. Stewart (Columbus, OH: Charles E. Merrill, 1978).

WORDS OF ADVICE IF YOU HAVE A CHILD WHO IS GIFTED

1. Remember that each gifted child is a unique individual rooted in a certain family, community, and culture. Gifted children cannot be stereotyped. Although certain general principles apply to their guidance, gifted children all differ from each other.

2. Recognize that gifted children are, first of all, children. They can only be expected to behave appropriately according to their age. They need the following:

   ➤ Love, but also controls
   ➤ Attention, but also discipline
   ➤ Parent involvement, but also self-dependence and responsibility

3. Respect your child and his/her knowledge, which at times may be better than your own. Because gifted children are sometimes impatient with authority:

   ➤ Assume that your child means to do right.
   ➤ Allow as much liberty as you can on unimportant issues.
   ➤ Try to give general instructions to carry out in the child's own creative way rather than specific commands to carry out in yours.
   ➤ Provide clear expectations for behavior.

4. Talk with your child about the importance of conventions such as politeness, manners, courtesy, and regard for others. Otherwise, a gifted child's impatience may cause problems.

5. Discuss discipline with the child. Gifted children seem to understand rational arguments and usually have a well-developed sense of duty.

6. Try to set as few limits as possible and only those that are truly necessary, but when you do set them, follow through. Gifted children are particularly curious to see whether you will be consistent. Gifted children, however, may need fewer constraints than others.

(continued)

7. Encourage your child to participate in developing limits for himself / herself. Because gifted children are highly verbal, they tend to argue and to defend their reasoning and viewpoint with clear logic. Try to see this as a strength to be put to good use in establishing limits rather than as a threat to enforcement of rules.

8. Allow your child to *choose* in as many situations as possible. Gifted children thrive on choices. Make sure, though, that the choices are agreeable to you.

9. Try to respond to your child's needs, not to his / her negative behavior. Understanding the child's needs, however, does not mean that you must accept or even tolerate his/her poor behavior.

10. Convey trust that your child will act wisely.

11. Praise your child. Even if something doesn't work, praise the effort. Curious minds take risks, and that requires support.

12. Take time to be with your child, listen to what he/she has to say, and discuss ideas with him/her. Be a good example yourself.

13. Emphasize early verbal expression, such as reading, discussing ideas, poetry, and music.

14. Read to your young child. Provide good books, magazines, and other media.

15. Emphasize doing well in school.

16. Encourage your child's questions, but insist that he/she not ask them at inappropriate times.

   ➤ When needed, have the child sharpen or rephrase questions to clarify them.

   ➤ Occasionally reply to a question with a question that will send the child searching in larger directions.

   ➤ When you cannot answer a question, direct the child to a resource who can.

17. Stimulate and widen your child's mind through suitable experiences with books, recreation, travel, people, museums, and the arts. Provide the stimulation of lessons in a

special skill, an able companion with whom to spend time, and special experiences outside the home.

18. Encourage the child to follow through and strive for real mastery rather than going through a lot of hobbies or collections in a short time. Gifted children usually have a wide, versatile range of interests but may have problems concentrating in one area for long.

19. Avoid overstructuring the child's life so that there is too little free time. A child cannot be expected to perform at top capacity at all times. Allow time for him/her to daydream, be silly, and contemplate. Gifted children are usually creative, and being creative on schedule is difficult.

20. Laugh with your child; seek to develop his/her sense of humor. Most of all, enjoy your child.

Source: Adapted from *Counseling Parents of Exceptional Children* by J. C. Stewart (Columbus, OH: Charles E. Merrill, 1978).

SELECTING DOCTORS FOR CHILDREN WITH SPECIAL NEEDS

Any time parents get together, whether it's sitting in a clinic waiting room or picking up a child at school, the conversation almost inevitably gets around to doctors. Special needs children spend a lot of time with doctors—pediatricians, orthopedists, neurologists, ear specialists, pulmonary specialists, and the list goes on and on. The suggestions below will help you in choosing the best medical specialists for your child.

1. Ask around, especially people with whom you feel confident, and perhaps families with children who share a similar handicap.

2. First, check to make sure the doctor will take new patients, kids with your child's handicap, and that the caseload (the wait for an appointment is a clue) is not too heavy. Ask if you can talk with a family whose child is a patient.

3. Explain your child's special needs to the office staff or clinic, and schedule an interview with the doctor.

4. When you visit the office, check out the waiting room. A cheery (and not necessarily fancy) waiting room can say a lot. How long must you wait? And how long does it look like others have waited? Is there a play area for kids — one the kids are actually using?

5. In your interview with the doctor (leaving your child in the play area), ask why he or she chose to work with children with special needs. What is his or her experience in working with kids who have the disability that your child has. If the doctor lacks specific experience with this disability, is he or she able to refer you to a more appropriate doctor? If the doctor accepts patients similar to your child, what is his or her philosophy of treatment—medication, surgery, discussion with you and others, a policy of going slowly and trying something in moderation first? How does he or she handle emergencies?

You will come up with other questions, too. Keep in mind that you, the parent, are doing the interviewing and making the choice.

6. If you decide to take it a step further, bring in your child from the play area to meet the doctor. Observe how the doctor approaches your child and your child's reaction to the doctor, and the subsequent interaction.

7. What are the nurses and other staff people like? Chances are that you often will deal with them rather than the doctor. Ask them what hospitals the office uses so you will know if they are convenient and acceptable to you.

Obviously, many more questions and factors go into the decision of choosing a doctor. And, last but not least, don't overlook your personal rapport and comfort level with the doctor, the staff, and the office environment. These intangibles are important.

Adapted in part from *PRO Newsletter.*

TALKING WITH MEDICAL PERSONNEL

1. Identify a medical professional with expertise in your child's specific disability as your primary source.
2. Ask all medical personnel involved with the child to meet together with you at some point to discuss progress, future goals, and plans.
3. Ask medical questions you have about your child's health and care. If you don't understand the jargon, don't hesitate to ask for clarification.
4. If you want to ask sensitive questions and your child or other people are present, ask to speak to medical personnel in private.
5. If your questions require complicated answers, arrange for a special appointment rather than a simple phone call or a question during a school conference.
6. Discuss the child's strengths. Medical personnel most often discuss the problems, and sometimes the child's progress is not emphasized.
7. Discuss the next logical milestones of change to expect.
8. Search for information on the disability:

   ➤ Read anything you can find on the topic.
   ➤ Surf the web for information on the disability.
   ➤ Write or e-mail anyone who has information.
   ➤ Ask medical personnel who work with your child if they know of any relevant materials that could help you understand your child's disability.

9. Between contacts with medical personnel, make a list of questions that occur to you; sometimes they are hard to remember during a conference or discussion.
10. List any questions your child may have. This is one good way to reinforce your child's role in his/her own care.

This list has been adapted from one originally compiled by Betty Anderson, Federation for Children with Special Needs, Boston, and first published in the *SLD Gazette.*

QUESTIONS TO ASK YOUR CHILD'S DOCTORS

Before going to see your doctor or medical specialist to whom your child has been referred, be sure to write down your concerns and questions and take them with you. These questions may include the following:

> ➤ Does my child's problem have a medical cause?
> ➤ Can it be treated?
> ➤ Does my child need special equipment (such as glasses, hearing aid, a brace)?
> ➤ Does my child need medication?
> ➤ If my child is on medication, what is it, what is it for, and what are some of the side effects?
> ➤ Is there any special medical treatment that my child's teacher, therapist, or social worker needs to know about?
> ➤ Can I watch or observe any special behaviors at home that will help me understand my child better?
> ➤ Will you please send a copy of your report to my child's special program?

If your child with special needs is referred to an audiologist (a professional who tests your child's hearing ability), these are some questions you should ask after your child is tested:

> ➤ Does my child have a hearing loss?
>   - If so, please explain to me about the type of hearing loss my child has.
>   - Is the hearing loss in only one ear or both ears?
> ➤ How does the hearing loss affect my child's speech and language skills, learning abilities, and social and emotional skills?
> ➤ Does my child need a hearing aid or other devices to help his or her hearing?
> ➤ What should my child's teacher or therapists know about his or her hearing?
> ➤ What can I do to help my child?
> ➤ How can teachers and therapists help?
> ➤ Will you please give me a copy of your recommendations?
> ➤ Will you please send a copy to the program that works with my child?

WHAT PARENTS SHOULD LOOK FOR IN A PROGRAM FOR CHILDREN WITH SPECIAL NEEDS

Whatever the teaching model—an infant stimulation, preschool, or public school program for children with disabilities—parents should look for the following good practices in the child's program.

➤ A teacher or therapist who is certified to work with children with special needs should be involved in the child's testing, program planning, teaching, and parent training.

➤ Whatever the program, it requires written permission from the parent to test the child, to obtain other records about the child, to release information to other agencies about the child, or take pictures of the child.

➤ The parent and other family members should be involved in helping choose what kind of program and services the special needs child receives, and also in setting goals for the child. You should not feel inferior when you are around specialists and professionals.

➤ The parent should be given copies of individual program plans and other confidential information, such as assessments and evaluations.

➤ Specially trained professionals (such as a physical therapist, speech and language therapist, occupational therapist, audiologist, psychologist, or low-vision specialist) should work closely with the parent and the child's teacher if the child needs help from one or more specialists.

➤ A parent group should be available for support. Groups of parents of special needs children sometimes invite guest speakers to their meetings to talk about things that parents want to learn more about. These meetings also provide needed support to parents who have many things in common and can share their feelings and help each other.

➤ A lending toy and book library should be available to the family. Many parents cannot afford the special books, toys and helpful materials they and their special needs children need.

➤ If the child is going to go to a preschool, public school, or vocational program, the parent should visit the program and ask himself or herself:

- Does the classroom or workshop seem cheerful and relaxed?
- Does the staff seem interested in the children?
- Will my child fit in?
- How many children will be in my child's class, workshop, or therapy group?

➤ The program should have special materials and equipment to help the child learn.

➤ The specialists should show a genuine interest in you and your child and should be willing to work with you. You should never feel you need to apologize for asking professionals to help you in developing training programs for your child.

➤ Some time should be set aside for the child to be involved in "fun" activities (such as swimming, music, art, field trips, and playtime).

Note to parents: *There is no such thing as a perfect program.* If you would like to talk about possible changes, talk to the program staff and see how you can work together to make your child's program the best possible.

GETTING ALONG WITH YOUR CHILD'S PROGRAM STAFF

You and the professionals who are responsible for your child's program have the same goal: To make sure that your child's program meets his or her needs! Effort is required on the part of the staff and you as the parent. Here are some suggestions on how to strengthen your relationship with those who work with your special needs child:

➤ Keep your child's records in a notebook and keep it up to date.

➤ Visit your child's program as often as possible.

➤ Introduce yourself to your child's teacher, therapist, educational assistants, and any other people who work with your child.

➤ Use different ways to communicate with the teacher at your child's school:

– Phone the teacher or therapists often.

– Send notes to the teacher (in your child's school bag).

– Ask your child's teacher to start a notebook to send back and forth to school. You and the staff can write down important messages or progress daily or weekly.

➤ Meet with your child's teacher often.

➤ Be constructive. Always try to be assertive but not aggressive.

➤ Say "thanks" once in a while. Your child's teacher and other staff members will appreciate a pat on the back.

➤ Listen carefully to what the teacher and specialists have to say about your special needs child.

➤ Even if you don't agree with those who work with your child — which can be difficult at times — be polite and try to stay calm. Getting angry only makes things worse!

➤ Always seek to know what your special needs child's teacher and specialists expect your child to learn and what you can do at home to help.

WHEN YOUR CHILD CHANGES PROGRAMS

Parents of children with special needs have told us that when there is a change in their children's services or special programs, they feel particular emotions, sometimes all at once. You may experience some of these feelings when there are changes in your child's program. They may include the following:

FEAR—You may be afraid of how your child will do in the new program. You may be afraid of how the new staff will act with your child. You may want to ask, "What kind of services will be offered?", "Will they have enough special help?", "Who will be my child's teacher?", and/or "Will he/she be safe there?" You may also be afraid of how other children may act toward your child.

ANGER—You may be angry or mad for a while because your child cannot remain in the program he or she is currently in. You have probably come to know and trust those who have worked with your child and may become upset that your child cannot stay in that program.

PRIDE/HAPPINESS—You may feel proud that your child has done well and needs different services. You may feel happy that your child with special needs will be able to attend another program to learn new skills.

What can you do as a parent whose child is changing programs?

- ➤ Talk to the program staff that are helping your child presently about what your child needs and what services he or she will need in the future.
- ➤ Collect all records and recommendations that have been given to you about your child to share with your child's new program staff.
- ➤ Go visit and observe the new program. Write down your questions or concerns to ask the staff at the time of your visit.
- ➤ Request a parent/staff conference with the new program staff as soon as possible. (See parent conference tips on next page.)
- ➤ Talk to someone you trust about how you are feeling about the change in your child's program.

PREPARING FOR A PARENT–TEACHER CONFERENCE

Here are some suggestions that relate specifically to the preconference, conference, and postconference.

Preconference

1. Write down questions you want to ask (see next tip sheet).
2. Write down information you would like to share.
3. Write down suggestions you have.
4. Check the time of the meeting.

Conference

1. Be on time.
2. Find out how much time has been allowed for the meeting. It will help you pace yourself.
3. Introduce yourself to other attendees, if any.
4. Take notes during the meeting, especially items that school personnel say they will do and things you agree to do.
5. Ask the teacher to explain anything you do not understand.
6. Be sure to bring up your questions and concerns.
7. Share information that will help the teacher know your child better.
8. Cooperate on things you like, and follow up on the things you agree to do.
9. If time runs out and you still have questions, ask for another meeting.
10. Sign only the papers you clearly understand.
11. If you appreciate what your teacher is doing, tell him/her so. Teachers are just like everyone else and appreciate compliments.

Postconference

1. Check your notes. See whether you understand what you agreed to do and what the school has agreed to do.
2. If you think of more questions, feel free to request another appointment with the teacher.
3 Share the information with your partner (if applicable) and child.
4. Plan to keep in touch with the teacher.
5. If you were satisfied with the conference, write a note to the teacher. Say thank you for what they are doing, if you agree.

QUESTIONS TO CONSIDER BEFORE A PARENT–TEACHER CONFERENCE

At conferences, you are encouraged to ask questions and express concerns you may have about your child. Before attending a parent–teacher conference, think of questions you want to ask your child's teacher. Ask your child if he or she has questions for the teacher. Also try to anticipate questions the teacher may ask you. Because the time allowed for these meetings is often limited, this is a way for you to plan ahead and get the most from the meeting.

Questions You May Want to Ask

_____ 1. In which subjects does my child do well? Is my child having trouble with any subject in particular?

_____ 2. Does my child get along with the other children?

_____ 3. Does my child obey you?

_____ 4. How can I help you at home?

Questions the Teacher May Ask You

_____ 1. What does your child like best about school?

_____ 2. What does your child do after school? (What are his/her interests?)

_____ 3. Does your child have time and space set aside for homework?

_____ 4. How is your child's health?

_____ 5. Are there any problems that I should know that may affect your child's learning?

_____ 6. What type of discipline works well at home?

CONSIDERING A BABYSITTER OR RESPITE CARE PROVIDER

When you need some time away from your special needs child, you will want to find someone you can trust to watch your child and who understands any unique needs. Some people who can help you find the right person to care for your child are the following:

➣ Family members
➣ Friends
➣ Staff member of your child's special program or school
➣ Other parents of special needs children
➣ Your child's doctor

When you are satisfied that you have found the right person, explain as clearly as possible to the babysitter or caregiver everything he or she needs to know about your child's special needs or handicap while caring for him or her.

Have the babysitter take care of your child at least once while you are at home so you will be available to answer any questions. This will also make the babysitter feel more comfortable.

Fill out the form entitled "Information Form for Babysitters" (in Appendix C) in order to give your babysitter as much information about your child as possible. Put it on the refrigerator or near the telephone.

SPENDING QUALITY TIME WITH YOUR CHILDREN

1. *Plan* for quality time. It doesn't just happen.
2. Develop shared interests with your child.
3. Really listen to your child.
4. Occasionally be willing to change your daily schedule so you can attend activities involving your child.
5. Accept your child's feelings. You don't have to agree or encourage—just accept.
6. Be consistent and trustworthy by following through on what you say you will do.
7. Emphasize the positive. Try to convey the message to your child that you love him/her unconditionally.
8. Enjoy your child and yourself. Have fun together!

HELPING CHILDREN FEEL GOOD ABOUT THEMSELVES

Children's views of themselves are often influenced by the way other people who are important in their lives feel about them. We, as parents and teachers, must make sure we are doing all we can to help children feel good about themselves.

1. Treat children with respect, and expect the same from them.
2. Help children find their strengths. They know their weaknesses.
3. Encourage children in areas of both strengths and weaknesses.
4. Find ways to recognize each child as special. Try to avoid comparing one child to another.
5. Try to listen to children and understand their points of view.
6. Encourage children to express their feelings, both good and bad, without their fear of losing your love.
7. When you are displeased with something children have done, discipline them for a specific behavior, not because they are "bad."
8. Help children discover acceptable ways to behave in areas in which they are having difficulty.
9. Let children know you have confidence in them by giving them ways to be successfully independent.
10. Hug and praise children at every opportunity.

Children model many adult behaviors. They will notice if you feel good about *yourself* and your place in the world. Therefore, we need to work on building our own self-esteem as well as that of our children.

HELPING YOUR CHILD DO WELL IN SCHOOL

Building Good Study Habits

1. Provide a quiet work space.
2. Determine a set time for study. Immediately after school or after dinner are good times.
3. Keep the study time the same even if the child doesn't have homework for that day. The time can be spent reading, doing math, or working on something you assign. (Many times, students are rewarded with free time when they don't bring their work home. This builds poor study habits.)
4. Begin by setting 20 to 30 minutes of study time, depending on the child's age. If more time is needed, add it gradually.
5. If the child is having trouble getting started with homework, help with the first problem or give an example.
6. If the child wastes study time, set limits on how long he/she has to complete a task.
7. Work *before* play is still a good rule.
8. Check with your child's teacher to see what schoolwork is to be done.
9. Praise and reward the child when he / she is being successful.
10. To build good habits, provide consistency.

Parent-Child Learning Activities

1. Read *with* your child 20 to 30 minutes each day or several times a week. Often, if a parent and child trade off reading paragraphs or pages, the child won't get tired and will stay interested in the story.
2. Read *to* your child. Children can understand and enjoy material they can't read by themselves.
3. Have your child read *alone* 15 or 20 minutes each day— or more if he/she wants to. Make a graph charting minutes

of reading each day. (The child can do the charting.) Build in rewards for *x* number of minutes of reading each week. Rewards might be money, a movie, extra TV, a computer game, special times with parent, etc.

4. Take your child to the public library to check out books.
5. Make sure your child sees you reading.
6. Discuss things that are happening in the news or what the child is doing in school. This might be done during mealtimes.
7. Take your child on short trips around the city or state. This will help your child grow in knowledge and experience.
8. Play games with your child. Games can help children learn to think, and they give you a chance to spend some fun time together.
9. Be realistic about what you expect.
10. Give praise instead of punishment. Successful experiences lead to more success.

HELPING YOUR CHILD BUILD GOOD STUDY HABITS

Share these tips with your child.

Getting Ready

1. Start with *positive thinking*. *You* can do it if you want to.
2. Know what you have to get finished. Set goals for yourself.
3. Know yourself. Know when and how you work best.

WHERE?

1. Organize your work space. Somewhere quiet is best. Be sure you have good lighting and the materials you need to complete the assignment.
2. If your home is too crowded or noisy, ask your mom or dad's help to find another place.

WHEN?

Ask yourself these questions:

1. Do I work best before or after meals?
2. Do I work best in the morning, afternoon, or evening?

Set a study schedule for the time you have the most energy. This will help you finish more quickly.

HOW?

1. Avoid distractions. Turn off CD and DVD players, radios, TVs.
2. Ask friends to come back at another time. Unexpected company can keep you from getting your work done.
3. Let someone else answer the phone and take messages for you. You can return calls after you're finished.
4. Set up a study schedule. This can save you time and energy and keep you from forgetting important things or from constantly having to decide what to do next.
5. To help you get good results from your studies, fit in the four health essentials

   ➤ Schedule time every day to *exercise*.

➤ Get plenty of *rest.*
➤ Eat *balanced meals.*
➤ Have *fun.*

Digging In

1. Study your text, especially the table of contents, to get an *overview* of the subject. Before each chapter, look over the major terms, which often are printed in boldface type.
2. *Find another book* on the same subject in the school library, especially a book written for younger readers. You will recognize that this level stresses the main ideas more than in your own book. Don't bother reading every page. What you want is a general idea.
3. Be selective when *underlining.* Use your brain more than your pencil. Pick out *key words, dates, definitions,* and *names* to underline. If a section seems important to you, draw a vertical line next to it in the margin. Words such as *because, in addition, later, also, therefore, along with, in spite of* are keys to the relationships between the ideas the author is presenting.
4. Use o*utlining* when you're reviewing for a test. Group the ideas so their relationships are clear. This means identifying main categories under the general topic and organizing the specific facts under them.
5. *Take notes* in your own words. Write down the important ideas, not just facts. *One notetaking technique:* Divide notebook paper into three vertical columns. Use the large middle section for classroom notes, the left column for key ideas, and the far right column for textbook notes or a brief summary of the page you're studying.
6. Keep a small assignment notebook to r*emember assignments.* Assign a page for each day that work is due.
7. *Break assignments into smaller tasks* with one due each day, week, or month. Don't try to do a large assignment all at once.

(continued)

8. Use the computer to study if you wish, taking notes, making outlines, and reviewing the material.

The Big Test and How to Take It

If you can, think of the test as a learning experience and a chance to show how much you know about a subject.

1. Think positively.
2. Begin early. Study and review regularly.
3. Study by self-testing. Write down the questions you would ask if you were the teacher. Try to answer the questions after you close your book. Try different ways of answering, such as aloud, making a list, writing a paragraph, or outlining. Check yourself. This shortens study time and builds confidence.
4. Get plenty of sleep the night before.
5. Eat breakfast.

Taking the Essay Test

1. Read the test all the way through before beginning.
2. Notice instruction words such as *trace, list, compare,* and *discuss.* Be sure to do exactly what the directions tell you.
3. Choose one question with which to begin. It should be the one you find the easiest to answer. This will help you start remembering facts and give you confidence.
4. Begin with an introductory statement and end with a concluding statement.
5. Plan enough time to proofread your answers.

Taking Short-Answer Tests

1. Read each question carefully.
2. Move along at a steady pace.
3. Skip over any questions you're not sure of, and come back to them later. Mark them in some way so you won't forget.
4. Plan enough time to proofread your answers.

"STREET-PROOFING" YOUR CHILD

1. Teach your child who a *stranger* is. Children might think a "stranger" means someone who acts strange.
2. Teach your child not to take rides, candy, money, or bribes from a stranger. Often children are bribed into being helpful or accepting help. A lost dog, kitten, or toy may be a way to interest the child.
3. Teach your child never to accept an alternative way home. Children need to know that any change in plans will be relayed to them only through school personnel.
4. Teach your child that he/she has a private space that everyone must respect.
5. Teach your child that any area covered by a bathing suit or underwear should not be touched by strangers.
6 Don't allow children to break the rules in your presence. Don't allow strangers to give them candy or ruffle their hair, even when you are with them.
7. Provide "safe places" for your children on their way home. Show them places they can go if they need help, such as a neighbor's home or a certain store.
8. Teach your child things to do if they are approached by a stranger, such as ignoring, walking away, using the "safe places" in the neighborhood, or, if approached by someone in a car, heading the opposite direction.
9. Encourage your child to tell you if he/she has encountered a situation that makes him/her uncomfortable.
10. Practice and repeat these tips so that your child will form good safety habits. Role-play possible situations.

Adapted by Roger Kroth from remarks by Dr. Marion Sheldon.

DISCIPLINING YOUR CHILD

1. Even when you are unhappy with your child's behavior, be sure he/she understands that you love him/her but not the behavior.
2. Know how you want your child to behave, and tell him/her what you expect.
3. Make the rules clear and simple. Tell your child ahead of time what the rules are.
4. Know what can be expected of children at certain ages. Try not to give your child more responsibility than he/she can handle.
5. Set an example for your child. Children learn from watching others, especially their parents.
6. Catch your child being good and make sure he/she knows you've noticed. Examples: Smile a lot, give hugs, praise the child for being good.
7. Be consistent when you discipline your child so the expectations are clear.
8. Try to change only one behavior at a time. You can't change everything at once.
9. Expect children to behave, and most times they will.

SELECTING AND PLAYING GAMES

Children need to be actively involved in the learning situation if they are to benefit from it. Games—whether purchased commercially or made at home—are good tools for getting the child involved. When choosing and playing games with children, parents (and teachers) should do the following:

➤ Select games that provide practice the children need and that are of interest to them. Remember—each child is an individual with unique needs.

➤ Play simple games with young children. Primary children or slow learners at higher levels may find that games that use concrete materials (beanbags, balls, cards, etc.) are easier to learn to play than games requiring only mental processes.

➤ Teach game playing as you would teach other activities. Demonstrate as necessary. To include language practice, have children occasionally give the directions for games orally.

➤ Protect children's feelings in games as in other activities. Children who are timid should not be forced to play a game against their will; perhaps giving them a game to play individually will help them feel accepted until they gain enough security to take part willingly in a group game.

➤ Help children understand that they must play games according to the rules. If boys and girls do have suggestions for improving the directions, do not implement the changes during a game; start over again or save the change for the next time. Emphasize that people can have permanent satisfaction as well as immediate enjoyment only if they play honestly and fairly.

➤ Discuss and agree upon who is to take responsibility for putting away game materials in good order.

➤ Accept only good work in games as in other activities. Let the children know this before they begin a game.

SETTING GOALS FOR YOUR CHILD

Setting goals is one of the most important components in planning your child's educational and therapeutic program. Think seriously about what things are important for your child to learn and how these goals will affect your family. Then discuss these with the professional staff who will be working with your child.

A goal should have the following characteristics:

➤ *Be important to you, the parent, and to the child's progress.* Because the goal is important to the entire family, talk to all family members before setting goals.

➤ *Be realistic.* In developing the goals for your child, balance your hopes for your child with the reality of the child's existing strengths and weaknesses.

➤ *Be set with knowledge* of the services available to accomplish the goal.

➤ *Be specific.* Try to develop goals that you can observe (see) and measure (count).

➤ *Include suggestions for how to reward your child for making progress toward the goal.* As the parent, you know your child better than anyone else, and what will be most rewarding.

➤ *Be flexible.* As the child accomplishes the goals, come up with new goals to continue the progress your child is making. Be prepared to change the goal if it is too difficult for your child to accomplish.

➤ *Be able to be broken down into steps.* The child should be able to work on the goal one step at a time.

Praising Your Child: 99 Ways to Say "Very Good"

1. You've got it made.
2. That's right.
3. You're on the right track now!
4. That's good!
5. You're very good at that.
6. That's coming along very nicely.
7. That's *much* better!
8. Good work!
9. You're doing a good job.
10. You've just about got it.
11. That's it!
12. Congratulations!
13. I knew you could do it.
14. That's quite an improvement.
15. Now you've figured it out.
16. Now you have it.
17. Not bad at all.
18. Great!
19. You're learning fast.
20. Good for you!
21. You make it look easy.
22. You really make my job fun.
23. That's the right way to do it.
24. You're getting better every day.
25. You did it that time!
26. That's not half bad!
27. Wow!
28. That's the way!
29. Nice going.
30. Now you've figured it out.
31. Sensational!
32. You haven't missed a thing.
33. That's the way to do it.

(continued)

34. Keep up the good work.
35. That's better.
36. Nothing can stop you now!
37. There's first-class work.
38. Excellent!
39. Perfect!
40. That's the best ever.
41. You're really going to town.
42. Fine!
43. Terrific!
44. That's better than ever.
45. You did very well on that.
46. Outstanding!
47. You did very well.
48. You're really improving.
49. Right on!
50. Good remembering!
51. I'm happy you're working like that.
52. You've about mastered that.
53. You're working hard today.
54. I'm proud of the way you worked.
55. That's the best you've ever done.
56. You're doing a lot better.
57. Keep working—you're good.
58. I couldn't have done it better.
59. That's a fine job.
60. You've been practicing!
61. You're doing beautifully.
62. Superb!
63. Keep it up!
64. You did a lot of work.
65. You've got that down pat!
66. You did well today.
67. Tremendous!
68. You're doing fine.
69. Good thinking!
70. You're learning a lot.

71. Keep trying!
72. You outdid yourself!
73. I've never seen it done better.
74. Good for you!
75. Good going!
76. I like that.
77. One more time and you'll have it.
78. I'm very proud of you.
79. That a way!
80. I think you've got it.
81. Good job!
82. You figured that out fast.
83. You remembered.
84. That's really nice.
85. It's a pleasure to be with you.
86. You're right.
87. Clever!
88. That makes me feel good.
89. That's really great!
90. Way to go.
91. Well, look at you go!
92. Now you've got it!
93. Top notch work!
94. Your brain is in gear today!
95. Much better!
96. Wonderful!
97. Super!
98. Marvelous!
99. Awesome!

LEARNING THE TRAITS OF
TYPICAL ADOLESCENT BEHAVIOR

➤ Strengthening self-identity
➤ Concern with physical changes
➤ Confusion about independence versus dependence
➤ Mood swings, quick changes in feelings
➤ Not confiding, talking over problems, or discussing feelings or ideas
➤ Impulsive behavior
➤ A need not to be with the family
➤ Anxiety about growing up
➤ Influence of, and devotion to, peer group
➤ Conflict with parents

DEALING WITH YOUR FEELINGS
ABOUT YOUR CHILD WITH SPECIAL NEEDS

Many parents have written or talked about the feelings they have after learning that their child has a disability or special needs. The shock may set in at birth or upon diagnosis during childhood. These feelings are normal and should not cause you to feel guilty. Feelings that parents of a child with special needs have include the following:

Denial

➤ You may understand what someone has told you about your child but cannot accept it as truth.

➤ You may say, "I just don't believe my child is handicapped," or ask, "What did I do to make this happen to my child?"

Guilt

➤ You might say, "It's my fault this happened."

Anger

➤ When doctors, nurses, family members, school staff, or friends do not understand your feelings, you may feel angry and frustrated and lash out.

➤ You may ask, "Why did this happen to me?"

Resentment

➤ You may feel burdened by the added responsibilities that come with a child with special needs.

➤ Seeing parents with a child who is nondisabled may be upsetting to you.

(continued)

Fear

➤ You may be afraid about what will happen to your child and how the disability will affect his or her life.

➤ You may worry abut how you are going to deal with the responsibilities of having a child with special needs.

➤ You may feel alone and that no one understands your situation.

➤ You may be afraid to leave your child with someone else, even if only for a few hours.

Grief

➤ You may feel a great sadness about having a child with disabilities.

➤ You cry or feel like crying often.

➤ You may say, "This is not the child I expected or wanted."

➤ You may feel tired and worn out. Every day may seem like a lifetime.

Acceptance

➤ All children, with or without disabilities, give pleasure as well as pain to their parents.

➤ Accepting and coping with a child's disability is an ongoing process.

When you have come to accept your child's disability, you may experience feelings of

hope

joy in small successes

pride

satisfaction

CONSIDERING YOUR OTHER CHILDREN

If you have other children in your family, keep the following in mind:

- ➤ Try to explain your child's disability to your other children in language they can understand. Keep it simple. Answer their questions honestly.
- ➤ If your child with special needs is in a special program or receives special help, take your other children to visit the program. The more your children understand and learn about their sister or brother, the easier it will be for them to accept him or her. If a teacher or therapist comes to your home to talk about your special needs child, include your other children, too.
- ➤ You may find that your other children are having many of the same feelings about their brother or sister that you are having. These feelings could include guilt, anger, embarrassment, resentment, and sadness. Try to talk with them often about how they are feeling. And listen.
- ➤ If possible, introduce your children to other children who have a brother or sister with a disability. They may find that these children relate to their feelings.
- ➤ Try to do something special with your other children as often as you can. Your child with special needs will take up much of your time and energy, but remember that your other children need your attention, too.
- ➤ Your other children may be willing to help you in many ways with your special needs child. Try not to give them too much responsibility in caring for their brother or sister, but involve them to whatever extent you think will help them feel needed.
- ➤ Whenever your child with disabilities makes you happy or proud, share your feelings with your other children. They need to feel the joy and happiness that is possible in having a special needs child in their family.

HOW TO SURVIVE

1. Be realistic about what your child can do.
2. Make the rules in your home and stick to them.
3. Model the kind of behavior you would like to see in your children. Examples speak louder than words.
4. Discipline your children clearly.

   ➤ Be brief and to the point without lecturing, nagging, or using put-downs.
   ➤ Don't give children too much room for discussion. When you're in charge and in the right, why argue?
   ➤ Compromise when necessary.

5. Deal with problems as they arise; don't postpone dealing with them.
6. Use "Grandma's Rule": The child works before play.
7. Present a consistent, united front with your spouse or mate.
8. Establish a daily study hall/quiet time Sunday through Thursday.
9. Assign chores with an allowance that depends upon their completion.
10. Be aware of your children's social activities; know their friends, where they're going, time they will return, and the friends' phone numbers.
11. Establish and maintain physical and emotional closeness with your child.
12. Keep in touch with your child's teacher and school.
13. Work together and play together.

Adapted by Roger Kroth from comments by Dr. Tom Carey.

HOW TO MAKE IT EASIER ON YOURSELF

➤ Remember—a child with special needs is a child *first* and a child with special needs *second*.

➤ Recognize and understand your own feelings about children with special needs or disabilities.

➤ Recognize and understand that society often reacts with rejection, pity, embarrassment, and guilt at seeing and interacting with special needs children. *How the parent handles these reactions is what is important!*

➤ Seek out other parents who have special needs children with whom to exchange thoughts and feelings about children with special needs.

➤ Find a parent support group or a group of parents of children with disabilities who meet in your community. You will be surprised what you can learn and share with others who understand your concerns.

➤ Don't neglect other children in the family, who may have feelings of guilt, embarrassment, or anger at the special needs child. Try to change the climate to one that reflects your own love and caring for all children in the family.

➤ Keep in mind that parents are the key people in the care and growth of the special needs child.

➤ Institute a routine to alleviate the extra work or responsibilities surrounding the special needs child.

➤ Loving your special needs child is not enough! Learn all you can about the child's disabling condition. Talk with the professionals who work with your child. Read books and or articles related to your child's special needs.

➤ Keep the communication line open with professionals who work with your child. Don't wait for a problem or crisis!

➤ Become familiar with the special language or "lingo" that professionals use when talking about your special needs child.

(continued)

➤ Keep a notebook containing all records and program notes given to you about your child. Those who work with your child may request this information.

➤ Learn from your child's teachers or therapists what activities and therapeutic toys you may use at home to improve this child's skills.

➤ Find special resources and special services available in your community.

➤ Find time for yourself! It is important for parents to have time away from their child with special needs.

HOW TO BE GOOD TO YOURSELF

➤ Make time regularly to do something you want to do. Try to take time away from your duties as a parent (such as exercising, going to lunch or dinner with a family member or friend, reading, or going on a weekend trip).

➤ Talk to someone you trust about your feelings about your handicapped child.

➤ Find a good babysitter who will take care of your child when you need help.

➤ Accept your good and bad feelings about your handicapped child. Keep in mind that most parents who have a child with special needs have had some feelings just like yours.

➤ Find and get to know other parents who have children with a disability. You will appreciate the support of others who share your problems.

➤ Read books or other materials about your child's disability.

➤ If you don't understand something a professional has told you about your child, ask questions until you understand.

HOW TO COPE WITH STRESS

1. Concentrate on breathing with a steady rhythm.
2. Love thy neighbor.
3. Seek variety.
4. Change "can't" to "won't."
5. Take responsibility for yourself.
6. Make no big moves.
7. Don't be hassled by small stuff.
8. Find your own stress level.
9. Know that health beats stress.
10. Maintain an optimistic bias—accentuate the positive.
11. Exercise regularly.
12. Eat regularly.

LEARNING A NEW VOCABULARY

As a parent of a special needs child, you will run across some unfamiliar terms. Doctors, psychologists, teachers, therapists, and other professionals who work with your child have their own terminology. Below are some of the words you will need to understand.

Achievement test — A test designed to measure a child's knowledge, skills, and understanding in a specific subject area. Achievement tests may measure your child's reading, math, and spelling levels compared to other children in the same grade or age.

Adaptive behavior — The ability to function in nonacademic skill areas, such as social living and self-help.

Age/grade equivalent — The scores from tests given to your child, defined in years and months that are equal to the average score for children of that age group.

Ancillary services — Special programs that your child could receive if he or she needs special help or support in the learning program; may include speech and language therapy, occupational therapy, physical therapy, audiological services, psychological services, interpreter services, and orientation and mobility training, among others.

Assessments — Tests to determine your child's special needs; may include mental, social, emotional, educational, physical, hearing, or speech / language tests.

Audiological services — Services that include, among others, evaluation of a child's hearing ability in which an audiologist may recommend hearing aid equipment and / or other aids for a child, and possibly, counseling for parents and teachers who work with children who have a hearing problem.

Baseline — A record of observations of the child's specified behavior before initiating treatment or services.

(continued)

Battery of tests — A group of tests given to a child to find out his or her strengths and weaknesses; may be administered by professionals such as an educational diagnostician, speech/language pathologist, occupational therapist, physical therapist, and/or psychologist.

Behavior disorder — A disability in which a child's behavior may interfere with his or her getting along with others, and the behavior is so severe that it causes the child to have trouble learning at the level expected for his or her classmates.

Case history — Combined information gathered by people who work with your child that will help them understand the child's background, personal history, physical development, medical history, and educational history.

Central nervous system — The brain and the spinal cord.

Cognitive — A term referring to mental abilities, such as memory, ability to solve problems, understanding, and ability to make judgments.

Communication disorder — A disability in which a child has trouble understanding or using speech and/or language.

Criteria — A measure against which to see whether the child's goal is met. For example, a teacher may set the criteria for stacking blocks as: "Stacks four or five blocks."

Cumulative record — All of the child's educational and related records, beginning with entry into school; includes information about evaluations, health, progress notes, and special programs in which the child has been involved.

Curriculum — The plan for what the school is going to teach the child, using special techniques and activities and materials to help the child learn and live to the best of his/her ability.

Developmental disability — A disability that is manifested before adulthood, such as mental retardation, epilepsy, cerebral palsy, autism, physical disabilities, and emotional disorders, that results in the impairment of general intellectual functioning.

Differential diagnosis — The conclusion reached as a result of tests given by a professional (diagnostician, psychologist, speech/language pathologist, etc.) to try to learn the child's abilities in various learning areas rather than only one problem area.

Due process — A legal guarantee of certain rights and privileges that neither the government nor anyone else can take away.

Educational diagnostician — A professional who is qualified to give tests to find out the child's pre-academic, academic, and mental level, to be used in placing the child in a program designed to meet his or her specific needs.

Expressive language — Spoken, written, or sign language a person uses to communicate with others.

Eye–hand coordination — Ability to use the eyes and hands together; eye-hand coordination is needed to eat with a spoon, pick up objects, copy designs with a pencil, cut with scissors on a line, and paint with a brush, for example.

Fine motor — Refers to skills that require small-muscle coordination, such as cutting with scissors, painting, handwriting, drawing, playing with puzzles and blocks, and so on.

General education — The school program offered to students without disabilities; children with special needs are included in these programs to the extent possible.

Gross motor — Refers to skills that use large muscles, including rolling, crawling, walking, running, throwing, jumping, and similar activities.

Hearing loss — A disability in which a child has hearing problems that delay or stop the development of speech, language, or pre-academic or academic skills.

Implementation — The stated *who, how, what, when,* and *where* of providing special services.

(continued)

Inclusion — A program provided for children with disabilities that allows them to be with typical children as much as possible; the included children receive as many support services as necessary while being included in as many general education activities as possible.

Individualized Education Program (IEP) — A written plan of instruction for each child receiving special services, as required by law. An IEP gives a statement of the child's present levels of educational performance, annual goals, short-term objectives, specific services needed by the child, dates when these services will begin and be in effect, and related information. The program is undertaken by a team that includes the child's parents.

Individualized Family Service Plan (IFSP) — An expanded IEP that is written for preschool children with disabilities and their families. The plan outlines the family's strengths and needs related to enhancing the child's development.

Individuals with Disabilities Education Act (IDEA) — PL 94-142, Education for All Handicapped Children Act, was renamed IDEA in 1990. IDEA carried forth all the provisions of PL 94-142 and included additional elements. Simply put, it guarantees a free and appropriate public education for all students, regardless of disability, in the public school system and allocates funds to states to help with services. There have been two reauthorizations of IDEA since 1990, one in 1997 and one in 2004.

Infant stimulation program — Special activities offered to children under 2 years of age, usually provided in the home and can include training in feeding, social skills development, self-help skills, and motor development.

Interpreter services — Special help for children who are deaf or hard of hearing; for example, if a child uses sign language to communicate with others, a person who hears and can use sign language may be assigned to the hard-of-hearing or deaf child to help communicate with teachers or students who do not understand or use sign language in the school.

IQ — Intelligence quotient, a score on a test that attempts to measure mental development level from the ability to solve a group of verbal and nonverbal problems; an "average" IQ score is considered to be between 80 and 119.

Learning disability — A condition in which a child with average or above-average intelligence has significant problems in one or more of the areas of reading, writing, spelling, or math.

Least restrictive environment — A legal requirement stating that individual special needs children should receive services in the best possible setting for them, and if they can function with less help, they should have the chance to do so, which may be in the general education classroom.

Long-range goals — A group of goals set by a child's parents and the professionals who work with the child; usually set and reviewed at least once a year and could include the areas of academic, social, physical, language, and behavior development.

Mental age (MA) — The level of a child's mental ability compared to children of the same chronological age; for example, a child who has an MA equal to the average 10-year-old would have an MA of 10 years no matter what his/her real chronological age.

Mild to moderate disabilities — Includes learning disabilities, emotional/behavioral disorders, speech and language impairments, and physical and health disabilities. Mild to moderate disabilities are identified as high incidence.

Moderate to severe disabilities — Specific disabilities related to a student's ability level and need for specialized services. This group includes cognitive and developmental disabilities, autism spectrum disorders, hearing loss, and visual impairments and is considered low incidence.

Multidisciplinary team — More than two professionals working together to evaluate and help a special needs child; the team could consist of, for example, a medical doctor, special education teacher, speech/language pathologist, physical therapist, and psychologist.

(continued)

Neonatologist — A medical doctor specializing in newborn infants, especially those who are premature (born early) or must stay in the hospital after birth.

Occupational therapy — A service provided by an occupational therapist that promotes the child's motor development and identifies equipment to help a child in everyday activities and self-help skills, such as special feeding equipment.

Ophthalmologist — A medical doctor who evaluates and treats diseases of the eye.

Orientation and mobility training — A service that helps blind children move and live in their surroundings.

Orthopedist — A medical doctor who works with problems of the bones; if working specifically with children, this specialist is called a pediatric orthopedist.

Physical disability — A condition that involves problems of the bones, joints, or muscles, or long-term illnesses that affect a child's ability to perform in school or prevent school attendance.

Physical therapy — A service that includes evaluation of motor skills (fine and gross) and therapy to help the child develop normal motor patterns, sometimes involving special equipment.

Psychological services — Evaluation of the child's social and emotional behaviors and any needed therapy to the child, his/her family, and support to the professional staff that works with the child.

Public Law 94-142 — The Education for All Handicapped Children Act, passed by the U.S. Congress in 1975, guaranteeing a free and appropriate education to all children with disabilities in the public school system and providing monies to states to help provide these services.

Public Law 99-457 — A 1986 amendment to the Education for all Handicapped Children Act, providing help and services for special needs children and their families from birth to 5 years of age.

Receptive language — The form of language that refers to how a child receives and understands information from others.

Reinforcement — The praise or other forms of rewards (stickers, food, toys, free playtime) given to children after they do something you want them to do more often.

Respite care — Services provided for special needs children and their parents, in which the child may spend a limited amount of time in someone else's care to allow rest or time away for parents or family.

Self-help skills — Skills that a child uses in daily living, such as eating, dressing, and toileting.

Short-range goals — Steps used to achieve the child's long-range goals; usually described in words that are easy to observe and measure.

Special education — Services additional to, or different from, those provided in a program for children without disabilities; includes special materials, techniques, and equipment for children with special needs.

Visual impairment — A condition in which the child, after the best possible correction of the visual problem (glasses, surgery) is not able to perform well in a general education program without special help; partially seeing children have a visual acuity of 20/60 or less in their better eye, after the best possible correction, and can still read print; blindness is defined as central vision of 20/200 or worse in the best eye, with the best possible correction, or field (side) vision of no more than 20 degrees.

Exercises

The exercises in this appendix are intended for you to practice with and use. The first nine activities are perception and values exercises. The tenth activity is a personal stress test. The last activity deals with case histories for role playing, and there are four components within that last exercise.

ACTIVITY 1: WHO AM I?

Dr. Manford Kuhn, sociology instructor at the University of Iowa, developed a free response instrument called "Who Am I?" One of the activities consisted of having the students take out a sheet of paper, head it "Who Am I?" and write down 20 statements about themselves. Dr. Kuhn related the responses to various personality types. At one time he was interested in the proportion of "consensual" statements to "subconsensual" statements. Consensual statements were those with clear boundaries that could be substantiated fairly easily by others, such as "I am a man"; subconsensual statements were much more subjective. The analysis that Dr. Kuhn proposed may have value for the researcher, and the activity itself can be meaningful to any individual.

Modified Procedure

Take out a sheet of paper, write down the date, and head it "Who Am I?" Now list as many answers as you believe the question poses. For analysis purposes, you may want to reflect on the following questions:

1. Was this task difficult to do?
2. Are you relatively satisfied with the things you listed?
3. Which items would you like to change? (Place a checkmark by these.)
4. Would you like to add things to your list? (Jot these down.)
5. How many items relate to: job? family? social life? personal accomplishments?
6. From your list, can you tell anything about what you value?
7. If you were to give your list to a friend, would he or she recognize you and agree with your list?

Take your list and the analysis you made of it and put it away for a year. After a year has passed, do the activity again and compare the old list with the new one to see if you have changed. Reflect on why you have or haven't changed.

ACTIVITY 2: THE BALANCE SCALE

Justice often is depicted as a blindfolded woman holding an old-fashioned balance scale. In life, you probably like to do a number of things and do not like to do a number of things. Although you hope the scales of justice are tipped in favor of the "likes," you may want to check this out.

Simon, Howe, and Kirschenbaum (1972) developed a strategy called "Twenty Things You Love to Do." The individual is asked to list things he/she really likes to do, and then code them as to when they were done last, whether they cost money, are done alone or with other persons, etc. The main question that should be posed, of course, is "Are you actually doing the things you really enjoy doing in your life?"

In 1892, William James said:

> Be systematically ascetic or heroic in little unnecessary points, do every day or two something for no other reason than you would rather not do it, so that when the hour of dire need draws nigh, it may find you not unnerved and untrained to stand the test. (p. 149)

You undoubtedly engage in a number of behaviors daily that you do not enjoy. You do them but probably not for the heroic reasons James suggested.

Procedure

Draw a line down the middle of a sheet of paper, separating it into two parts. If you feel artistically inclined, you may want to draw a balance scale at the top, or cut out the zodiac sign for Libra and glue it at the top of the paper. On one side of the paper, write the heading "Things I like to do." On the other side, write "Things I don't like to do that I am currently doing." Now start listing activities in each of the columns. When you have finished, consider the following questions:

1. Which column was the easiest to do?
2. Is your "like" column equal to or longer than your "don't like" column?

3. Are you doing, or have you done recently, those things you like to do?
4. Put a W for "work" beside items in each column that are associated with your job. Then look to see whether your job has more things you like than you dislike.
5. Write a K beside items that involve some interaction with kids. Were there any? Should you be working with children?
6. How many of the "don't like" behaviors could you eliminate and still keep your job?
7. Put a P beside items that involve physical activity or are health-oriented. Are you keeping physically fit? Carkhuff and Berenson (1976, p. 22) indicated that the "helper must have a high level of physical energy if he or she is to discharge the demanding responsibilities of helping."
8. What "don't like" behaviors are you doing that are good for you (e.g., jogging or practicing a new skill that is difficult)?

You might do the balance scale activity from time to time to see if you are changing or maintaining any behaviors. In analyzing the lists, you may want to change some behavior. A program can be developed to deal specifically with certain items on the list. For instance, you may have listed playing tennis as a "like to do" activity but realize that you have not played for months or years. Working out a schedule with a friend to play tennis regularly could help reestablish the behavior.

In some respects, having to program pleasurable activities seems like a shame; yet, organization, planning, and structuring often allow more free time rather than less. Many writers set aside a fixed time to write, and musicians a time to practice. Some people plan to ride horses, bicycles, or motorcycles every day. Others read for a while before they go to sleep. You should be able to learn new ways of behaving based on an analysis of your lifestyle and your knowledge of how to organize and plan for behavioral change.

ACTIVITY 3: ARE YOU A TEACHER WHO . . .

A number of years ago, Joel Goodman and Patty Bourexis devised an activity in which teachers were to check items that pertained to them in their interaction with children. This instrument could be used for self-analysis, or to check a person's self-concept against another's perception of his or her behavior. Similar exercises are provided in *Discovering Your Teaching Self* by Curwin and Fuhrmann (1975).

Procedure

The accompanying chart is an adaptation of the instrument developed by Goodman and Bourexis. The format is the same, but the items have been changed to help you reflect more on your relationships with your parents. In Column A place a checkmark beside the items that pertain to you. Then, if you want to check on how others see you, cover Column A or fold it under, give the chart to someone who knows you well (another teacher or supervisor), and have that person mark in Column B. This form of evaluation is not as accurate as actually taking behavioral data on yourself, but if you are aware of your values, others usually are aware of them, too. Column C can be used by a third person, or you can use it later to see whether you have changed in any way.

You could employ a number of variations to the marking system suggested. For instance, in marking Column A, you might use a U for "usually," S for "seldom," and N for "never." The chart could be used by staff members in a school, responding individually. The aggregate results could be used for an in-service session on parent–teacher interactions. Teachers often like to discuss the relative merit of some of the items and say they sometimes cannot do things they personally value. One teacher commented, "I really think it's important to visit in parents' homes, but we have a school board policy against it." Another said, "I don't think teachers should try to conduct parent group meetings with parents of children in their own classes. They can't open up because we [control] their children's consequences."

Are You a Teacher Who . . .

A	B	C	
____	____	____	1. Never admits to a parent that you're wrong?
____	____	____	2. Has a sense of humor in a conference?
____	____	____	3. Lets parents smoke in a conference?
____	____	____	4. Offers coffee to parents during a conference?

_____ _____ _____ 5. Doesn't have any favorites?

_____ _____ _____ 6. Shows expression and emotions during a conference?

_____ _____ _____ 7. Shows expression and emotions in parent groups?

_____ _____ _____ 8. Starts conferences and parent meetings on time?

_____ _____ _____ 9. Stops parent meetings at a scheduled time?

_____ _____ _____ 10. Has contacts with parents?

_____ _____ _____ 11. Has conferences in parents' homes?

_____ _____ _____ 12. Compares students with their older siblings?

_____ _____ _____ 13. Has trouble saying "I don't know" to parents?

_____ _____ _____ 14. Talks less than 50% during each conference?

_____ _____ _____ 15. Talks about your own problems and solutions in parent–teacher conferences?

_____ _____ _____ 16. Sits behind a desk during conferences?

_____ _____ _____ 17. Enjoys parent conferences?

_____ _____ _____ 18. Shows parents examples of children's work?

_____ _____ _____ 19. Calls parents when things go well with their child?

_____ _____ _____ 20. Sends notes home when children have behavioral problems?

_____ _____ _____ 21. Uses grades to keep students in line?

_____ _____ _____ 22. Has ever had a principal sit in on one of your conferences?

_____ _____ _____ 23. Finds yourself criticizing more than praising parents?

_____ _____ _____ 24. Has ever had dinner at a student's home?

_____ _____ _____ 25. Has ever had a parent over for dinner or a meeting at your home?

_____ _____ _____ 26. Thinks parents have lost the respect of their children?

_____ _____ _____ 27. Thinks parents have lost control of their children?

_____ _____ _____ 28. Feels physically drained at the end of a series of conferences?

_____ _____ _____ 29. Has parent group meetings?

_____ _____ _____ 30. Has strong negative feelings about certain racial or sexual groups?

_____ _____ _____ 31. Prefers to have conferences with fathers rather than mothers?

_____ _____ _____ 32. Studies a child's folder and past achievements prior to a conference?

_____ _____ _____ 33. Argues with parents?

_____ _____ _____ 34. Feels intimidated by parents?

_____ _____ _____ 35. Demonstrates to parents effective ways to work with their child?

_____ _____ _____ 36. Likes to problem-solve with parents?

_____ _____ _____ 37. Involves parents in planning for their child?

_____ _____ _____ 38. Encourages parents to visit during class sessions?

_____ _____ _____ 39. Uses parents as aides in the classroom?

_____ _____ _____ 40. Does not want parents to teach their own children?

_____ _____ _____ 41. Is honest with parents?

_____ _____ _____ 42. Listens to parents?

_____ _____ _____ 43. Dreads conference time?

_____ _____ _____ 44. Invites parents to phone your home in the evening?

_____ _____ _____ 45. Is positively reinforcing?

_____ _____ _____ 46. Sends home daily or weekly report cards?

_____ _____ _____ 47. Prepares handbooks or handouts for parents?

_____ _____ _____ 48. Has a good attendance record at conferences and group meetings?

_____ _____ _____ 49. Has students sit in on conferences with their parents?

_____ _____ _____ 50. Talks about other teachers to parents?

You may want to ask yourself some of the following questions:

➤ Am I really doing what I think I should be doing in my work with parents?

➤ Does any research or objective data support or reflect the choices I have made?

➤ Would the parents of the children I work with see me the same way I see myself?

➤ Could I teach another teacher how to explore his/her attitudes and values in regard to working with parents?

Activities such as "Are You a Teacher Who..." are easy to carry out and can be done independently. The list in the chart is not exhaustive, and you may want to add or substitute other items. Or you may want to develop your own list of behaviors that relate to consultant and teacher relationships. For many of the items, you could take behavioral data on yourself to test the validity of your responses or to modify your behavior if change is desirable.

You may want to share this activity with another teacher. Anyone concerned with teaching should find the chart itself to be a source of discussion. Feedback from a colleague about the usefulness of this technique should be valuable to you as a teacher.

ACTIVITY 4: THERE OUGHT TO BE A LAW

You frequently hear someone say, "There ought to be a law against..." In a society that uses the law to guarantee rights rather than relying on dictatorial fiats, value systems are reflected in the laws that are enacted. Citizens write and call their representatives, form lobby groups to promote values they feel strongly about, and try to get them transformed into action. The rights of minority groups are ensured; the will of the people speaks. People are working all the time to get thousands of laws enacted at national, state, and local levels.

Some laws reflect a moral philosophy that crosses national and cultural lines. The commandment "Thou shalt not kill," for instance, is fairly well respected in many nations, but it is seldom regarded as absolute. We in the United States consider killing permissible during times of war, in the line of duty, for self-protection, and so on. Some say that education should be mandatory; others say it should be optional. Some believe certain books and movies should be censored or banned; others defend freedom of the speech and the press. Some are for capital punishment; others are against it. The disagreement in values continues with support from both sides.

Chances are that the laws you would like to see enacted reflect some of your strongest values. Suppose you could write at least four laws. What would they be?

Procedure

Take out a sheet of paper. Write "Be It Hereby Resolved," and then write a law you would like to see enacted. It can be a new law or one that is already on the books. Try to write at least four laws, but feel free to come up with more. After you have completed the task, analyze your work by answering the following questions:

➤ Would you allow any loopholes in your laws? For instance, if you wrote, "All children between the ages of 3 and 21 shall be provided a free public school education," does this mean that a child who tries to stab a teacher should still be provided an education? Does it extend to the provision of textbooks? yearbooks?

➤ Do your laws group themselves into certain areas of concern, such as health, education, or economics?

➤ Do you think you could drum up much support for your laws from your friends? Can you identify any existing laws in agreement with your proposed laws?

➤ Do you know of any laws that you think should be abolished?

This activity is a good one for starting group discussions. You will find yourself defending or decrying a position such as legalized gambling, decriminalizing marijuana, or compulsory education. You will begin to ask yourself how you formed the values you hold.

Helping Others Assess Their Values

In addition to clarifying your own values, you should be prepared to help others with this clarify their own values. You might share the previous activities with co-workers, or use them in in-service sessions. But no one should be put in the uncomfortable position of having to do this before he/she is ready, or intimidated by a few people who are domineering.

A number of enjoyable activities support the idea that members of more or less homogeneous groups have different values. Two of these activities, "Values Voting" and "Alligator River," are in *Values Clarification* (Simon et al., 1972).

In "Values Voting" the leader reads a series of statements preceded by the words "How many of you..." If the participants agree with the statement, they raise their hands; if they disagree, they put their arms by their sides; and if they have no opinion or do not want to commit themselves, they fold their arms across their chest. If the activity is carried out quickly, with a little humor and without discussing any of the items, it can demonstrate the diversity of opinion in even a homogeneous group.

"Alligator River" is a story involving five characters, all of whom have some undesirable behaviors. The leader tells the story and then has the large group break into several small groups to arrive at a group consensus on how the characters should be ranked according to their desirability. After 10 minutes or so, the groups report back to the group as a whole and discuss how they arrived at the consensus.

These exercises reveal that the teachers and parents with whom you work come to conferences and meetings with a wide range of values. To work effectively, you must be aware of this phenomenon. Individuals may become resistant if others ignore, refute, or put down their values.

The following activities are designed to be used by parents, family members, and others with whom you are working for the benefit of the child. Some of them can be used as individual exercises, and others may be used to compare the values held between husband and wife or parent and teacher. In most cases they have been adapted from existing activities with some modification.

ACTIVITY 5: ARE YOU A PARENT WHO. . .

This activity utilizes the same format as Activity 3. The items, however, deal often with the parent–teacher relationship from the parent's point of view. In some cases, the other people involved in the activity may have to get inside the parent's head in responding to the question.

Procedure

In Column A place a checkmark beside the items that pertain to you. Then, if you want to check on how others see you, cover Column A or fold it under, give the chart to someone who knows you well (another parent or a friend), and have that person mark in Column B. Column C can be used by a third person, or you can use it later to see whether you have changed in any way.

Are You a Parent Who . . .

A   B   C

____ ____ ____ 1. Attends PTA meetings?

____ ____ ____ 2. Argues with teachers?

____ ____ ____ 3. Never admits to a teacher that you're wrong?

____ ____ ____ 4. Compares siblings with each other?

____ ____ ____ 5. Feels intimidated by school personnel?

____ ____ ____ 6. Admits to your child when you're wrong?

____ ____ ____ 7. Can listen to your child without interrupting?

____ ____ ____ 8. Dreads or puts off conference time?

____ ____ ____ 9. Calls the teacher when things are going well?

____ ____ ____ 10. Sends notes of appreciation to school personnel?

____ ____ ____ 11. Argues with your children?

____ ____ ____ 12. Displays your child's good work in prominent places?

____ ____ ____ 13. Feels in control with your child at home?

____ ____ ____ 14. Reinforces Board of Education members?

____ ____ ____ 15. Has attended a workshop for parents?

____ ____ ____ 16. Volunteers as an aide in your child's class?

____ ____ ____ 17. Has invited your child's teacher to your home?

____ ____ ____ 18. Enjoys parent–teacher conferences?

____ ____ ____ 19. Criticizes the teacher or school to other parents?

____ ____ ____ 20. Thinks school personnel have lost control of the children?

____ ____ ____ 21. Participates in educational planning at school for your child?

____ ____ ____ 22. Arrives at conferences on time?

_____ _____ _____ 23. Tells teachers how to educate your child?

_____ _____ _____ 24. Agrees with your mate on child rearing practices?

_____ _____ _____ 25. Reinforces positively?

_____ _____ _____ 26. Trusts teachers?

_____ _____ _____ 27. Is fairly consistent in dealing with your child?

_____ _____ _____ 28. Takes your child on field trips?

_____ _____ _____ 29. Has trouble sleeping because of worry about your child?

_____ _____ _____ 30. Feels physically drained after a weekend with your child?

_____ _____ _____ 31. Says "wait until your father (or mother) comes home"?

_____ _____ _____ 32. Thinks parents [you? other parents?] have lost the respect of their children?

_____ _____ _____ 33. Has a sense of humor with respect to your child?

_____ _____ _____ 34. Attends "special interest" parent meetings (ACLD, ARC, etc.)?

_____ _____ _____ 35. Runs or helps run parent meetings?

_____ _____ _____ 36. Tells your child about your own problems when he/she tries to tell you about his/her problems.

_____ _____ _____ 37. Thinks school personnel are not entirely honest about children?

_____ _____ _____ 38. Tells the principal when the teacher has done a good job?

_____ _____ _____ 39. Calls the school if your child is going to be absent?

_____ _____ _____ 40. Listens to the teacher during conferences?

_____ _____ _____ 41. Attends activities for and with your child (e.g., school events, Scouts, athletics, music)?

_____ _____ _____ 42. Enjoys playing games with your child?

_____ _____ _____ 43. Has a picture of your child with you?

_____ _____ _____ 44. Thinks that few people other than you really understand your child?

_____ _____ _____ 45. Asks the teacher what you can do to help your child at home?

Parents may be asked to consider the following questions:

> ➤ Why are the columns discrepant?
> ➤ Are the discrepancies causing a lot of friction?
> ➤ Should specific behaviors be changed?
> ➤ Do I know how to change the behaviors, or do I need additional help?
> ➤ What have I learned about myself?

ACTIVITY 6: WHOM WOULD YOU TELL?

This activity is similar to the Privacy Circle strategy discussed by Simon et al. (1972). It provides an opportunity for parents to consider how open they are in discussing disabilities and other personal matters. No value is attached to openness or closedness. As one mother said, "I might not mind talking about some of these things, but I must consider that my family has a right to privacy, too."

Benefits to children with disabilities resulted from President John Kennedy speaking out about his sister who was mentally retarded, but this does not mean that all individuals should do the same thing. Each family must consider its individual needs and other factors. The exercise gives the respondent an opportunity to explore his/her own value system with respect to a limited number of family matters.

Procedure

This activity can be done individually or in a group. It can be analyzed by the individual through introspection, by the individual with a teacher or counselor, or used for group discussion.

Whom Would You Tell?

1. Your child is a bed wetter? _____
2. Your child lies? _____
3. Your child is gifted?_____
4. Your child has experimented with drugs? _____
5. Your child has temper tantrums?_____
6. Your child watches too much TV? _____

7. Your child is mentally retarded? _____
8. Your mate is under psychiatric care? _____
9. Your child is brain damaged? _____
10. Your mate is alcoholic? _____
11. Your child has homosexual behaviors? _____
12. Your unwed daughter is pregnant? _____
13. You are having an extramarital affair? _____
14. Your child was suspended from school? _____
15. You slapped a child? _____
16. Your salary? _____
17. You have a blind child? _____
18. Your exact weight? _____
19. You smoke marijuana? _____
20. You have a deaf child? _____
21. Your method of birth control? _____
22. Your child had run away? _____
23. Your child has an emotional disability? _____
24. You have a new car? _____
25. Your child has a learning disability? _____

This activity need not take long. After the task is completed, have the respondents consider the following questions:

➤ Why do some disabilities seem easier than others to talk about?
➤ How open am I in comparison to others (if shared in a group)?
➤ Have I learned anything new about myself as the result of this activity?

Using this instrument for research would be interesting. Some have suggested that fathers seem to be a bit more reserved than mothers in discussing various disabilities.

ACTIVITY 7: DISABILITY RANKING SCALE

Barsch (1969) developed a disability ranking scale that he used with more than 2,000 people, including teachers, parents, and others working with children and youth with disabilities. The list included polio and heart conditions, along with the more traditional categories. He asked the respondents to rank the conditions from most severe to least severe as to how the condition would affect the individual. Interestingly, parents did not tend to rank the disability that their own children had as most severe, and teachers of children with a disability often did not rank the condition that they worked with as most severe. It was almost as if they were saying, "I know this condition, and it can't be as bad as _____."

A blind student in graduate school marked blindness as 10 (least severe). When asked about it, she said, "I'm blind and I'm getting along fine. I'm just glad I don't have any of those other conditions." For purposes of this activity, we have used the more traditional categories.

Procedure

Hand the respondent(s) the disability ranking scale, and have them fill in the information for their child. Then give the following instructions. Do not discuss the degree of disability within the category; just ask them to respond from their own frame of reference:

Categories of disabling conditions are listed below. Please rank these, from 1 to 7, according to your *own feelings,* on the basis of severity. Which disability do you think is the most severe problem a child could have? Which disability do you think is second most serious? Which do you think is third most serious, (and so forth)? Consider only the individual and his/her problem in adjustment to school and life.

Disability Ranking Scale

_____ Elementary Age   Type of Disability _____
_____ Secondary Age   Sex: M_____ F_____

Disability	Rank
1. Blindness	_____
2. Physical impairment	_____
3. Deafness	_____
4. Emotional disturbance	_____
5. Learning disability	_____
6. Mental retardation	_____
7. Speech/language impairment	_____

After completing the task, discuss the following questions:

➤ Was this task difficult? Why?

➤ How did you go about reaching your conclusions?

➤ Have you ever known anyone in the category you marked with a 1?

➤ Do you think your ranking is fairly typical of how society at large would rank the categories?

➤ Do you think society's ranking would have any effect on the funding of programs for people with disabilities?

This activity can be used with a PTA or any parent group, to explore attitudes.

ACTIVITY 8: RELATING DOMESTIC VALUES

In the late 1950s Farber, Jenne, and Toigo (1960) investigated the effect that a child with mental retardation had on the marital integration of husband and wife. One aspect considered in measuring marital integration was the ends the parents were striving for. This, the investigators believed, could be measured by looking at the consensus of husband and wife in their ranking of domestic values.

Both husband and wife ranked a list of 10 domestic values in order of their perceived importance to family success. The list consisted of the following (pp. 20–21):

a. A place in the community
b. Healthy and happy children
c. Companionship
d. Personality development
e. Satisfaction in affection shown
f. Economic security
g. Emotional security
h. Moral and religious unity
i. Everyday interests
f. A home

As parents show an interest in exploring their own value system, a domestic values ranking activity might be explored.

Procedure

This activity can be carried out in a number of ways. One is to have the values listed on separate pieces of paper and have each partner put a number from 1 to 10 beside each of the values. When both are finished, you could take the lists of domestic values and on one sheet put the husband's ranking in one column and the wife's ranking in another, then compare the differences.

Another way would be to have each of the values printed separately on a card. Have each partner rank the value cards from most important to least important. When this is finished, take the original list and put each partner's rankings in separate columns for comparison. The card technique has the advantage of not implying an order at the beginning of the task. If you are so inclined, performing a correlation between the rankings is easy (Siegel, 1956) so the parents can see the overall relationship between their rankings, as well as focusing on individual items that differ.

After the data have been compiled, discuss the following questions:

1. What are your thoughts about this activity?
2. Were you surprised at the results (e.g., the degree of agreement or disagreement)?
3. Have you ever discussed your differences or similarities on these values?
4. What have you learned about yourself and your partner?
5. Are you satisfied with the results, or do you want to change? If you want to change, how might you go about it?

The activity can be unsettling, so you should be sensitive to the feelings of the participants before, during, and after the activity. And you have to be ready to help the parents form a plan of action if they so desire. Agreements, one should remember, can be as important as differences. For some reason, many of us have become problem-oriented rather than strength-oriented. As parents, we respond to the lowest grade on the report card; as school psychologists, we respond to the valleys of the test profiles; and as teachers, we respond to bad behavior rather than appropriate classroom behavior. In working with significant adults, we must be constantly aware of the strengths that can help form the building blocks of a solid foundation for improved performance.

ACTIVITY 9: TARGET BEHAVIORS

The Q-sort was developed a number of years ago as a way of comparing people's perception of their real selves with their ideal selves (Stephenson, 1953). It since has been used to compare perceptions of the significant others in a child's life (Kroth, 1973). The technique is simple, easy to explain, and quick to do.

Procedure

Look at the forms on the next pages and pick one to use. One form lists 25 target classroom behaviors. The second form is blank so that you can write out your own target behaviors if you wish (especially if they are more related to home).

Referring to the scale at the bottom of the form, Participant #1 should write in the value number associated with the behavior. For example, for Item No. 1, "Gets work done on time," Participant #1, the teacher, might think the child is "very much like me," and would write the number 2 in the first box under "Real Sort."

After recording the value for each item on the "Real Sort," Participant #1 follows the same procedure for the "Ideal Sort," or how the participant would like the child to be—reflecting the value placed on each behavior. Then Participant #2 (say, the child) follows the same steps. (Two separate forms might be utilized, if the first participant's results might influence the other's. Then the numbers from one form could be transferred to the other form so they could be readily compared.)

Finally, to compare perceptions and values, subtract the lesser numbers from the higher numbers and record the differences in the "Difference" column. The larger the number, the greater the difference. Items showing a great deal of discrepancy are targets for discussion or action.

The comparisons that can be made are innumerable: How the father sees the child versus how he would like to see the child, how the mother sees the child versus how the teacher sees the child; how the father would like to see the child versus how the mother would like to see the child; and so on. After the activity has been completed, the following questions may be asked:

1. Are we in overall agreement in how we perceive the child?
2. Are there similar goals (ideal sorts) for the child?
3. Where are the areas of greatest discrepancy?

Target Behaviors

Item No.	Behavior	Real Sort			Ideal Sort		
		Participant #1	Participant #2	Difference	Participant #1	Participant #2	Difference
1.	Gets work done on time						
2.	Pokes or hits classmates						
3.	Out of seat without permission						
4.	Scores high in spelling						
5.	Plays with objects while working						
6.	Scores high in reading						
7.	Disturbs neighbors by making noise						
8.	Is quiet during class time						
9.	Tips chair often						
10.	Follows directions						
11.	Smiles frequently						
12.	Often taps finger, foot, or pencil						
13.	Pays attention to work						
14.	Works slowly						
15.	Throws objects in class						
16.	Reads well orally						
17.	Talks to classmates often						
18.	Scores high in English						
19.	Talks out without permission						
20.	Rocks in chair						
21.	Scores high in math						
22.	Asks the teacher questions						
23.	Uses free time to read or study						
24.	Works until job is finished						
25.	Walks around room during study time						

1 = most like me
2 = very much like me
3 = like me
4 = a little like me
5 = undecided
6 = a little unlike me
7 = unlike me
8 = very much unlike me
9 = most unlike me

Target Behaviors

Item No.	Behavior	Real Sort			Ideal Sort		
		Participant #1	Participant #2	Difference	Participant #1	Participant #2	Difference
1.							
2.							
3.							
4.							
5.							
6.							
7.							
8.							
9.							
10.							
11.							
12.							
13.							
14.							
15.							
16.							
17.							
18.							
19.							
20.							
21.							
22.							
23.							
24.							
25.							

1 = most like me
2 = very much like me
3 = like me
4 = a little like me
5 = undecided
6 = a little unlike me
7 = unlike me
8 = very much unlike me
9 = most unlike me

4. Are the differences easily explained, or are they going to be difficult to reconcile?
5. What have we learned about our perceptions by engaging in this activity?
6. What, if any, specific courses of action should be taken?

As with the other activities that compare the values of participants, you should be ready to discuss similarities and differences. The participants may become defensive, which leads to difficulty in exploring and understanding each other's point of view. The teacher particularly should be wary of defensiveness as it relates to value sorting. The tendency is to become authoritarian rather than understanding. For instance, a teacher may take the position that it is most important for the child to "smile frequently" and of little importance for the child to "score high in reading" at this stage of development, whereas the parent may take the opposite point of view. The teacher must take the lead in exploring and understanding these differences.

ACTIVITY #10: PERSONAL STRESS: SOCIAL READJUSTMENT RATING SCALE

Use this social readjustment scale by Holmes and Rahe to figure out the level of personal stress in your life.

Procedure

Look over the events listed below. Place a check in the space provided if it has happened to you within the last twelve months. When finished, add up the number of points next to each of your checkmarks. Place the total in the space below the list to interpret your personal stress results.

1. Death of a spouse   1._____100
2. Divorce   2._____73
3. Marital separation   3._____65
4. Jail term   4._____63
5. Death of a close family member   5._____63
6. Personal injury or illness   6._____53
7. Marriage   7._____50

8. Fired at work   8._____47
9. Marital reconciliation   9._____45
10. Retirement from work   10._____45
11. Change in health of family member   11._____44
12. Pregnancy   12. _____40
13. Sex difficulties   13._____39
14. Gain of new family member   14._____39
15. Business readjustment   15._____38
16. Change in financial state   16._____37
17. Death of a close friend   17._____36
18. Change to different line of work   18._____36
19. Change in number of arguments with spouse   19._____35
20. Mortgage or loan for major purchase
    (home, etc.)   20. _____31
21. Foreclosure of mortgage or loan   21._____31
22. Change in responsibilities of work   22._____29
23. Son or daughter leaving home   23._____29
24. Trouble with in-laws   24._____29
25. Outstanding personal achievement   25._____28
26. Spouse begins or stops work
    outside the home   26._____26
27. Begin or end school   27._____26
28. Change in living conditions   28._____25
29. Revision of personal habits   29._____24
30. Trouble with boss   30._____23
31. Change in work hours or conditions   31._____20
32. Change in residence   32._____20
33. Change in schools   33._____20
34. Change in recreation   34._____19
35. Change in church activities   35._____19
36. Change in social activities   36._____18
37. Mortgage or loan for lesser purchase
    (car, TV, etc.)   37. _____17
38. Change in sleeping habits   38._____16
39. Change in number of family get-togethers   39._____15
40. Change in eating habits   40. _____15
41. Vacation   41._____13
42. Christmas   42._____12
43. Minor violations of the law   43._____11

My score: _____

How to interpret your score:
0–149 = No significant problem
150–199 = Middle stress, think about ways to slow down
200–299 = You are experiencing moderate stress
300 or over = Major stress!

Source: From *Journal of Psychosomatic Research*, Vol. 2, 213-18, by Thomas H. Holmes and Richard H. Rahe, "The Holmes and Rahe Social Readjustment Rating Scale," Pergamon Press, Ltd., 1967. Used by permission.

ACTIVITY 11: CASE HISTORIES FOR ROLE-PLAYING EXERCISES

Four case histories are presented in this section. You can read the case histories and attempt to answer the questions that follow. You may not know all the answers, but you can give educated guesses. In terms of role playing, you can practice giving answers by yourself or talking to another person as if he or she is a parent, educator, counselor, or administrator. These exercises are to help you learn how well you listen and interpret.

Case History #1

Present Status

Jed is a 10-year-old white male whose mother is requesting placement for him in a program for children with disabilities. Jed has been evaluated and recommended for placement in an intermediate class for children with learning and behavior disorders. The family has just moved from another state, where Jed was in a general third-grade class. His teacher was Mrs. Turner, who is now being treated for stress-related disorders.

Physical Appearance

Jed was not present for the conference, so this information is from the mother's report: "He's just all boy... He's very active—can climb to the roof of the school in Louisburg even though he doesn't have a right arm.... He doesn't sleep well at nights and still wets the bed occasionally."

Educational Status

Jed has been in four different schools since he started school 5 years ago. As a Navy man, his father traveled around. Jed failed first and third grades. A psychologist said his ability to learn is normal.

Personal Traits

Jed doesn't get along too well with the kids in the neighborhood. He'd rather play basketball or watch TV. He never misses *The Simpsons*. His favorite food is peanut butter and banana sandwiches. He wants to be a Navy man like his dad.

Home and Family

The family has five children. The two girls are the father's, the two boys are the mother's, and Jed is a product of both mother and father. Jed gets along best with the older girl, who is in 10th grade.

The probation officer sees a ninth-grade stepbrother once a month. The Louisburg Mental Health Center says the mother and father need to be more interested in what their children are doing. The parents' response: "...but how can we when we have so many kids?"

"Jed likes dogs, but last summer he put kerosene on a cat and lit it on fire. He says he doesn't know why he did it. He's usually pretty good with animals. When his dad got back from his 2-week tour of duty in Norfolk, Virginia, he really tanned Jed for that."

Test yourself:

1. What is the child's name?
2. How old is he?
3. Has he been in special education before?
4. How many children are in the family?
5. Does the child have any physical problems? If so, what?
6. Has school been a successful experience for the child? Why do you draw the conclusion you have?
7. Has the child or family been in contact with any social agencies? If so, which ones?
8. What might be good reinforcers for the child?
9. Does the child have any unusual personality traits?
10. From whom would you like reports? Why?

Case History #2

Present Status

Maria is an 8-year-old girl. Her mother moved to Osage from Remus, California, where she was enrolled in third grade. The mother has taken a job as a counselor in a nearby junior college. The father has remained in California with his car-wash business.

Physical Appearance

Because of her poor vision, Maria can barely see to put the batteries in her hearing aid. Her mother has set up an appointment with an ophthalmologist next month because the school nurse believes that Maria's vision can be corrected with glasses. She has had perfect attendance at school ever since she started first grade.

Educational Status

Maria has been in the low reading group and low math group. She was in a summer remedial reading program, which the mother concluded was of questionable value. The girl always tries hard to complete her tasks and often cries if she cannot finish. Her teachers have always gotten along well with Maria, and the mother thinks her daughter might have received "social promotions" in school. The mother doesn't know what books the California schools used with her.

Maria's achievement test scores consistently have been in the 10th–15th percentile. She has never had an individual evaluation by a psychologist.

Personal Traits

Though she is fairly quiet, Maria seems to get along with other children. Most of her friends are two or three years younger. She likes to play house, Four Square, Mother May I?, and other games. She watches TV but sits so close and turns it up so loud that her mother discourages her watching television. Maria likes to fingerpaint, but her mother thinks it's "pretty messy" and doesn't encourage it.

Since the family moved to Osage, Maria doesn't like being in her room alone at night. The mother can think of no food that her daughter particularly likes or dislikes.

Home and Family

Maria is an only child. The parents are separated, at least temporarily; whether the separation will become legal is still speculative. The family income is modest but adequate. Maria is cooperative at home and is somewhat of a "mama's girl."

Additional Information

Her mother thinks Maria needs additional individual testing and wonders whether her repeating third grade might be a good idea.

Test yourself:

1. How old is the child?

2. Does she have any physical problems that will require special teacher attention? If so, what?
3. How is the child's general health?
4. What books were used with her in the previous school?
5. From where did she move?
6. Was the child a good, average, or poor student?
7. Does she get along with other children? Teachers?
8. Who is her favorite brother or sister?
9. What reinforcers are available in the home?
10. With what personality problems should the teacher be concerned?

Case History #3

Present Status

Ricki is 6 years old. Her father is a migrant worker who was born in Mexico and is applying for citizenship this year. Her mother is a Native American. The family lives in a trailer court on the outskirts of Caywood.

Physical Appearance

A pretty girl, Ricki has big brown eyes with a sort of sad look. Her mother reports that she is no trouble around home and that she doesn't talk much. Actually, her infrequent speech usually revolves around something she wants or needs. She is a slight child who tries to fade into the background whenever possible. She has had a lot of colds and earaches but has never been to a doctor.

Educational Status

Because of the itinerant nature of her father's job, Ricki's family moved several times last year. Some of the school systems did not have a kindergarten, but she attended school regularly when a class was available. She can print her name and recognize the letters in it, but she does not know other alphabet letters consistently. Her mother has tried to teach her to write numbers, but she hasn't seemed interested. As far as the mother knows, Ricki has taken no standardized tests. Her mother has not had a conference with any of her teachers before, and Ricki has never expressed an opinion about any of her teachers.

Personal Traits

Ricki doesn't like to play much with other children, though she gets along with them. She prefers to draw—something she does a lot, covering everything from brown paper grocery sacks to newspaper margins with drawings of miniature people that have a lot of detail. Her mother, who is proud of her daughter's artistic products, has a sample drawing in her purse, which she shows the teacher. She thinks Ricki may turn out to be an artist. The family has a television set but not a computer.

Home and Family

Ricki's father was tired of moving around, so he found a job as a stocker in a supermarket and hopes to live here permanently. Besides Ricki, the family has two other children—a boy 4 years old and a baby girl. Ricki likes to care for the baby, but she tends to ignore her brother, an active child who spends much time playing outside with neighborhood friends.

A big help to her mother, Ricki likes to do all kinds of chores, which mostly involve running errands and helping her clean. She doesn't do much with her father, who isn't inclined to spend time with Ricki anyway, preferring to take Ricki's little brother with him when he goes fishing. English is the only language spoken in the home, and the father is quite proficient at it.

Test yourself:

1. What is the child's ancestry?
2. How old is she?
3. Does she have any physical problems that may need attention? If so, what?
4. Does she have any unusual personality traits with which the teacher should be concerned?
5. How many children are in the family?
6. What are the child's social relationships?
7. What reinforcers are available in the home?
8. What is the family's socioeconomic status?
9. Is it likely that the child has been successful academically?
10. Are there any unusual circumstances in the child's family life?

Case History #4

Present Status

Jay is a 7-year-old white male who has not attended school before, except for a brief period in a special class in a closed psychiatric ward in a Detroit hospital. He was evaluated there, and residential placement was recommended at that time, nearly one year ago. Since then, his mother has married and moved to Sawyer. She now wants Jay to attend a public school, possibly in a special class, though she isn't sure.

Physical Appearance

For his age, Jay is large and also strong physically. His mother has had quite a bit of trouble controlling his temper outbursts and lately has given up trying. She thinks Jay is just unusually stubborn. His new stepfather has somewhat more success in discipline attempts, but it's still too early to say whether he will remain effective in this. In addition to his aggressive behavior, Jay seems to be a nervous child and stutters considerably, though usually with just the initial word in a sentence.

Educational Status

The boy has had little or no exposure to academic work, either formally or informally. He has never attended school on a regular basis, and his mother thinks he wouldn't pay attention if she were to try to teach him. Jay has no concept of numbers or letters, even though he was briefly introduced to them during his short stay in the hospital school. His records during this hospitalization may be available, but the mother hasn't seen them. She thinks they tested him extensively.

Personal Traits

Jay doesn't play much with children his own age. He is destructive of other kids' property, and after he destroys a toy or two, they won't play with him anymore. He also has torn up most of his own belongings and other things in the home that weren't under lock and key. He likes to play with matches and lighters, so these must be kept from him. He likes all kinds of food and will eat almost anything available, including bugs.

Home and Family

Jay is an only child. His father's whereabouts are unknown—he was never married to Jay's mother and left town soon after finding out that she was pregnant. From the time Jay was 2 years old, his mother worked as a waitress and dancer in a bar until recently, when she married for the first time. Because she worked nights, she slept most of the day and left Jay to his own devices. She feels guilty about this and now thinks that "things will be different" and wants to "start over with Jay."

On two separate occasions, firemen put out fires that Jay had started in an old garage behind his apartment building. After being called for the second time within a month, they took him to the hospital's psychiatric receiving center. Jay's mother feels responsible for his behavior because he had little or no supervision from her. She believes that now that she won't be working, "things will get straightened out."

Jay's new stepfather is a pharmaceutical salesman who recently was transferred to this area. His sales territory is large (three states). He was married once before but has no children of his own. Both parents emphatically do not want residential placement for Jay.

Test yourself:

1. What is the child's age?
2. How many other children are in the home?
3. Does the child have any physical problems? If so, what?
4. Has contact been made with any social agencies? If so, which ones?
5. Does he have any unusual personality traits?
6. Would you like to see any of his previous records? If so, which ones?
7. What possible reinforcers could be used in the classroom or at home?
8. Would you advise special class placement? Why or why not?
9. Have the child's interpersonal relationships been satisfactory? Explain.

REFERENCES

Barsch R. H. (1969). *The parent of the handicapped child: A study of child-rearing practices.* Springfield, IL: Charles C Thomas.

Carkhuff, K. J., & Berenson, S. G. (1976). *Teaching as treatment: An introduction to counseling and psychotherapy.* Amherst, MA: Human Resource Developmental Press.

Curwin, R.L.. & Fuhrmann, S. S. (1975). *Discovering your teaching self: Humanistic approaches to effective teaching.* Englewood Cliffs, NJ: Prentice-Hall.

Farber, S., J., Jenne, W. C., & Toiso, R. (1960). Family crisis and the decision to institutionalize the retarded child. *CEC Research Monographs,* series A (1).

James, W. (1982). *Psychology: A briefer course.* New York: Holt.

Kroth, R. (1973). The behavioral Q-sort as a diagnostic tool. *Academic Therapy, 8*(3), 17–33.

Siegel, S. (1956). *Nonparametric statistics for the behavioral sciences.* New York: McGraw-Hill.

Simon, S.D., Howe, L. W., & Kirschenbaum, H. (1972). *Values clarification: A handbook of practical strategies for teachers and students.* New York: Han.

Stephenson, W. (1953). *The study of behavior: Q-technique and its methodology.* Chicago: University of Chicago Press.

Forms, Surveys, and Questionnaires

CLASSROOM DATA FORM

1. What percentage of the children in your class or school live in a single-parent family?
    _____ out of _____ = _____%

2a. Tally the primary guardians for the students:
    _____ Both parents
    _____ Father   _____ Mother
    _____ Uncle   _____ Aunt
    _____ Grandfather   _____ Grandmother
    _____ Other relative (specify the types:_____)
    _____ Other person (specify the types: _____)

2b. Translate those figures into percentages, depending on how many students you asked:
    ____% Both parents
    ____% Father   ____% Mother
    ____% Uncle   ____% Aunt
    ____% Grandfather   ____% Grandmother
    ____% Other relative (specify the types: _____)
    ____% Other person (specify the types:_____)

3a. How many students are living with the following people, in addition to or instead of parents?
    _____ Uncle   _____ Aunt
    _____ Grandfather   _____ Grandmother
    _____ Cousin(s)   _____ Other family members

3b. Translate those figures into percentages, depending on how many students you asked:
    ____% Uncle   ____% Aunt
    ____% Grandfather   ____% Grandmother
    ____% Cousin(s)   ____% Other family members

(continued)

4a. How many other children are living in the same home as your students?

_____ 0   _____ 1   _____ 2

_____ 3   _____ 4   _____ 5+

4b. Translate those figures into percentages, depending on how many students you asked:

____% 0   ____% 1   ____% 2

____% 3   ____% 4   ____% 5+

5a. How many of your students were born in the following months?

_____ January   _____ April   _____ July   _____ October

_____ February   _____ May   _____ August   _____ November

_____ March   _____ June   _____ September   _____ December

5b. What is the most frequent month of birth for the children in your class? _____

6a. How many families have the following items:

___ Telephone   ___ Computer

___ Cable TV   ___ Washer/dryer

___ DVD player   ___ Video game system

___ Dishwasher   ___ Mail delivered to the home

___ Car   ___ Magazines delivered to the home

___ VCR   ___ Newspaper delivered to the home

6b. Translate those figures into percentages, depending on how many students you asked:

___% Telephone   ___% Computer

___% Cable TV   ___% Washer/dryer

___% DVD player   ___% Video game system

___% Dishwasher   ___% Mail delivered to the home

___% Car   ___% Magazines delivered to the home

___% VCR   ___% Newspaper delivered to the home

STUDENT CENSUS FORM

Student's First Name_____

Age: _____ Birthday: _____ (mo) _____ (day) _____ (yr)

Male _____   Female _____

Program or Class _____

___Hispanic   ___Native American
___African American   ___Asian American
___Caucasian   ___Other (specify) _____

Parents:

_____ Lives with both natural parents
_____ Lives with single parent
_____ Lives with parent and stepparent
_____ Lives with uncle, aunt, grandparents, or other relative
_____ Other (specify) _____

Number of parents/guardians or other adults
living with the student who work outside the home: _____

Number of children living in the home (other than the student):

_____ younger   _____ older   =   _____ (total)

Number of siblings placed in special education classes: _____

Is there a phone in the house?   _____ yes   _____ no
Is there a TV in the house?   _____ yes   _____ no
Is there a VCR in the house?   _____ yes   _____ no
Is there a computer in the house?   _____ yes   _____ no
Is mail delivered to the house?   _____ yes   _____ no

Name two things the family enjoys doing together:

1. _____

2. _____

Survey for Parents/Guardians: Interest in Parent/Guardian Group Meetings

Please check the five topics that would be of most interest to you in a small-group meeting of parents and guardians.

General Topics for Parents/Guardians of Students K–12

      _____ 1. The Challenge of Being a Single Parent

      _____ 2. Assertive Discipline: Creating a Positive Atmosphere at Home

      _____ 3. Divorce and Separation: Effects on Families

      _____ 4. Parent Roles in Sex Education

      _____ 5. Stepfamilies: How to Navigate Successfully

      _____ 6. Parent–Teacher Conferencing: Tips for Parents

      _____ 7. Helping Children Build Good Study Habits

      _____ 8. Getting the Help You Need When Your Child Has Problems in School

      _____ 9. Self-Esteem: Helping Kids Feel Good About Themselves

      _____ 10. Freedom and Control: Setting Limits for Children

Topics for Parents/Guardians of Students K–5

      _____ 1. Communicating With Children

      _____ 2. Helping Your Child's Language Development

      _____ 3. Spending Quality Time With Children

      _____ 4. Home Activities for the Young Child

Topics for Parents/Guardians of Middle School and High School Students

      _____ 1. Living With Your Adolescent

      _____ 2. Drug and Alcohol Use and Abuse

      _____ 3. Helping Your Child Plan His or Her Future

Special Topics for Parents/Guardians of Special Education Students

_____ 1. Parenting an Exceptional Child

_____ 2. Helping Siblings of a Child With Special Needs

_____ 3. Sex Education for Students With Disabilities

_____ 4. Helping a Child With a Learning Disability

_____ 5. The IEP Process: Legal Issues and Parent Roles

_____ 6. Behavior Management Techniques for Difficult Children

_____ 7. Dealing With Professionals: Teachers, Therapists, Diagnosticians, Principals

THANK YOU FOR YOUR TIME AND PREFERENCES!

SURVEY FOR PARENTS/GUARDIANS OF CHILDREN WITH DISABILITIES: STRENGTHS AND NEEDS

Age of child_____ Program/Teacher _____

To plan parent/guardian programs, we need to know what kinds of topics are of interest to you. Would you please take a few minutes to let us know how important you consider each of the following topics *and* how much you already know about that topic. When you've completed this form, please return it to_____.

How much do you know about this?		**Would you like to learn more about this?**
1= not much, 5 = expert		1 = no, 5 = definitely

1 2 3 4 5 (1) How infants/young people grow and develop. . . what's normal?   1 2 3 4 5

1 2 3 4 5 (2) Relationships between brothers, sisters, and other children   1 2 3 4 5

1 2 3 4 5 (3) How does language develop? Can I help?   1 2 3 4 5

1 2 3 4 5 (4) Setting limits, discipline, and home responsibilities.   1 2 3 4 5

1 2 3 4 5 (5) What can I do to help my child's motor development?   1 2 3 4 5

1 2 3 4 5 (6) Can anything be done to make mealtimes easier?   1 2 3 4 5

1 2 3 4 5 (7) Understanding standardized tests and evaluation procedures   1 2 3 4 5

1 2 3 4 5 (8) What can I do at home to help my son /daughter in school?   1 2 3 4 5

1 2 3 4 5 (9) What services are available in the community?   1 2 3 4 5

1 2 3 4 5 (10) How can I work more effectively with the professionals who serve my son/daughter?   1 2 3 4 5

1 2 3 4 5 (11) Parent–teacher conferences: How can I get the most out of them?   1 2 3 4 5

1 2 3 4 5	(12) Impact of a new child on the family	1 2 3 4 5
1 2 3 4 5	(13) Ways of explaining disabilities to children, relatives, and others	1 2 3 4 5
1 2 3 4 5	(14) Medical, dental, and nutritional needs of children with disabilities	1 2 3 4 5
1 2 3 4 5	(15) Legislation for children with disabilities	1 2 3 4 5
1 2 3 4 5	(16) Single-parent and stepparent concerns	1 2 3 4 5
1 2 3 4 5	(17) Effective parenting and communication	1 2 3 4 5
1 2 3 4 5	(18) How children/adolescents change adult relationships	1 2 3 4 5
1 2 3 4 5	(19) Drug and alcohol use	1 2 3 4 5
1 2 3 4 5	(20) Sexuality and children with disabilities	1 2 3 4 5
1 2 3 4 5	(21) How to work more effectively with the school system	1 2 3 4 5
1 2 3 4 5	(22) Social relationships	1 2 3 4 5
1 2 3 4 5	(23) Hearing from other parents who have children with similar disabilities	1 2 3 4 5
1 2 3 4 5	(24) Understanding more about my child's disability	1 2 3 4 5

I know something about the following and can help out by applying these skills (e.g., music, carpentry, puppetry):

_____

_____

Any other suggestions, ideas, or concerns:

_____

_____

Thank you for taking the time to respond. Your suggestions will be used to plan future parent/guardian meetings.

SURVEY FOR PROFESSIONALS: EVALUATING PARENT AND FAMILY INVOLVEMENT

Receiving services that emphasize parent and family involvement may include many ways to involve families and professional together.

Is home communication used? (Circle those used.)

staff letters   teacher/therapist notes
bulletin boards   home–school book
telephone   home visits
school visits   newsletters

_____ Do parents observe or participate regularly in activities?

_____ Is there one-way glass for observation, or an area for observation?

_____ Does a staff member join a parent during observation?

_____ Are parents free to observe without prior notice?

_____ Does the faculty or school hold family celebrations (holiday parties, etc.)?

_____ Is there a special parent resource area?

_____ If yes, does the area have up-to-date parenting materials?

_____ Is there a loan library for parents?

_____ Is there a mothers/fathers/siblings group?

_____ Is there a parent support group?

_____ Are parent training sessions held regularly?

_____ Do parents choose training topics?

_____ Are staff members available for family emergencies?

_____ Does the staff provide referral services for family support needs?

_____ Does the program honor ethnic and cultural family differences?

_____ Are parents or other family members encouraged to join committees and policy-making boards of the agency/program/school?

REINFORCEMENT QUESTIONNAIRE FOR STUDENTS

Name_____Date_____

Class _____ Age_____

Completed by _____

1. The thing I like to do best after school is _____
   _____
   _____

2. If I had $10, I'd _____
   _____
   _____

3. My favorite TV program is _____

4. My favorite game is _____

5. My best friend is _____

6. My favorite time of day is _____

7. My favorite toy is_____

8. My favorite CD or tape is _____

9. My favorite subject at school is_____

10. I like to read books about_____
    _____

11. Some places I'd like to go are _____

_____

_____

12. My favorite food is _____

_____

13. My favorite indoor activity is_____

_____

14. My favorite outdoor activity is_____

_____

15. My favorite hobby is _____

_____

16. My favorite animal is _____

_____

17. The three things I like to do most are:

    a. _____

    b. _____

    c. _____

18. The three things I like to do least are:

    a. _____

    b. _____

    c. _____

19. The three things I would like to have most are:

    a. _____

    b. _____

    c. _____

INFORMATION FORM FOR BABYSITTERS

Child's name _____

Parent's name _____

Parent's address _____

Parent's home telephone _____

I will be (place, address, phone number) _____

_____

_____

If you cannot reach me, please call _____

_____

Other Important Telephone Numbers

My child's doctor: _____

Fire department: _____

Police: _____

Ambulance: _____

Poison control center: _____

Special Things to Know About My Child:

Mealtime or snacks: _____

_____

Bathtime: _____

_____

Playtime: _____

_____

Naptime or bedtime: _____

_____

Other special instructions: _____

_____

_____

_____

Line Drawing From the Fourth Activity in Chapter 4

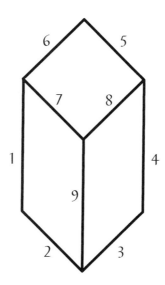

National Service Organizations and Technology Centers

Adamlab, LLC
http://www.adamlab.com/

Alexander Graham Bell Association for the Deaf and Hard of Hearing
http://www.agbell.org/

Alliance for Technology Access (ATA)
http://www.ataccess.org/
Find ATA centers across the United States at http://www.ataccess.org/community/centers.lasso

ALS Association
http://www.alsa.org/

American Association on Mental Retardation
http://www.aamr.org

American Council of the Blind
http://acb.org/

American Foundation for the Blind
http://www.afb.org/

American Lung Association
http://www.lungusa.org/

American Occupational Therapy Association, Inc. (AOTA)
http://www.aota.org/

American Printing House for the Blind
http://www.aph.org/

American Speech-Language-Hearing Association
http://www.asha.org/

The Arc of the United States (formerly Association for Retarded Citizens of the United States)
http://www.thearc.org

An Association for Children and Adults with Learning Disabilities (AC-ACLD, Inc.)
http://www.acldonline.org

Bloorview MacMillan Children's Centre
http://www.bloorviewmacmillan.on.ca/

Boulevard: A Disability Resource Directory of Products and Services for the Physically Challenged, Elderly, Caregivers and Healthcare Professions
http://www.blvd.com/accent/

Candlelighters Childhood Cancer Foundation
http://www.candlelighters.org/

Carroll Center for the Blind
http://www.carroll.org

Catalyst: A Resource for Technology in Special Education
http://www.thecatalyst.us/

Center for IT Accommodation (CITA)
http://www.gsa.gov/cita

Cornelia de Lange Syndrome Foundation
http://cdlsusa.org

Council for Exceptional Children (CEC)
http://www.cec.sped.org

CEC's Technology and Media Division
http://www.tamcec.org/

Crossroads Ruth Lilly Assistive Technology Center
http://crossroads.easterseals.com/site/
PageServer?pagename=INCN_
assistive_technology

Curative Care Network's Rehabilitation Services
http://www.curative.org/page/reha.asp

DEAFTEK.USA
http://www.deaftek.org/

Disability and Business Technical Assistance Centers
http://home.earthlink.net/~dawwn/
dbtac.htm

Easter Seals Disability Services
http://www.easterseals.com

Education and Library Networks Coalition
http://www.edlinc.org/

Epilepsy Foundation
http://www.epilepsyfoundation.org/

Family Resource Center on Disabilities (FRCD)
http://www.frcd.org/

Helen Keller National Center for Deaf-Blind Youth and Adults
http://www.helenkeller.org/national/

Information Center for Individuals with Disabilities
http://www.disability.net/

International Dyslexia Association
http://www.interdys.org/

Laurent Clerc National Deaf Education Center at Gallaudet University
http://clerccenter.gallaudet.edu/
InfoToGo/

Learning Disabilities Association of America
http://www.ldanatl.org/

Life Span Institute
http://www.lsi.ku.edu/lsi/centers/

March of Dimes Birth Defects Foundation
http://www.modimes.org

Muscular Dystrophy Association
http://www.mdausa.org/

National Association for Visually Handicapped
http://www.navh.org/

National Association of the Deaf
http://www.nad.org/

National Ataxia Foundation
http://www.ataxia.org

National Cancer Institute Cancer Information Service
http://cis.nci.nih.gov/

National Down Syndrome Society
http://www.ndss.org

National Hemophilia Foundation
http://www.hemophilia.org/

National Multiple Sclerosis Society
http://www.nationalmssociety.org/

National Rehabilitation Association
http://www.nationalrehab.org/

National Rehabilitation Information Center
http://www.naric.com/

National Spinal Cord Injury Association
http://www.spinalcord.org/

National Tay-Sachs & Allied Diseases Association
http://www.ntsad.org/

Neurofibromatosis, Inc.
http://www.nfinc.org/

Osteogenesis Imperfecta Foundation
http://www.oif.org/

Parents Anonymous
http://www.parentsanonymous.org

Prader-Willi Syndrome Association (USA)
http://www.pwsausa.org

Recording for the Blind & Dyslexic, Inc.
http://www.rfbd.org/

Spina Bifida Association of America
http://www.sbaa.org/

The Association for Persons with Severe Handicaps (TASH)
http://www.tash.org/

Tourette Syndrome Association, Inc.
http://www.tsa-usa.org/

Trace Center, College of Engineering, University of Wisconsin-Madison
http://trace.wisc.edu/

Tuberous Sclerosis Alliance
http://www.tsalliance.org/

United Cerebral Palsy
http://www.ucp.org/

World Institute on Disability
http://www.wid.org/

Index